THE CRAFT OF THE
COCKTAIL

THE CRAFT OF THE COCKTAIL

EVERYTHING YOU NEED TO KNOW TO BE
A MASTER BARTENDER, WITH 500 RECIPES

DALE DEGROFF

PHOTOGRAPHS BY GEORGE ERML

CLARKSON POTTER / PUBLISHERS
NEW YORK

Published by Clarkson Potter/Publishers, New York, New York
Member of the Crown Publishing Group, a division of Random House, Inc.

CLARKSON N. POTTER is a trademark and POTTER and colophon are registered
trademarks of Random House, Inc.

Printed in China

Design by Jan Derevjanik

Library of Congress Cataloging-in-Publication Data
DeGroff, Dale.
   The craft of the cocktail / Dale DeGroff.—1st ed.
   Includes bibliographical references and index.
   1. Cocktails.   2. Bartending.   I. Title.
TX951 .D39   2002
641.8'74—dc21   2001057791

ISBN 0-609-60875-4

10 9 8 7 6 5 4 3 2 1

First Edition

My life has unfolded like a day behind the bar. The regulars, the unexpected guests, the solitary drinker methodically working toward his end, the group spontaneously celebrating another day on the planet. I fell in love with bars because of the uninhibited, disordered, and surprising way life unfolds at the bar. The only logical progression in my life has been the wealth of characters who have crossed my path, leaving their sweet, sour, strong, and weak for me to ponder. I dedicate this book to all the friends and strangers who took a moment to tell a great story and send me on my way.

CONTENTS

INTRODUCTION

By age twelve, I knew exactly where I wanted to live when I grew up: Big things happen in big places, and New York City was the biggest. Luckily, my father had instilled in me an unreasonable supply of optimism, which buoyed me through learning a city that could swallow you up without a trace. This optimism, along with a few good friends and dumb luck, was about all I had when I arrived in New York in 1969.

Within a year, I went to work for my best friend's brother, Ron Holland, a principal in a small creative ad agency called Lois, Holland, and Callaway. Everyone's favorite account at the agency was Restaurant Associates. Besides affording Ron and his partners the golden opportunity to work with the legendary restaurateur Joe Baum, it also enabled them to dine and entertain their clients at the very best restaurants in town. In short, a dream account. My chief occupation at the agency was to get in on as many expensive free meals as was humanly possible, which was easy given Ron's generosity. It did not take long to get hooked.

Every Sunday we'd meet for brunch at Charley O's at Forty-eighth Street and Rockefeller Plaza in the heart of Manhattan, assembling just before noon. The old blue laws forbade serving alcohol before noon on Sundays, so the stroke of midday was much anticipated. Ron Holland and his partner, the legendary art director George Lois, had worked closely with Joe Baum creating Charley O's. It was a terrific room, full of dark mahogany and leaded glass, with a long bar along the east wall and a beautiful oval window looking out on Rockefeller Plaza. On the walls hung photographs and quotes from great writers and great drunks; Ron's own Grandma Holland, who pronounced on her death bed, "I'll keep drinking them as long as they keep making them," was on the wall too, her wisdom right alongside Robert Benchley and Errol Flynn. Charley O's was a bar for everyone from writers to gamblers, secretaries to politicians, all drawn there by solid drink, hearty food, and tremendous good cheer. Charley O's was where Pat Moynihan threw his yearly St. Paddy's-day breakfast; it was where Bobby Kennedy announced his candidacy; and it was the beginning of my love affair with the New York Bar & Grill.

If there was one single pivotal day in my life that determined my future, it was when I volunteered to fill in for a bartender who failed to show up for a party that Charley O's was catering at Gracie Mansion, the home of New York City's mayor. The manager was frantic and asked whether anyone knew how to tend bar. None of the old-time barmen wanted to work a thankless, tipless gig; I lied and said I was a bartender. But before dashing off to the mansion, I rushed over to Mike Flynn, the head bartender, and asked, "By the way, how do you tend bar, anyway?" There was very little time, but Mike was a kind and sympathetic soul. He wrote out a list of common drinks and how to make them, and gave me some pointers on how to pour. In what seemed like seconds later, I was behind the bar at Gracie Mansion. Mayor Abe Beame was presenting the keys of the city to Rupert Murdoch, so all the top people in the Beame administration and a number of other prominent New Yorkers were attending. All of a sudden, it dawned on me that I was center stage and this was a captive audience. It was only a makeshift, poorly stocked bar, and I never really had to make anything that fancy, but there was something about being behind that bar that felt just right. I don't know how Muhammad Ali felt the first time he climbed into a ring, or how Louis Armstrong felt the first time he picked up a trumpet, but for me, I knew I was standing in a very familiar and cozy place. I was home.

In 1987, when Joe Baum opened the Promenade Bar in the newly restored Rainbow Room, I was offered the unique opportunity to create a classic bar in the old style. I was ten years into my bartending career with two great bars on my résumé, the original Charley O's and the Hotel Bel-Air. I had an intuitive

THE
RAINBOW
ROOM

The Classic Cocktail Dinner
Monday, November 17, 1997

HORS D'OEUVRE

WILD MUSHROOM TARTELETTES
OSETRA CAVIAR IN TINY POTATOES
SMOKED SALMON CANAPÉS
CURED DUCK RAVIOLI
ROASTED OYSTERS ROCKEFELLER

BULL'S BLOOD AND MARTINIS

SAUTÉED HUDSON VALLEY FOIE GRAS
grilled citrus & sherry vinegar

CENTURY SOUR

GRILLED DIVER SCALLOPS
fennel & dill

MONKEY GLAND

MINT JULEP GRANITÉ

MEDALLION OF VEAL
roasted apples & pears

BIG APPLE MANHATTAN

"TROPICAL FRUIT CRUISE"
3 desserts & 3 cocktails

*Chef Waldy Malouf
Pastry Chef Martin Howard
Master Mixologist Dale Degroff
& Staff*

understanding of what a great bar could be, but I still had much to learn about what made a great drink. What followed was a journey back in time to learn how to re-create the classic cocktails in the classic style. There wasn't anyone around who remembered how to do it. Using only fresh and natural ingredients meant doing away with fast and easy pre-made mixes and figuring out how to achieve just the right amount of sweet and sour, strong and weak. It meant searching for out-of-print cocktail books and experimenting with hundreds of recipes, adjusting them to a modern palate and today's larger portions.

And so began my quest for *just* the right cocktails with *just* the right recipes. What I learned while rediscovering the lost art of bartending is what I will share in this book: a treasure of recipes that will tantalize your palate, enliven your parties, and inspire you to embark on your own journey to discover new and exciting ways to mix drinks.

Cheers!

PART 1

THE CRAFT OF THE COCKTAIL

THE

HISTORY

OF THE

COCKTAIL

I learned about cocktails much the same way I learned to tend bar. Certainly through research, but mainly through experience. My fellow bartenders taught me how to treat people, my customers taught me about life, and most important, my mentor, the great restaurateur Joe Baum, taught me how little I knew. Joe sparked my curiosity to find out what makes a great cocktail.

The cocktail is, in a word, American. It's as American as jazz, apple pie, and baseball; and as diverse, colorful, and big as America itself. Indeed, it could even be argued that the cocktail is a metaphor for the American people: It is a composite beverage, and we are a composite people. Let's begin by looking at what preceded its invention.

THE EARLY DAYS

Before Europeans settled in America, they had been cultivating beverage traditions for centuries. Southern Europeans, around the Mediterranean, produced wine and brandy, while distilled-grain spirits were part of the tradition and culture of the peoples who inhabited the northern tier of Europe, where it was too cold for wine grapes to grow. Interestingly, the distillates produced with fermented grape and grain mash were also revered for their "medicinal" qualities, and came be known as *aqua vitae* in Latin, *eau-de-vie* in French, *usquebaugh* in Gaelic, and "water of life" in English. Naturally, as the technology of distilled spirits from grain and grape advanced, water of life could be produced more cheaply and in greater quantities, and eventually it was used to produce flavored cordials and liqueurs.

Once the Europeans established themselves on this side of the Atlantic, they put to good use the beer- and wine-making skills they had brought with them from the Old World. They also brought the Old World opinion that drinking water was unwholesome, even dangerous. The early colonists were voracious experimenters, fermenting beverages from practically everything they could get their hands on: pumpkins, parsnips, turnips, rhubarbs, walnuts, elderberries, and more. They flavored their beer

with birch, pine, spruce, and sassafras. They planted apple orchards everywhere from Virginia northward to produce cider and, more important, applejack, which provided the base for many early colonial drinks. Applejack was also popular because it could be made without the use of expensive distilling equipment. Fermented apple juice, or hard cider as it was called, was left out in the cold in late fall and early winter. As layers of ice formed on the surface of the cider, they were skimmed off, removing the water content and thus concentrating the alcohol in the remaining liquid.

Conversely, as trade between the Old and New worlds increased, Europe in turn discovered the plants and botanicals that the colonists were well on their way to exploiting. As early as 1571, a Spanish doctor named Nicolas Monardes published a document describing plants and medicines from the Americas that were being assimilated into daily life all over Europe. In Italy and France, these plants eventually found their way into fortified and flavored wines, such as vermouth and other apéritif wines. Ironically, these products made their way full-circle across the Atlantic, where they later played a pivotal role in the growth of the cocktail tradition.

That cocktail tradition began with rum. Distilling spirits began commercially in the New World in 1640 when Wilhelm Kieft, the director-general of New Amsterdam (now Manhattan), erected the first still in which to distill gin and a tavern in which to sell it. When Manhattan fell into the hands of the English, the still was used to make rum, the

COCKTAIL TRIVIA

On more than one occasion when I was behind the bar, I offered a bitters-soaked lime or lemon wedge dipped in sugar to bite into for a hiccup cure. Remarkably, most (but not all) of the time it worked. Try it.

first internationally accepted spirit of the New World. But truth be told, rum was sort of an accident. Christopher Columbus introduced sugarcane to our hemisphere on his second voyage for the purpose, of course, of making sugar. Rum was made by the ever-industrious colonists as a way to utilize the molasses left over from sugar production—that is, rum was a by-product of sugar. But by the end of the seventeenth century, rum production dwarfed sugar production to such an extent that the British enacted laws requiring that a certain proportion of all sugarcane crops must be used to make actual sugar. Rum had become the base for many colonial beverages, especially punches, and was produced throughout the Caribbean, South America, and to a great extent even in New England.

The production of rum fueled the growing economy. By 1733 it surpassed all other exports from the colonies. At the time, New England rum distillers were purchasing the molasses from the cheapest sources in the Caribbean, which were more often than not French and Portuguese. As a result, the British rum distillers who were sourcing their own molasses were losing a market share to the upstart colonial distillers and their cheaper molasses, and hence cheaper rum. In retribution, the British passed the Molasses Act of 1733 to control and tax the flow of molasses into the colonies. The Sugar Act followed, and then in 1765 the Stamp Act, which required the use of a tax stamp on all transactions. These acts led to the founding of the First Continental Congress, and eventually to the Revolutionary War. So, you see, it was rum, not tea, that precipitated our break from Great Britain. (Well, maybe there were a few other minor concerns, but this is a book about cocktails, not textiles.)

The American victory over the British left the new republic deep in debt. To the astonishment of most of his colleagues in the new government, Alexander Hamilton, our first Secretary of the Treasury, decided to pay our war debts quickly by way of a federal excise tax on rum and spirits, which was passed by the Congress in 1791 and signed into law by President George Washington. Thus began the tradition of paying for our wars by taxing our spirits. This would prove handy when, just twenty years later, the new nation found itself at war again with Great Britain in 1812. For the second time in the nation's brief history, the British blockaded our coastline, cutting off trade with molasses producers in the Caribbean and all but finishing the dwindling rum distilleries. This led to a tidal increase in the domestic production of grain spirits, and eventually to the birth of the second American spirit, bourbon, our all-American corn whiskey.

COCKTAIL TRIVIA

Although Angostura Bitters has an alcohol base, like vanilla extract, it is considered a food additive and flavoring agent, not an alcoholic beverage. When used by the drop, it won't affect the alcohol content of a drink. Only persons with severe allergic reactions to alcohol should avoid flavoring with bitters..

It was also during the period between these two wars that the word *cocktail* seems to have come into use. If you ambled into a colonial New England inn for a cold one, or just as likely a hot one, you'd probably order a ratafia, shrub, turnip wine, posset, pope, bishop, sack, flip, or an ale. Are any of these cocktails? Not really. But they were the progenitors of the cocktail, which made its official debut in print in 1806 in a publication called *The Balance and Columbian Repository*. In a letter to the editor, a reader had queried the meaning of a new word, *cocktail*. The editor wrote back:

"Cocktail is a stimulating liquor, composed of spirits of any kind, sugar, water and bitters. It is vulgarly called a bittered sling and is supposed to be an excellent electioneering potion, in as much as it renders the heart stout and bold, at the same time that it fuddles the head . . . It is said also, to be of great use to a Democratic candidate because, a person having swallowed a glass of it, is ready to swallow anything else."

The sarcastic last line of that reply addresses the practice of plying voters with alcohol, a tradition said to have begun with George Washington that did not end officially until Prohibition. The editor's reply also gives us for the first time a clear distinction between what constitutes a cocktail and separates it from all the concoctions that came before it: the addition of bitters. *Bitters* is a generic term for alcoholic beverages distilled or infused with plant or root extracts. Native Americans taught the early settlers how to use indigenous plants for flavorings in beverages and for

medicinal purposes. Eventually, Old World plants were incorporated into these heady infusions, some of which included gentian root, colombo root, cinchona bark (quinine), ground ivy, horehound, cassia, wormwood, and angostura bark and root. Historically, these infusions were promoted as medicine to beat the tax on alcohol, though they did serve as effective digestifs. What they really did, however, was enhance the flavor of mixed drinks to which they were added.

The first commercially produced bitters was probably Peychaud's, made by Antoine Amédie Peychaud, a Creole immigrant to New Orleans who operated a pharmacy on the French Quarter's Royal Street from around 1793 through the 1830s. Peychaud himself made his bitters on a small scale but in 1840 the product was manufactured and sold nationally and internationally. With his background as an apothecary, Peychaud was a natural mixologist who delighted the friends who gathered for late-night revelry at his pharmacy. Peychaud would mix cognac and a dash of his secret bitters for his guests in a two-sided eggcup called a *coquetier*, pronounced "cock-tyay." Sound familiar? It is very likely that this word evolved into the word *cocktail* in English, but there are countless other tales with the same claim. Regardless of what Peychaud called his concoction, it evolved into the anise-scented Sazerac—sans absinthe, of course.

The transition from rum to whiskey was well under way long before the British again tried to choke off America's molasses supplies. The immigrants who fled the famines in the British Isles in the early eighteenth century found the New England states less than welcoming, and many of them settled along the frontier of western Pennsylvania. While the Quaker and Dutch colonists settled early on in Pennsylvania to escape the Puritan intolerance of New England, the hardy Scots pushed even farther west, opening up new wilderness and clearing lands for small farms. Naturally, many of them were schooled in the art of distilling whiskey from the old country, and brought small stills with them. Others simply built their own stills out of necessity, as whiskey was used in commerce in place of cash. Goods were purchased and debts were settled with Monongahela, as the whiskey came to be known, named for the river that marked the western frontier at that time.

Later, Hamilton's heavy tax on spirits drove many distillers out of the colonies altogether and to the frontier territories that would become Kentucky, Tennessee, Ohio, and Indiana. These territories were ideal for whiskey production: The soil was rich, crop yields were higher than in the east, and there was a plentiful supply of pure mineral water bubbling up through the limestone shelf. Savvy settlers cleared the land and planted corn, which was indigenous and offered greater return per acre than other grains. From corn they made corn whiskey, which they barreled and sent down the river by barge to New Orleans. Depending on the distance and the water level of streams and rivers, the barrels of whiskey were sometimes in transit for many months. Completely by accident, whiskey makers discovered the benefits of barrel aging. Prior to the invention of the steam engine, all barge traffic on the river went in one direction only—south toward the gulf—on flatboats and barges, very slowly. But with the advent of steam-powered riverboats and canals, in the middle of the nineteenth century, northern routes were opened to the lucrative eastern market. Whiskey production benefited from easier access to the big markets of the north and east. This development was followed by revolutionary advances in the technology of distilling (brilliantly documented in Michael Kraft's important book, *The American Distiller*, 1804), that led to the growth of large distilleries that replaced small farmers as the main source of whiskey from "the West." It was also at this time, around 1833, that the word *Bourbon* first appeared on whiskey labels, a tribute to the French who fought side-by-side with Americans in the Revolution. French names were popular throughout the colonies and the frontier. Everything from streets in New York City to cities on the frontier like Louisville and Lafayette were renamed to honor our French allies.

THE GOLDEN AGE

When the war with Britain ended in 1815, spirits were heavily taxed again to pay for the war, but not for too long. In 1817, with the debt settled, all excise taxes on domestic spirits were repealed, and for over forty years—up until the Civil War—the spirits industry enjoyed a tax-free growth period. This finally set the stage for what would become known as the golden age of the cocktail. Bars and saloons flourished during this period. In 1832, the Pioneer Inns and Taverns Law created a new type of license that allowed inns to serve alcoholic beverages without being required to lease rooms. This made official what had been happening ever so quietly after colonial-era regulations relaxed after the Revolutionary War: The bar was officially open for business. The floodgates were now open.

The Industrial Revolution that swept the western world in the nineteenth century had a powerful impact on every facet of American life, and the alcoholic-beverage industry benefited greatly. Factories lured people to urban centers around the country and fostered a sea change in the way people ate and drank and gathered. As cities grew larger, restaurants—without inns—became an important part of the urban landscape. Mass immigrations took place between 1820 and 1855, bringing people from Scotland, England, and Ireland and from Germany and other Central European countries directly to the bustling cities. Like the colonists before them, these new Americans brought with them their distilling and brewing skills and their love of the communal tradition of the public house and taproom.

BARMAN AS POWER BROKER

Of the late-nineteenth-century barkeepers, Theodore Roosevelt said, "Bartenders form perhaps the nearest approach to a leisure class that we have at present on this side of the water. Naturally they are on semi-intimate terms with all who frequent their houses. There is no place where more gossip is talked than in bar rooms, and much of this gossip is about politics…that is the politics of the ward, not of the nation."

The new immigrants typically lived in the worst areas of these urban centers. But many prospered by creating their own social clubs, stocked with gallons of illegal spirits that they occasionally sold to the neighborhood at large. These unlicensed establishments were a phenomenon referred to as "blind pigs" or "blind tigers." The gimmick was that you paid a certain amount of money "to see the blind pig," and as a bonus you were served a free drink. The goal of these wily merchants,

of course, was to get enough people to pay to see the pig so that they could open *legit* establishments. These neighborhood bars and saloons, often two or three to a block, were central to community and precinct politics, serving as community living rooms where men gathered to talk politics.

The emergence and popularity of neighborhood bars in New York had the blessing of Tammany Hall, the city's notorious political machine. The political bosses of the day were happy to grant the Irish and German immigrants licenses to operate saloons, not for the financial return but because they could control the ward politics by controlling the saloons, where for the most part the voting males spent their free time. With time, the saloon owners became the power brokers in their precincts.

By the 1870s, the bar business was big business, in full swing, and cocktail books and manuals were flooding the market. Cocktail bars of every description were flourishing in the big cities, from neighborhood haunts to the fancy palaces in big hotels. One of the most stunning bars in New York was the Hoffman House, with towering ceilings and a fifty-foot ornate mahogany bar, marble floors and walls, cigar counters, and oyster bars. The barmen, pristine in their starched white jackets, were skilled practitioners trained in every aspect of beverage and service. Somehow, all the elements fell into place: the technology of refrigeration, charged water (just another word for soda water, water is literally charged with gas), tap beer systems, and the

perfecting of mechanical ice systems; the amazing variety of bottled spirits available, both imported and domestic; a large, motivated, and well-trained work force; and a growing industrial economy fueling consumer spending. This was the height of the cocktail's golden age, when many of the classics were either born or perfected: the Martini, the Manhattan, the sour, the fizz, the old fashioned, the Pousse Café, the sling, and the julep. Many remain classics today.

This was the era of the consummate professional—the Barman. Service became as important as what was being served. The competition was intense, with bars opening on every corner. What separated success from failure was quality and service. In his 1888 *Bartender's Manual,* Harry Johnson wrote a chapter entitled "How To Attend Bar," in which he chides the novice to supply ice water immediately with every drink, to mix drinks above the counter where the guest can see, and to mix them in such a way as to be "neat, clean, and scientific." He also says that professionalism affords a bit of showmanship when he instructs to "mix in such a way as to draw attention." Finally, Johnson instructs the bartender to be a caring friend: "If you think a customer is about spending for a beverage, when it is possible that he or his family needs the cash for some other more useful purpose, it would be best to give him advice rather than a drink, and send him home with an extra quarter instead of taking the dime for a drink from him."

PROHIBITON AND REPEAL

Early into the twentieth century, however, teetotalers were gaining momentum across the country to kill the production and sale of liquor. By 1912, Prohibition was already in place in many states. Then in 1919, the Eighteenth Amendment to the Constitution was passed, and Prohibition became the law of the land, outlawing the sale of alcohol in every way, shape, and form. In retrospect, Prohibition is universally acknowledged to have been a gigantic failure. Speakeasies, the nickname for covert bars and private clubs where liquor could be found, not only flourished, they thrived. Even city officials and policemen were involved in the ruse of abstinence. But while booze continued to flow, and cocktails remained a staple of society, the profession of barman suffered immensely. It was no longer a respectable position to tend bar, or at least one could not discuss it publicly. Because many bars were makeshift—if you could call them bars at all—the arena for showmanship and excellence proved futile, and practically disappeared.

By the time Prohibition ended in 1932, two generations had passed, and the image of the bartending profession was badly tarnished by organized crime's control of bars and speakeasies. Of course after Prohibition there was great demand for bartenders, but the level of craftsmanship and respect for the profession as a serious pursuit had waned. One of the few pre-Prohibition bartenders who returned after Repeal was Patrick Gavin Duffy, who worked at the Ashland House in New York City. He became one of the most respected bartenders of his day, credited with having created the first highball in the 1890s, by mixing whiskey with club soda over ice in a tall glass.

Though the recovering liquor industry was glad to see Prohibition go, Repeal proved to be another series of obstacles, many of them still in place today. Under new laws, individual states—and even the individual counties within states—were granted enormous power over the alcohol industry. The results were a Byzantine maze of local laws and regulations that make doing national business in the liquor industry a nightmare. Some states require liquor to be served only in small 50-milliliter "airline" or "nip" bottles, which basically discourages cocktails that require a dash of this or a half a shot of that. In other states, customers have to buy whole bottles of booze, and then leave behind the remainder if they can't finish. And rigorous registration procedures for individual brands severely limit the range of spirits available in many states simply because of too much red tape. States like Pennsylvania and Washington own the liquor stores, and choice of brands is made by state authority. This leads to a dearth of smaller brands that don't sell in volume and that dramatically impacts on the cocktail possibilities.

COCKTAIL TRIVIA

Adrian Barbe, who owned and ran Hurley's Saloon at Forty-ninth Street and Sixth Avenue in New York City for twenty years, attributed much of his success to the men he put behind his bar. He would say about his bartenders, "I don't care what nationality they are, as long as they are Irish behind my bar."

COCKTAIL TRIVIA

Bartenders returning to the trade, or just getting started, were put at a severe disadvantage by these laws. And the Great Depression didn't help energize the business, either. Perhaps the proverbial bottom of the barrel was hit, however, during the peacetime era of the fifties, when cocktails suffered the ultimate insult: time-saving measures for a go-go society. Pre-prepared and processed food products designed to make life easier flooded the market; TV dinners, baby formula, Kool-Aid, Jiffy Pop, and Tang were the rage. Americans happily abandoned the fresh and natural, scooping up all that was processed and canned. The cocktail bar was not spared. Pre-sweetened, artificially flavored sweet-and-sour mixes, in the form of liquids or powders, made the scene. A product called 7-11 Tom Collins Powdered Mix, developed in the thirties, heralded the beginning of the end of the fresh-fruit cocktails of the pre-Prohibition era. Then, after World War II, several more of these products flooded the market, and a generation of bartenders learned the "Kool-Aid" style of making drinks: ice, liquor, water, and the mix.

A RETURN TO THE
CLASSIC COCKTAIL

Though James Bond championed the vodka Martini in the sixties, it wasn't until the late eighties that the rebirth of the cocktail really took shape. I am proud to say that I was there to act as midwife. In 1985 I went to work for legendary restaurateur Joe Baum at a fine restaurant in Manhattan called Aurora. Joe was the first president of Restaurant Associates, a company that operates restaurants and institutional food-service outlets throughout the United States and abroad. When Joe took over the company in the fifties, America was a meat-and-potatoes country with iceberg lettuce and Tommy Tucker Dinners thrown in for the kids. Joe began a series of bold innovations that over the years had a huge impact on the way Americans ate and drank. He started in the fifties with The Newarker at Newark Airport in New Jersey, the first fine-dining restaurant in an international airport. That was followed in

1959 by The Four Seasons restaurant in New York City's Seagram Building, considered by many to be one of the first world-class American restaurants. Then, in 1960, Baum single-handedly introduced tequila to New York at La Fonda Del Sol, where his innovative cocktail program included Pisco "Sawers," Batidas, Margaritas, and one that's experiencing a rebirth today, the Mojito Criollo.

In 1987, Joe afforded me the opportunity to play an important role in reviving the great American cocktail. At the newly restored Rainbow Room, atop the Art Deco masterpiece at 30 Rockefeller Plaza, Joe was determined to implement his dream of a nineteenth-century-style bar that used all fresh ingredients and no mixes. When Joe explained his plan for a beverage program that utilized only fresh juices with no commercial mixes, I gently complained that if the bar were very busy, it might be difficult to maintain the fresh-squeezed routine. Joe snapped back that it had been done for a hundred years, and if I couldn't figure out how to do it, he would find someone who could. So I enthusiastically replied, "I think it's a great idea, and I know we'll have no problem with it!"

But there were problems with it. As it was, I used fresh juice only to enhance an occasional Margarita or Whiskey Sour to accommodate a demanding guest. Like most young bartenders back then, I relied on mixes not just as a shortcut, but to give a drink sweetness and balance.

I found a copy of Jerry Thomas's *How to Mix Drinks* or *Bon Vivant's Companion*, 1862, and some other treasures from the mid-nineteenth century which proved invaluable in helping me reconstruct the methods of the classic era. Thomas's recipes were simple and direct: a base ingredient combined with modifiers. He demonstrated the absolute necessity of using simple syrup in a cocktail program that utilized freshly squeezed lemon and lime juice. This was how he mastered the sweet and sour cocktails like fizzes, sours, and fixes. It was enlightening to read about the methods barmen like Jerry Thomas and Harry Johnson had used to master ingredient, recipe, and technique. The superb craftsmanship and wide variety of exotic ingredients they employed inspired me to approach the profession of bartending like a chef. And what better place to reinvent the classic cocktail than the pinnacle of New York's nightlife, the historic Rainbow Room. There's no reason why you can't do it in your own kitchen. So roll up your sleeves, and let's explore the ingredients that we need to make great cocktails.

THE INGREDIENTS OF THE COCKTAIL

I am a firm believer that spirits are gifts from the gods. How could man ever have figured out how to make them on his own? The process is not necessarily easy, and it would be impossible if not for the help of magical organisms called yeast. Spirits are the distillation of fermented sugars. In fermentation, sugars (and starches that can be converted into sugars) are mixed with water. Then that magical yeast takes over and consumes the sugar, letting off a little gas in the form of carbon dioxide, and producing ethyl alcohol. As the sugar is converted, the alcohol content rises and eventually kills the yeast. Removing the alcohol from the water, finally, is the process called distillation.

Basically, anything can be fermented, and consequently distilled, as long as it contains sugar. People have fermented and then distilled every kind of fruit, and most kinds of vegetables, known to man for thousands of years. The starches found in grain, potatoes, agave plants, rice, and dozens of other starchy plants are converted to sugar and then to alcohol. Even beets are high in sugar, and are a huge source of alcohol production.

Distillation creates neutral spirits, which are then flavored by myriad sources. The best place to start is with the still (the devise for distillation) itself. The complex flavor of finer premium gins, for instance, is achieved by passing the high-proof spirit through a final distillation in a pot still, with botanicals that flavor the gin and provide that unique aroma. Producers of fine Cognac wouldn't consider using anything other than an alembic still, because it is a single-batch still that distills at a lower temperature, retaining more of the character of the original fruit or grain. The type of still, producers know, affects the complexity of the flavors.

Flavoring alcohol is easy, because alcohol is a most hospitable organic compound. Alcohol bonds naturally with other organic compounds, and this produces most of the flavor and aroma that we enjoy in spirits. Alcohol can be diluted with pure water to produce vodka, or flavored with botanicals to make gin. It takes on the smoke flavor of scotch that's lifted during fermentation from barley malt that was exposed to peat smoke while drying. The vanilla and caramel flavors that sweeten bourbon are the dividends returned as the spirit passes season after season through the layer of caramelized wood sugar (created by charring the wood), just under the charred oak inside a bourbon barrel. Unfortunately, alcohol molecules don't distinguish between good and bad flavors when they link with other organic compounds, so the distiller must be a brilliant matchmaker and introduce only the desired flavors and aromas.

What flavors and aromas do you prefer? Choosing the spirits for a home bar, tasting them, and using them to make great cocktails can be a daunting task, but it is not at all impossible. But there are a few fundamentals we should get out of the way before we start flipping cocktail shakers around.

One of the most important ingredients: ice.

ICE

Ice is the soul of the American cocktail. Cocktails are shaken, stirred, and blended with ice. We Americans share a penchant for ice-cold drinks that is unique; Americans traveling in Europe are often vexed by the stingy amount of ice used in drinks. This wasn't always the case: As far back as the sixteenth century, ice was used to chill everything from water to red wine in Continental Europe. But ice never made the jump to the British Isles, where the Brits didn't warm up to cold drinks until after World War I. Consequently, the use of ice to chill beverages grew slowly in the British colonies. What made ice eventually attractive to us was our extreme climate—scorching-hot summers and frosty-cold winters.

Sadly, like the art of making cocktails before Prohibition, making ice cubes that are fit for cocktails has suffered. The big square ice cubes Grandma used to pop out of those hand-cranked ice cube trays lasted forever. Today, ice has been redesigned: modernized for speed of production and increased surface area, and redesigned to fill the space inside a glass more completely, giving the illusion of more liquid. But the "new" ice fails to chill a beverage without over-diluting. The new shapes—little boxes with holes inside, discs, trapezoids, some so fragile that they crumble when handled—may achieve more surface area, but they melt so quickly that the beverage becomes diluted and warms too quickly.

Nineteenth-century beverage recipes called for four kinds of ice: block, lump or cubed, cracked, and snow. Block ice was the standard through the nineteenth and early twentieth centuries. Tools were designed to create the other kinds from the blocks, such as the ice pick, to break up the blocks into lumps; an ice hammer, to break lumps into cracked ice; and an ice rasp, to shave the block into snow ice. Lump or large cubes are best when serving spirits on the rocks or in a highball, because they melt more slowly, chilling but not over-diluting.

You won't need cracked ice too often, but when you do, just crack large cubes by hand by folding them in a clean dish towel and whacking them with the bowl of a heavy serving spoon. They are perfect in very sweet drinks, juices, and soft drinks, and in some specialty drinks like a Caipirinha or a Daiquiri on the rocks. Cracked ice should be used in a blender for frozen drinks; it creates the slush you're looking for without straining your blender in the process. (Lump ice does not completely break down and could ruin the blender, and snow ice will turn to water in a blender.) Crushed or snow ice is for just plain fun. If you think about it, frozen fruit Daiquiris are really adult snow cones.

WATER IS THE KEY

To illustrate how important water is to a cocktail, try the following experiment: Place a bottle of gin in the freezer and a bottle of vermouth in the fridge. Chill your glasses and your olives, get everything very cold. Prepare a Martini without ice by simply mixing the cold ingredients in the chilled glass and dropping in the olives. Take a sip, and what you will experience will not resemble a Martini—it will be too strong. The water does many things to a cocktail. Besides diluting it, it also mellows the alcohol burn and introduces the 80- or 90-proof spirit gently to the tongue, by opening flavors and aromas that would be missed otherwise.

SPIRITS

A well-stocked bar should offer one or more selections from the "Big Seven" categories: gin, vodka, whiskey (bourbon, scotch, rye, blended, and Irish), rum, tequila, brandy, and liqueurs.

Where to begin? Start by assessing your needs—not for a single drink, but for setting up your home bar.

Price

Price doesn't guarantee quality, but in most cases you get what you pay for. If you plan to make mixed drinks, choose the best ingredients you can afford. But there's no need to overspend on super-premium spirits—after all, it's totally unnecessary to use a Cognac above the V.S. (very superior) category to make a Sidecar. But don't grab the cooking brandy either! There are three price levels to refer to when considering the brands in the big seven categories: call or value brands, premium brands, super-premium brands.

Label and Proof

Though the information on bottle labels can range from minimalist-chic to the Gettysburg Address, the most important information, mandated by law, is who makes it, where it's from, and its alcoholic strength or proof; these are the bare basics. Better labels tell you the process by which the spirit was made, and if it's been aged, how long and under what conditions. All of this information will determine its price. Proof describes the alcohol strength in a spirit as the percentage of alcohol (for example,

40 percent alcohol by volume) or a proof number. The proof number is double the alcohol volume number, so that 40 percent alcohol equals 80 proof. The standard proof required by the controlling agency of the U.S. government for most full-strength spirit categories such as vodka and gin is 80 proof. (The agency is the BATF, or Bureau of Alcohol, Tobacco and Firearms; the grouping of alcohol with firearms is more of the fallout from Prohibition.) Flavored and spiced spirits are often 35 percent, or 70 proof. Apéritifs are much lower, usually between 16 percent and 30 percent; and liqueurs range widely from 24 percent to 55 percent.

Age

The barrel-aging of spirits adds flavor and finesse, and rounds out the harsh notes present in young spirits. And most spirits are usually aged in oak barrels. The size of the barrels, their preparation, and the number of times they have been used are all factors that affect the resulting spirit. For example, bourbon aged in warehouses in Kentucky, with its hot summers and cool, damp winters, will age differently than scotch aging in a warehouse on the Isle of Skye with damp cool breezes and very little hot weather. The bourbon may reach maturity in four to six years, whereas the scotch will need six to twelve. The aging of spirits is often used as a marketing tool, and may have little to do with quality. A twelve-year-old designation on a bottle of blended scotch that is aged in depleted casks or is poorly made means little. Don't rely only on age declaration when choosing a spirit; look also for established, well-respected brands. And in some cases, younger spirits are preferred. For example, Margaritas are best with unaged silver or lightly aged reposado tequilas, with the green vegetal flavor of the agave intact. Save the expensive, very old añejo tequila for sipping. The same applies with rum for a Daiquiri: Always use young or unaged silver rum because the older rums, with their oak and vanilla notes, get in the way of the clean lime flavor of a well-made Daiquiri. The Mai Tai, on the other hand, calls for an aged Jamaican rum when made according to the original Victor Bergeron recipe. Whiskey that is used in cocktails should come from an established producer and be properly aged. And with the exception of fruit brandies and eau-de-vie, all brandies are much improved with barrel age.

Style

Of all the considerations when buying spirits, the most important is style—also the most subjective. The Big Seven categories are a good general list to check when shopping, but what about the actual brands? One answer is to taste them yourself. If you are a gin drinker, you might buy small bottles of different brands and taste them straight and then in your favorite cocktails. This is a fun but slow approach. You could also do this research at a bar (preferably one that I'm standing behind). But, alas, if that's not possible, let me talk you through them as if you're sitting at my bar. Feel free to pour yourself something in my stead while we're at it.

TASTING: THE NOSE KNOWS

We have nine thousand taste buds in our mouths, but we have millions and millions of olfactory receptors in our nasal passages. Phillip Hills, author of the wonderful book *Appreciating Whisky,* illustrates the importance of scent in our perception of taste with a fun little experiment: Close your eyes and pinch your nostrils shut. Have a friend place a small piece of apple and then a small piece of onion on your tongue. Don't chew; just taste. Until the aroma has had a chance to travel through the nasal passages at the back of your mouth, it will be difficult to tell the two apart.

Now don't go out and thrust your nose into a glass of spirits and inhale deeply. You will succeed only in numbing the olfactory receptors for the next half hour. Begin by holding a glass under your nose, but breathing through your mouth, not your nose. This way, the strong vapors will not be drawn into your nasal passages, but the subtle aromas will rise. The glass that professional tasters use for spirit tasting is a small stem glass with a round bowl and a chimney-shaped top. The alcohol vapors are trapped in the glass, but the characteristic nose of the liquor rises. However, a simple wine glass will be fine for a cocktail-party tasting.

The next step, the actual tasting of cocktails, is also a bit different from tasting wine. Don't take a large sip and wash it around your mouth, especially if you intend to taste several more samples. It might be wise to go from sample to sample just enjoying differences in the nose or aroma before beginning the actual tasting. When you do finally taste, take a small amount of the spirit and cup it in the center of your tongue. Let it slowly roll around your tongue side to side and back to front, touching all the different taste receptors for sweet, bitter, salty, and sour located on different parts of your tongue. Since you took in so little, spitting is probably not necessary; but if you're tasting several samples, it's probably a good idea to spit until you've found your favorite...then of course it's time to make cocktails.

VODKA

Vodka is the easiest spirit to discuss stylistically. As defined by law in the United States, vodka must be a pure spirit with no additives except water, non-aged, and basically tasteless and odorless. Generally, vodka is made from grain or potatoes, with grain accounting for well over 90 percent of the production on the international market. Vodka is a rectified spirit, which means it is distilled at least three times, a fact that some brands like to remind us of in their advertisements. The final and very important step in vodka production is filtering through charcoal, though some brands claim to use diamond dust, glacial sand, or even quartz crystals.

The stylistic differences between vodka brands are subtle, since strong flavor is not a consideration. The first and most obvious difference is between grain and potato vodkas. The most distinctive of all the vodkas I tasted in either category was Luksusowa, a potato vodka from Poland that actually has pronounced flavor. I would definitely recommend it to vodka drinkers, but not in a Martini; it should be taken chilled and straight as a sipping vodka. Other potato vodkas readily available in the United States, such as Chopin and Teton (both made with potatoes) and Peconika (made with a potato and grain mix), are almost indistinguishable from regular grain-based vodka. Remember, this spirit is distilled to 190 proof—almost pure alcohol—and then filtered. The impurities that give lower-proof spirits their characteristic flavor, called congeners, are almost completely distilled out of vodka.

The second stylistic difference in vodka is its texture on the tongue, or mouth feel. I find that two of the very popular imported vodkas represent the two

The Cosmopolitan, an extremely popular vodka-based drink.

prominent styles: Absolut has an oily, almost viscous texture that is often described as silky with a sweet finish; and Stolichnaya has a clean, almost watery texture and a slight medicinal finish. Along with the texture, the Absolut-style vodkas have a hint of sweetness in the aftertaste that is missing in the Stolichnaya. That hint of sweetness and the oily texture are due in part to glycerin, a by-product of distillation present in trace amounts in all spirits. Scandinavian countries tend to produce vodka in the silky style with the hint of sweet in the finish; Russian and Eastern European countries produce vodkas with the clean, almost dry medicinal finish.

The third stylistic difference is heat. I find that vodkas are either hot, rough, and raw, or smooth, round, and finished. Most are 40 percent alcohol, but some reveal their proof on the tongue more aggressively than others. Usually, less expensive bulk vodka will burn in the mouth and throat, while vodka made by a master distiller feels smooth and round. The premium and super-premium brands are a good choice for the Martini or a straight shot of vodka to accompany caviar or other hors d'oeuvres.

Value Brands

* Smirnoff, United States, 80 proof
* Olifant, Holland, 80 proof
* Wyborowa, Poland, 80 proof
* Luksusowa, Poland, 80 proof (potato)

Premium Brands

* Absolut, Sweden, 80 proof
* Finlandia, Finland, 80 proof
* Skyy, United States, 80 proof
* Peconika, United States, 80 proof (potato/grain)
* Teton, United States, 80 proof (potato)

THE SMIRNOFF STORY

In the 1930s, Rudolph Kunett of Bethel, Connecticut, bought the name and formula for Smirnoff vodka, originally produced in Czarist Russia, from Vladimir Smirnoff in Paris. Kunett's father had supplied grain for the original vodka in Czarist Russia. In 1939, John Martin bought the whole ball of wax from Kunett for $14,000 plus a small royalty on every case sold. Martin was president of Heublein Inc., grandson of the founder. After World War II, Martin ceaselessly promoted his vodka with four main cocktails: the Bloody Mary, the Screwdriver, the Moscow Mule, and the Vodkatini. His most successful promotions established associations with Hollywood and well-known actors. He placed the Smirnoff bottle in movies, especially the hugely successful James Bond films. He hired the young actor and director Woody Allen for the Smirnoff print advertisements. His famous catch phrase to woo the lunchtime gin-Martini drinker was "Smirnoff...It leaves you breathless."

* Tanqueray Sterling, England, 80 proof
* Boru, Ireland, 80 proof
* Stolichnaya, Russia, 80 proof
* Frïs, Denmark, 80 proof

Super-Premium Brands

* Belvedere, Polish, 80 proof
* Chopin, Polish, 80 proof (potato)
* Grey Goose, France, 80 proof
* Rain, United States, 80 proof
* Cristall, Russia, 80 proof
* Mor, Estonia, 80 proof (potato)

FLAVORED VODKA

Although flavored vodkas are relatively new to Americans, the Russians have been flavoring their vodkas for hundreds of years. So do you need flavored vodka at your home bar? Sure. If you want to make a great Cosmopolitan, then you need citrus vodka. How about whipping up a fabulous Espresso Cocktail with Stolichnaya Vanil, Kahlúa, cold espresso, and cream? Choose your favorite flavor and have some fun with it.

Value Brands

* Gordon's Citrus, United States, 60 proof
* Gordon's Orange, United States, 60 proof
* Smirnoff Citrus, United States, 80 proof
* Smirnoff Orange, United States, 70 proof

GIN

Gin is made from a mash of cereal grain—primarily corn, rye, barley, and wheat—that is flavored with botanicals to give it a distinct taste. Though many botanicals can be (and are) used by individual producers, juniper is usually the most prominent fragrance and flavor note, the common factor that unifies all gins. Other botanicals include coriander, lemon and orange peels, fennel, cassia, anise, almond, and angelica.

A Dutch chemist named Dr. Franciscus Sylvius purportedly created gin at the University of Leyden in the mid-sixteenth century. He called it *genièvre,* for "juniper" in French, and declared it an attempt to enhance the therapeutic properties of juniper in a medicinal beverage. English soldiers fighting in the Lowlands of the Netherlands adopted the taste for gin, which they called "Dutch courage." The production of gin in London was encouraged by King William III (William of Orange) to fill the void created when he banned French imports, including wine and spirits. As a result, gin production soared from a half million gallons in 1690 to 18 million gallons in 1710. Gin, like many other spirits, changed in character in the early nineteenth century with the invention of "Coffey" or continuous still. Today, gin is made around the world, but the London Dry style is considered the benchmark for quality. Gordon's London Dry gin is made by special license in the United States, as are many other American gins designated London Dry, but I think Gordon's is the most authentic of the lot. Seagram's Extra Dry Gin, though not marketed as a London Dry, is also a very well made American gin in the London Dry style. Confused by terminology? Here's how to keep them straight:

Types of Gin

Dutch gin is 70 proof to 80 proof, though always 80 proof in the United States. Dutch gin, or genever—sometimes called Schiedam—is made from rye, corn, and malted barley in pot stills that produce lower proof. The juniper and other botanicals are added during fermentation and then distilled, and a barley malt flavor is usually apparent in the finish. Genièvre is aged in oak casks and probably tastes much more like the original gin than the highly rectified English gin. Holland gin is great for sipping cold with smoked fishes, but not for your Martini.

London Dry is a highly rectified spirit (80 proof to 94 proof) flavored during the second or third distillation, when the vapors pass through a specialized still with an attachment called the gin head, into which the botanicals are added to give the gin aromatic and flowery characteristics.

Old Tom is London Dry but sweetened with simple syrup, a style very popular in the nineteenth century. Old Tom was originally used to make the Tom Collins and other sweet cocktails, but in the twentieth century the sweetness quotient seemed to drop a few notches as styles changed. Old Tom was available in this country until the 1950s, and it is still available in England.

American gin producers, primarily Seagram's, have come out with a line of lower-proof flavored gins and bottled gin drinks. These products haven't set the market on fire, and none of the imported producers has followed suit.

Below are some old favorites and new arrivals that would be great additions to your bar. My advice is to lean toward the premium and super-premium levels if you enjoy your gin in the Martini cocktail, and value or call if you enjoy Tom Collins and Gin Sours.

Value and Call Brands
* Gordon's, United States, 80 proof
* Seagram's, United States, 80 proof
* Olifant, Holland, 80 proof
* Bols Genever, Holland, 80 proof

Premium Brands
* Beefeater, London Distilled, 94 proof
* Bombay, England, 80 proof
* Bombay Sapphire, England, 94 proof
* Boodles, England, 90.4 proof
* Tanqueray, England, 94.6 proof
* Hendrick's, Scotland, 88 proof
* Stolichnaya, Russia, 80 proof
* Frïs, Denmark, 80 proof

Super-Premium Brands
* Junipero, United States, 97 proof
* Tanqueray No. Ten, England, 94.6 proof
* Bafferts, England, 80 proof

WHISKEY

The first time someone walked up to my bar and said, "I'll have a whiskey and soda, bartender," I was stumped. Does he want Irish and soda, scotch and soda, bourbon and soda, rye and soda? At first I would ask for clarification, but finally I realized only the English ask for whiskey and soda, and they always mean scotch. (Now I just listen for the accent.) The bourbon drinker, on the other hand, never takes a chance; he or she always orders by brand, or at least specifies bourbon.

Irish and Scotch

All whiskey drinkers have their loyalties, but we must pay tribute to our Irish and Scottish brothers who invented the stuff. Lore has it that whiskey of some sort has been made in Scotland and Ireland for seven hundred years. Before the "whiskey missionaries" migrated to the New World and discovered corn, whiskey in Ireland and Scotland was made from barley, wheat, rye, and even oats. Two grains in particular, barley and sometimes rye, are malted, or encouraged to germinate, to produce a chemical change that helps turn the starch in the seed to sugar, which is converted to alcohol. The germination process has to be stopped in the malt to prevent the total loss of the starch. This is done by drying the malt in a kiln. This is where scotch and Irish diverge.

In the case of scotch, drying is the stage in the process that adds the flavor characteristic that separates scotch from all the other whiskies of the world. Part of the drying process takes place over a peat-fueled fire, with the peat smoke coming in direct contact with the drying malt. Later, during fermentation and distillation, the smoky flavor of the burned peat is carried along as "baggage" with the alcohol molecules to the final product. Irish whiskey, on the other hand, has no smoke flavor, even though it is partly pot-distilled malt, because the malt is dried in a closed kiln that is fired by coal or gas, and no smoke comes in contact with the malt. Irish whiskey has a subtle sweetness from the corn-based grain whiskey and a honey, toasty flavor from the barley and barley malt. Both scotch and Irish whiskey, however, have to be distilled at low temperatures in a pot still to avoid breaking the flavor links that provide their distinctive characters. Malted barley is important to all whiskey, and a certain amount of it is added to the mash of most whiskies around the world to get the fermentation process going.

American

On this side of the Atlantic, whiskey falls into two categories: straight or blended. Straight must be made from at least 51 percent of a grain, must not exceed 160 proof, must be aged in oak barrels for two years, and may only be diluted by water to no less than 80 proof. Blended whiskey is a combination of at least two or more 100-proof straight whiskeys blended with neutral spirits, grain spirits, or light whiskeys.

Straight whiskey is made in three styles: Bourbon, Tennessee, and Rye. Bourbon, which takes its name from Bourbon County, Kentucky, is made with a "mash" of grain that is ground or crushed before it's steeped in hot water, and then fermented. Two types of mash are used in bourbon: sweet mash, which employs fresh yeast to start fermentation; and sour mash, which combines a new batch of sweet mash with residual mash from the previous fermentation. Within the bourbon category, there are two distinctive styles: wheat and rye. Bourbon is made primarily with corn (up to but no more than 80 percent; higher than that and it must be labeled "corn whiskey"), but the remaining grain in the mash is either rye or wheat (and a small amount of barley malt to get the fermentation going). There is often great debate among bourbon makers over the question of which is better. If you're curious, sip Maker's Mark (wheat) and Jim Beam (rye) side by side. I am a wheat guy personally, but not to the extent that I would ever turn down a glass of good bourbon no matter what school the maker prefers.

Tennessee whiskey is similar to bourbon in almost every way, with the exception of the filtration process. Before the whiskey goes into the charred barrels to mature, it is slowly filtered through ten feet of sugar-maple charcoal. It takes from ten days to two weeks for a batch to pass through the charcoal, drop by drop. Jack Daniel's and George Dickel are two leading Tennessee sour-mash whiskies.

Rye is similar in taste to bourbon, but it possesses a decidedly spicy and slightly bitter flavor profile—like biting into a rye seed in rye bread. Though wheat and barley are commonly used to make rye whiskey, U.S. law mandates that it be made with a minimum of 51 percent rye.

STORING ALCOHOLIC BEVERAGES

Spirits that are 70 proof and above and liqueurs or cordials that are not dairy based can be stored at room temperature for an unlimited amount of time. Fortified wines like port, Madeira, and sherry should be refrigerated after opening. The sweetest wines will last up to four weeks when refrigerated. Vermouth and other aromatic fortified wines will last four weeks if kept refrigerated between uses and not left out for long periods. In all cases with wines of any type, refrigeration is crucial.

Belmont Breeze Punch.

Blended Versus Straight

Until the middle of the nineteenth century, whiskey was a straight unblended spirit with only water added to lower the alcohol strength. Sometimes it was bottled, but most often it was served right out of the barrel. At that time, whiskey consumption was confined to Ireland, Scotland, and the United States; in England it was considered the poor relation to fine French brandy, and the English found the malt scotch too strong in every way. All of that changed, however, when the phylloxera epidemic that wiped out Europe's grapes devastated Cognac in the 1880s. Scotch whiskey stepped up to the plate with the help of the Coffey still, which was able to produce a light, high-proof mixed-grain whiskey cheaply, and of Andrew Usher, a distiller from Edinburgh

who figured out a solution to the "too strong" complaint. Usher blended the light grain whiskey with the heavy malt whiskey to achieve a blended whiskey that had the good qualities of both spirits and could be produced with consistency at a very good price. Blending was further enhanced around this time when the grain-whiskey producers in Scotland discovered the sweetness of corn from their American cousins and started using it, too.

Blending in American whiskey was a result of Prohibition. Aged, straight whiskey inventory was nonexistent in the United States after Prohibition, and young whiskey was blended with older Canadian stocks until the production of aged straight whiskey could catch up to the market.

Whiskey in Cocktails

Really smoky scotches, like the Islay malts, are the hardest of all the whiskies to find a home for in cocktails, though it's not impossible: Gary Regan's Debonair Cocktail, matching ginger flavor with smoky scotch, is both successful and delicious. Blended scotch is a lot easier to integrate into a cocktail, and there are many classics that employ it successfully, like the Rob Roy, the Blood and Sand, and the Robbie Burns. American blended and straight whiskies are much more cocktail friendly and are found in sours, juleps, toddies, smashes, nogs, and

COCKTAIL TRIVIA

When you see the designation "100% Single Malt Scotch Whiskey," the whiskey is made with only malted barley, and the word "single" means the whiskey is the output of a single malt distillery in one season.

punches. I have explored some uncharted areas with American whiskey; see the Belmont Breeze and the Whiskey Peach Smash. Irish whiskey, because of its subtle and complex flavor profile, is another good mixer, but stay away from big tastes. I like to tinker gently, using dashes of flavor like Bénédictine or Peychaud's Bitters.

Value Brands

BLENDED SCOTCH
* Ambassador * Black and White * Grant's

SINGLE MALT SCOTCH
* Deanston 12 year * Aberlour Glenlivet 10 year
* Bowmore Legend

BOURBON
* Old Forester * Ancient Age
* Jim Beam * Benchmark

BLENDED AMERICAN
* Calvert * Four Roses
* Fleischmann's Preferred

RYE
* Jim Beam

CANADIAN
* Canadian Mist * Black Velvet

TENNESSEE
* George Dickel #8

IRISH
* Clontarf * Powers * Murphy's

Premium Brands

BLENDED SCOTCH
* Dewars * Cutty Sark
* Johnnie Walker
  Red & Black Label
* J & B
* Famous Grouse
* Chivas

SINGLE MALT SCOTCH
* The Glenlivet 12 year * Glenfiddich 12 year
* Highland Park 12 year * Macallan 12 year

BOURBON
* Wild Turkey 101 proof * Maker's Mark (Small Batch) * Old Forester Bonded * Old Rip VanWinkle Family Reserve 13 year * Jim Beam Black Label

BLENDED AMERICAN
* Seagram's Seven

RYE
* Wild Turkey Rye * Old Overholt

CANADIAN
* Canadian Club Classic 12 year * Seagram's VO
* Crown Royal * Tangle Ridge 10 year

TENNESSEE
* George Dickel Old #12 * Jack Daniel's Black

IRISH
* Bushmills * Jameson * Tullamore Dew

Super-Premium Brands

BLENDED SCOTCH
* Johnnie Walker Gold and Blue Label
* Chivas 18 year * Ballantine's 30 year
* J & B Ultima 86 proof

MALT SCOTCH
* Glenlivet 18 year * Macallan 18 & 21 year
* Bowmore 30 year * Bunnahabhain 1979
* Springbank Campbelton 1967

WHISKEY: SWEET OR SOUR MASH?

Sour mash is a designation that is used often to describe Tennessee whiskey, but actually most bourbon, too, is made by the sour-mash method. It's a fairly simple concept: A small amount of fermented mash is held back from the previous fermentation and added to the next batch. The sour-mash method ensures continuity in the yeast strain.

WHISKEY LINGO DISTILLED

* GRAIN NEUTRAL SPIRITS: Spirits distilled from mixed grain at above 190 proof and unaged.

* GRAIN SPIRITS: Spirits distilled from mixed grain at above 190 proof, then stored in oak containers instead of stainless steel, and bottled at not less than 80 proof.

* MALT SCOTCH: Aged in used oak barrels not less than three years, but in practice almost never less than five years, and usually between eight and fourteen years. Pot distilled from a mash of 100 percent malted barley, dried partially in peat-fired kilns for flavor. Made in Scotland.

* BLENDED SCOTCH: The malt and grain whiskies that are blended together must be aged in used oak barrels a minimum of three years. Blended from single-malt whiskies and mixed-grain whiskey made in Scotland. Distilled at less than 166.4 proof.

* IRISH WHISKEY: Made from a blend of triple-pot-distilled malted and unmalted barley whiskey and mixed-grain whiskey, mostly from wheat, oats, rye, and corn. Aged in used oak barrels a minimum of three years.

* CANADIAN: Aged in used oak barrels a minimum of three years. Distilled from mixed grains: rye, corn, wheat, and barley malt.

* BLENDED AMERICAN WHISKEY: A blend of at least 20 percent, 100-proof straight whiskey with neutral grain spirits, grain spirits, or other whiskies.

* AMERICAN LIGHT WHISKEY: Distilled between 160 and 190 proof and stored in new or used oak barrels.

* BOURBON: Aged in charred oak barrels for not less than two years. Made from a mash of 51 percent to 79 percent corn with wheat or rye and a small amount of malted barley. Distilled at not more than 160 proof.

* TENNESSEE WHISKEY: Aged in charred oak barrels a minimum of two years, but not usually bottled less than four to six years. Jack Daniel's makes a whiskey sold locally in Tennessee at only one year old. Made similar to bourbon with the exception of the charcoal filtration process.

* RYE: Aged in new charred oak barrels a minimum of two years, and made from a mash of 51 percent to 100 percent rye and/or malted rye.

* CORN (White Lightning): Aged in new or used oak barrels but sometimes just "rested" but not aged. Made from a mash of at least 80 percent corn.

* AMERICAN STRAIGHT WHISKEY: Rye, corn, and bourbon are American straights.

* BLENDED STRAIGHT: A blend of two or more straight whiskies.

BOURBON
* Booker's Small Batch 125.3 proof
* Blanton's Single Barrel 93 proof
* Pappy Van Winkle's Special Reserve 20 year 90.4 proof
* Woodford Reserve Single Barrel 90.4 proof
* Baker's Small Batch 107 proof
* Distiller's Masterpiece 18 year 99 proof

RYE
* Old Potrero Single Malt 123.5 proof

CANADIAN
* Crown Royal Special Reserve

TENNESSEE
* Gentleman Jack
* Jack Daniel's Single Barrel 90 proof
* George Dickel Special Barrel Reserve 86 proof

IRISH
* Black Bush
* Bushmills Malt 16 year Triple Wood
* Jameson Gold
* Tullamore Dew 12 year
* Midleton Very Rare
* Midleton 26 year

TEQUILA

Tequila is the distilled version of a drink originally made by the Aztecs in Mexico called *pulque,* which was made with the fermented sap of the maguey plant. Spanish conquistadores didn't much like pulque, so they introduced the Aztecs to the art of distilling. The first spirit to be produced from the maguey plant was called *vino mezcal,* and today the over-all category to which tequila belongs is known simply as *mezcal.*

Early mezcal was most likely a fairly rough spirit, not much better than pulque, just higher in proof. By the late eighteenth century, mezcal production was centered around the town of Tequila, where experimentation with different maguey types eventually led to the selection of the variety classified as Agave Tequilana Weber, known today as Blue Agave. Pulque, by the way, is still made in certain parts of Mexico by the ancestors of the Aztecs. Tequila, however, is produced only in and around the town of Tequila, in Mexico's Jalisco province. Mexican law decrees that in order to be classified tequila, the spirit must be produced from blue agave plants grown within a delineated region in the five Mexican states of Jalisco, Nayarit, Michoacán, Guanajuato, and Tamaulipas.

Tequila falls into two main categories: Mixto and 100 percent Blue Agave. Mixto is made from a mash of no less than 51 percent blue agave, with sugars from cane or other sources added during fermentation, and is often shipped in bulk and bottled elsewhere. Tequila designated 100 percent Blue Agave is distilled from the fermented sugars of the blue agave plants only, and it must be aged and bottled in Mexico. According to Mexican law, there are four types of tequila: blanco, joven abocado, reposado, and añejo. Blanco, also known as white, silver, or plata, can be mixto or 100 percent blue agave that is aged less the sixty days in wood and is usually stored in stainless-steel tanks during its resting period; this is the most common style of tequila. Tequila stamped joven abocado, also called gold, is a sort of non-category; it is almost always mixto tequila whose color does not come from aging, but from the addition of color and flavor, usually caramel. Reposado tequila, which means "rested" in Spanish, can also have color and flavor added, and is aged by law at least sixty days and up to a year in wood. Añejo, or aged, tequila is aged in wood for at least a year, more often longer. The best añejos, complex and elegant, are sometimes compared to fine Cognac.

The journey from mere plant to Cognac-like elixir begins with the heart, or *piña,* of the blue agave plant, which when separated from the outer leaves can weigh between fifty and one hundred pounds. The piñas, full of sweet juice called *aguamiel* ("honey water"), are taken to the distillery, where they are steamed or roasted in brick or concrete ovens for twenty-four to thirty-six hours (or in modern steel autoclaves that can cook the piña in seven hours) to extract their valuable sugar. The piñas rest and cool for another twenty-four hours, then are ground up or milled and washed to remove the remaining aguamiel for fermentation. During fermentation, the sugar level is tested and the important decision is made whether to add additional sugars to make mixto or to produce a 100 percent blue agave tequila. Distillation then takes place in either a pot still or a column still, depending on the producer, though handmade 100 percent blue agave tequilas are often distilled at lower temperatures in a pot still. Regardless, by law the tequila must pass through the still twice, the product of which results in a spirit with 55 percent alcohol that is ready for aging and subsequent rectifying with pure water to bring it to commercial proof, usually 80 proof.

MEZCAL: TEQUILA'S SIBLING

It's impossible to talk about tequila without mentioning mezcal. Mezcal is the Mexican spirit that was bottled with the infamous worm, or *gusano,* in the bottom of the bottle. Mezcal is produced mainly around the city of Oaxaca. Recently several premium and super-premium mezcals have been introduced to America, including Encantado and the Del Maguey village mezcals. Mezcal is made from a different type of agave than tequila; the primary source is the espadin species. But several other varieties of maguey are also used: pulque maguey and two wild varieties called maguey silvestre and maguey tobala. To confuse you even more: The word *mezcal* is used to define the over-all category, and tequila is a type of mezcal, but mezcal is not necessarily tequila.

Production of mezcal is almost the same as for tequila, with the exception of the cooking of the piñas. In mezcal production, the heat for the cooking comes from wood charcoal. And although the piñas do not come in direct contact with the charcoal, they are impregnated with the smoke during the baking process, which is a flavor that is apparent in the final product.

Tequila and Mezcal in Cocktails

Tequila is very mixable, combining easily with citrus and other fruit juices and with just tonic and ice. The vegetal character of tequila works well in savory drinks like the Bloody Mary and the traditional Tequila con Sangrita. Mezcal, on the other hand, is almost grappa-like in flavor, with a pronounced smokiness. The applications for mezcal in cocktails are more limited, but there are some good matches: Try ginger ale or ginger beer. Some tropical fruits, such as mango and passion fruit, work well. Mezcal is also good in strong coffee or espresso.

Value Brands (THE VALUE BRANDS ARE ALL MIXTO TEQUILAS)

* Pepe Lopez *Margaritaville * Capitán *Juarez

Premium Brands

* Cabo Wabo Blanco * Sauza Conmemorativo 4 year
* Sauza Hornitos (100% Blue Agave) * Cuervo Gold
* El Tesoro Silver (100% Blue Agave) * Herradura Silver

Super-Premium

* Patron Reposado & Añejo (100% Blue Agave)
* El Tesoro Reposado & Añejo (100% Blue Agave)
* Chinaco (100% Blue Agave) * Cuervo Tradicional
* Porfidio (100% Blue Agave)
* Sauza Tres Generaciones (100% Blue Agave)
* Tenoch

RUM

Historically, rum is the first spirit of the New World, initially produced in Brazil, Barbados, and Jamaica in the wake of Columbus's introduction of sugarcane to the West Indies in 1493. By the mid-eighteenth century, rum was being produced all over the Caribbean, in South America, and in New England, where it was the favorite spirit. The Rum Sling of that era (rum, sugar, water, and lemon juice) could have been in the running as the first example of an American cocktail, if only it had employed bitters.

Rum is made from molasses, sugarcane juice, or concentrated syrup made by reducing the free-run juice of the pressed sugarcane. There are three basic types of rum (well, actually four if we include the new flavored and spiced rums): **Light-bodied** rum, sometimes called white or silver, spends up to a year in barrels and is filtered before bottling, rendering it very subtle, such as Bacardi Light. **Medium-bodied** rum, sometimes called gold or amber, is richer and smoother in character as a result of the production of congeners (organic compounds produced during fermentation), or the addition of caramel, or occasionally through aging in wood barrels; fine examples include Mount Gay, Appleton Gold, and Bacardi 8. **Heavy-bodied** rum is a category shared by blended and colored dark rums like Myers's, Gosling's, and Bacardi Black, typically used in rum punches, and full-bodied, well-aged "brandy style" or sipping rums like Angostura 1824, Barbancourt 15 year, and Demerara El Dorada 25 year.

The new fourth category, spiced or aromatic rums, taste exactly as they're labeled because of the addition of spices or aromatics in the distillate. Flavored rums, however, were developed only a few years ago, with the introduction of spiced and coconut rums, and now they are surpassing vodka and gin in terms of flavor options. After the success of Bacardi Limón, several companies entered the flavor category aggressively. Cabana Boy, a maker of Trinidad rum bottled by White Rock Distillers of Maine, now offers eight flavored rums, and Cruzan Rum from St. Croix now offers seven flavors. Old standards like Malibu, Captain Morgan Spiced Rum, and Bacardi Spice are still best-sellers, too. Recently a new subcategory of juice-enhanced rums emerged with the release of Bacardi Tropico.

Value Brands

LIGHT
* Ron Castillo White, Puerto Rico
* Fernandes "Vat 19" White, Trinidad
* Rhum Barbancourt White, Haiti
* Angostura Old Oak White, Trinidad

MEDIUM OR GOLD
* Appleton Special Gold, Jamaica
* Palo Viejo Gold, Puerto Rico
* Fernandes "Vat 19" Gold, Trinidad
* Brugal Gold, Dominican Republic

HEAVY
* Coruba Dark, Jamaica
* Cruzan Estate Dark 2 year, St. Croix
* Fernandes Dark, Trinidad
* Ron Matusalem Classic Black Cuban Tradition, Florida

Premium Brands

LIGHT

* Bacardi Silver, Puerto Rico
* Bacardi Limón, Puerto Rico
* Mount Gay Premium White, Barbados
* Wray & Nephew White Overproof, Jamaica
* Rainbow Spirits White Rum
  (50 percent of Profits to AIDS Research)
* El Dorado White, Guiana

MEDIUM

* Mount Gay Eclipse, Jamaica
* Bacardi Gold, Puerto Rico
* Occumare, Venezuela
* Lemon Hart, Guiana and Trinidad
* Appleton Estate VX, Jamaica
* Barbancourt 3-Star 4 year, Haiti

HEAVY

* Bacardi 8 year, Puerto Rico
* Barbancourt Rum 5-Star 8 year, Haiti
* St. James Rhum Hors D'Age, Martinique
* Mount Gay Extra Old, Barbados
* British Navy Pusser's Rum, British Virgin Islands
* El Dorado 12 year, Guiana
* Myers's Dark, Jamaica
* Gosling's Black Seal, Bermuda (but made from
  rum purchased on other islands)

Super-Premium Brands

MEDIUM

* Rhum Barbancourt 15 year, Haiti
* Appleton Estate 21 year, Jamaica
* Sea Wynde, Jamaica
* Pyrat Cask 23, Anguilla
* Bacardi Reserve Baccarat Bottling, Puerto Rico
* Zaya 12 year Gran Reserva, Guatemala

HEAVY

* Angostura 1824, Trinidad
* Pyrat XO Reserve Planters Gold, Anguilla
* Pampero Rum Aniversario, Venezuela

Rum Around the World

* AUSTRALIA: Australia has been producing rum since the nineteenth century, making white, gold and black varieties. Stubbs white is one of the few brands that are exported to the United States.

* BARBADOS: Barbados rums are medium to heavy, led by Mount Gay Eclipse, the oldest and most well known, founded by Dr. William Gay in1663.

* BRITISH VIRGIN ISLANDS: Pusser's rum is the most famous brand, made with a blend of rums from Barbados, Trinidad, and Guyana. Its strong flavor blends well in punch-style drinks. The brand was created from the blend used by the British Navy from the eighteenth century until 1970, when run rations were discontinued.

* CUBA: Havana Club is the best example of Cuban rums, made from a blend of molasses and sugarcane juice in continuous stills and are sand filtered.

OVERPROOF RUM

"Overproof" rum is a potent spirit of 75 percent (that's 150 proof!) pure alcohol that is usually added as a float or a dash to finish a drink. Using overproof spirits of any kind without diluting can be very hard on the human body, but the overproof rums are especially powerful, as they are often of higher proof than other kindred spirits. They should *never* be used in cooking or around open flame.

* **DOMINICAN REPUBLIC:** These are just beginning to attract attention in the United States, mostly because they have been available for only a few years. The leaders are Brugal and Ron Bermudez.

* **GUIANA:** The rums of Guiana are medium to heavy in style, and much of the rum is sold for blending to companies like Lemon Hart in England, a tradition dating back to when the British Navy supplied every sailor with a ration of rum, made in Guiana and Trinidad.

* **HAITI:** Haiti is known primarily for Barbancourt, a wonderful sipping rum made with sugarcane juice instead of molasses. Aged eight to twelve years, it has a beautiful Cognac-like finish.

* **JAMAICA:** Jamaica is known for its heavier-bodied rums, made in a process similar to the sour-mash process employed in Tennessee whiskey production. The Wray & Nephew distillery, the largest in Jamaica, makes a range of medium rums and flavorful overproof rum under their own label and the Appleton label. Myers's Dark is a favorite in the United States and is the most important ingredient in Planter's Punch.

* **MARTINIQUE:** "Rhum" making in Martinique is influenced by French Cognac techniques, with sugarcane juice and molasses distilled in pot stills and aged in oak. Clément Rhum is one of the best from Martinique, but it is not easy to find. Rhum Vieux St. James is a full-bodied four-year-old that is much easier to find in this country.

* **PUERTO RICO:** Puerto Rico is the largest rum producer in the Caribbean, and Bacardi is the largest producer of rum in the world. Bacardi Silver is a good example, produced in a continuous still and charcoal filtered.

* **TRINIDAD:** Local producer Angostura has finally decided to produce rums under its own label, which happens to be one of the oldest continuous trademarked brands in existence. Look for Angostura Premium White as a terrific Daiquiri base.

* **U.S. VIRGIN ISLANDS:** Cruzan Rums are fine examples of the cocktail-friendly rums here, some of which are flavored. Of higher quality is Cruzan Estate Diamond, an older reserve aged four to ten years.

* **VENEZUELA:** Pampero makes the premier rums here, the best aged rum called Aniversario.

RUM: WHAT'S IN A NAME?

Where did rum get its name? One theory employs the Latin name for the species of grass we call sugarcane, *Saccharum officinarum*, both of which words end in "rum." The Spanish called it *ron*, the Swedes and Russians called it *rom*, the French called it *rhum*. The English, however, didn't mince words when they called rum "kill-devil." In his book *Rum, Romance, and Rebellion*, Charles William Taussig writes that the word *rum* was derived from the West Indian word *rumbullion*. But Anton Barty-King and Hugh Massel, authors of *Rum Yesterday and Today*, find the origin of the word in Chaucer, who writes of "a stormy people delitynge ever in rumbul..." Taussig cites a 1676 periodical describing the substance as *"made of sugar canes distilled; a hot, hellish and terrible liquor made on the island of Barbados."*

Rum in Cocktails

Though colonial America loved rum, the Revolutionary War and subsequent War of 1812 destroyed the rum industry here in the United States. It wasn't until Prohibition that we discovered rum again, but it wasn't in this country, it was in Cuba. Havana became *the* destination for bohemians, the well-heeled, and especially the Hollywood elite. The talented bartenders of Cuba were prolific in their rum creations, naming drinks after the stars, like the

Mary Pickford and the Dorothy (after Dorothy Gish). Ernest Hemingway's daiquiri at Havana's famous El Floridita Bar was christened the *Papa Doble* by a now famous barman named Constante Ribailagua, and it is still served to this day.

BRANDY

Brandy is a liquor distilled from wine or other fermented fruit juice. The name derives from the Dutch *brandewijn* ("burned wine"), referring to the technique of heating the wine during distillation. A number of subcategories fall under the broad definition of brandy, including fruit brandy, grappa, marc, pomace, and eau-de-vie (French for "water of life"). Eau-de-vie and fruit brandies can be made from almost any fruit. The finest grape brandies traditionally come from the two southwestern French regions of Cognac and Armagnac. Spain also produces some top-quality brandies, such as the Brandy de Jerez Solera Gran Reservas. And here in the United States, a surprising number of excellent examples come from several producers, including Bonny Doon, Carneros Alambic, Creekside Vineyards, and Germain-Robin.

Spanish Brandy

Spanish Brandy and Spanish sherry come from the Andalusia region of southwest Spain. Many of the towns in this area are qualified by the phrase "de la Frontera" because historically this was the frontier between Christian Europe and the Moors beyond. In the center of this area is the town of Jerez de la Frontera, settled by the Phoenicians, then the Greeks, Romans, Vandals, Goths, Moors, and finally Christians. The vineyards of this area prospered in ancient times, and though the Moors didn't drink alcohol, they developed an alembic still to distill alcohol for medicinal and cosmetic purposes. It is believed that the Moors, in fact, are responsible for the first distilling of any kind in Europe, in the town they called Sherisch, which later became the town of Jerez. (Note the similarity between *Sherisch* and *sherry*.) When the Spanish Christians recaptured the "frontier" in 1262 from the moors, they made wine to supply the large contingent of soldiers stationed there, and they also began to barrel wine for Spanish expeditions around the world. The wine was preserved for travel by the addition of alcohol distilled from grapes. This fortified wine, of course, came to be known as sherry.

Cognac

As early as the tenth century, English and Norse seamen came to this western region of France for salt. After repeated journeys they began to buy wine. Eventually, the wine was boiled down before the journey to save it from oxidation, economize on space, and avoid taxation, which was levied by bulk. The idea was to restore the wine to its original state by adding water after the journey. When Cognac was first distilled sometime after 1600, other brandies were already being produced in France. But until the invention of multiple distillation a century later, most brandy had to be doctored by herb and fruit flavors to hide its imperfections. Until the early nineteenth century, Cognac was shipped in barrel and aged and bottled at the destination. In the nineteenth century, the Cognac firms began to age and bottle the Cognac themselves.

The most common grape in Cognac is trebbiano, known in France as ugni blanc or Saint-Emilion. The wine produced is high in acid and low in alcohol, which gives Cognac its attractive flavor profile. The wine goes through a double-distillation process in an alembic or pot still, emerging as raw Cognac to be aged. Because the oak used for aging is so porous, an amount equivalent to what the French people consume on a yearly basis evaporates "to the heavens"; this loss due to the evaporation is romantically known as the angels' share. There are 175 Cognac firms that range in size from the small farmer to the multinational shipper. Each stage of blending is carried out slowly, so that the flavors of the Cognac marry properly. Rectification, which is the addition of distilled water, is done to bring the Cognac to its proper bottling strength. The *paradis* ("paradise") is the inner sanctum of the aging cellars, where the very oldest reserves, some from the mid-1800s, are kept. Vintage Cognac is uncommon but occasionally permitted by the French government under strict guidelines. Older, or *Three-Star,* Cognacs are labeled *V.S.* (Very Superior) and *V.S.O.P.* (Very Superior Old Pale). The terms *Extra* and *Reserve* usually indicate the oldest Cognacs produced by a particular house.

Cognac was there for the birth of the cocktail in Antoine Peychaud's apothecary shop, and it has been an important cocktail base ever since. Brandy, whiskey, and gin were the three base spirits for all the early cocktails, fancy cocktails, and crustas. The three were essentially the same ingredients: spirits, bitters, and a sweetener, usually curaçao. The difference was in the garnish and preparation. The original juleps were made with Cognac and peach-flavored brandy. All the Pousse Café and shamparelle recipes were topped with brandy. In the nineteenth century, many woke up to the brandy-based Morning Cocktail and went to bed with the Stinger. Before Prohibition, the Coffee Cocktail, made with brandy and port, was the after-dinner alcohol confection of choice. In recent years, Hennessy had some success when it promoted the Hennessy Martini. Cognac was well represented at the Rainbow Room with Between the Sheets, a revival cocktail that graced my menu for eleven years and sold well the whole time. Two years ago I was commissioned by Courvoisier to create a cocktail with their Millennium Cognac and made the best-tasting cocktail of my career: the aptly named Millennium Cocktail, using curaçao and pineapple juice.

THE SOLERA SYSTEM

Spanish brandies are aged in a particular way that distinguishes them from their French counterparts, using the *solera* system. Unlike Cognac and Armagnac, which age slowly in individual oak casks, Spanish brandy is moved through a series of oak casks arranged in rows on top of one another called *criaderas.* The bottom layer of this system is called the solera, and it contains the oldest brandies. The solera level is the last stop before bottling; the layer above the solera is called the first criadera, then the second criadera, etc. New brandy, after five years in oak, begins its trip through the casks at the top level. To move it through the criaderas, an equal amount is taken from each cask and transferred to the cask below. In this way, the new brandy is disciplined by the older brandy. The blending takes place horizontally as well, moving wine from the old barrels to even older barrels across the bottom row to ensure a good supply of very old wines for blending with the younger ones. In three years this system achieves an aging equivalent to that of brandy or Cognac held in individual casks for fifteen years.

Armagnac

The region is located in Gascony, in the southwestern part of France; the brandy known as Armagnac was first produced in the fifteenth century. As for Cognac, the grape variety used to make Armagnac is trebbiano, known in France as ugni blanc or Saint-Emilion. Other minor grapes used are picpoul, jurançon, and plant de grèce. The grapes are picked before they are fully ripe and mature to ensure high acidity, a key component in the finished product. The low-alcohol wine (9 to 10 percent) is immediately distilled in a continuous still, and all distillations must be completed by April 30 of the spring following the harvest.

Limousin oak and Tronçais oak are used for aging Armagnac, an element as important as the grapes or the soil in producing the distinctive flavor that makes Armagnac unique. Armagnac will continue to improve in oak for up to about fifty years, at which point the flavor of the fruit dries out. Once Armagnac reaches a desired age, which varies according to each house, it is put into glass demijohns covered with wicker to protect it from the light. Once the Armagnac goes into glass, like other spirits, it no longer changes. Armagnac may or may not be vintage dated. It may also be blended. If it is both vintage dated and blended, the vintage indicated will denote the youngest year in the blend. The designation of *Three Stars* on the label requires that the spirit age at least two years in wood; *V.S.O.P.,* at least four years in wood; *Extra,* at least five years in wood. The key element of Armagnac is not the vintage date but how long the Armagnac was aged in wood. Armagnac has a stronger flavor than Cognac or brandy, and it can't be substituted for all brandy cocktails. Armagnac would, however, enhance two brandy-based cocktails, the Alabazam and the D'Artagnan (see also pages 74 and 110).

Calvados

This dry apple brandy is a specialty of the Normandy region of France. The Calvados appellation comes from western Normandy and a small area east of Rouen. While apple brandy (called applejack in this country) is made in other parts of the world, Calvados is considered the best. It is made by double-distilling the fermented apple cider, then aging it in Limousin oak barrels for no less than one year, some as long as forty years. Truly good Calvados, however, should be aged between ten and fifteen years before it is considered drinkable.

Calvados does well in cocktails, especially the American applejack cocktails, like the Jack Rose. Frank Meier, the head bartender at the Ritz bar in the 1930s, has an impressive Calvados recipe in *The Artistry of Mixing Drinks* (1936) which he calls the Apple Jack Cocktail.

Other applications for Calvados include the trendy Sour Apple Martini, or with hot spiced cider, or in place of bourbon in the Apple Manhattan.

FORTIFIED AND AROMATIC WINES

Aromatic or flavored wines are one of the oldest alcoholic preparations known to man—Hippocrates, for example, steeped herbs and flowers in wine to make medicine in the fourth century B.C. In most cases, aromatic wines are fortified with grape spirit. Aromatic wine is highly processed, so the character of the base wine is not apparent in the finished product.

Vermouth

When it comes to cocktails, the most important of the aromatic wines is vermouth. The word *vermouth* comes from the German word *Wermut,* for wormwood. Wormwood-flavored wines are mentioned in the seventeenth century by Samuel Pepys in his diary. But Antonio Carpano of Turin, Italy, is credited with producing the first commercial vermouth in 1786, followed by the House of Cinzano, which was established in 1757 but didn't produce the Cinzano brand until several years later. The Martini & Rossi Company also participated in the pioneering of Vermouth, establishing Italian-style vermouths that were red and sweeter. In 1800, Joseph Noilly of Marseillan, France, introduced a new, white, dryer-style vermouth. Although Italian and French vermouth differ slightly, the basic formula consists of base wine and mistelle (sweetened grape juice and brandy) flavored with herbs, roots, bark, and flowers. The manufacturing process is fairly complex. Herbs and flavors are steeped in the base wine and in the brandy. After steeping, mistelle and brandy are blended mechanically in large vats. The mixture is blended, pasteurized, then refrigerated for two weeks to allow impurities to crystallize, then filtered and bottled.

Other flavored wines include Lillet, Dubonnet, Amer Picon, and Saint Raphael from France and Rosso Antico, Cocchi, Punt e Mes, Cynar, and Barolo Chinato from Italy. Chambéry, a premium dry vermouth from the French Alps, is made with a high-quality base wine and various mountain herbs, and it is the only vermouth with its own *appellation d'origine*.

Aromatic wines are found in the superstars of the cocktail world, the Martini and the Manhattan, and in countless other cocktails, modern and classic.

Sherry

Rupert Croft-Cooke, in his 1956 book *Sherry* writes, "There is sherry, and there are all other wines." Sherry is a versatile wine that fits the bill as an apéritif, a food wine, and a cocktail ingredient. Sherry is fermented like all wines, but after fermentation is complete there is an additional step in the production of sherry that separates it from other wines: It is fortified with unaged grape brandy. Like Spanish brandy, sherry is aged by the solera system. Though this fortified wine ranges widely in color, flavor, and sweetness, there are really only two distinct sherry categories: *fino* and *oloroso*. Fino is the drier style, on the surface of which a bacterium called *flor* is encouraged to grow (see below). Finos are lighter-bodied wines than oloroso because flor can't grow on a wine with alcohol content higher than 15.5 percent. And oloroso wines are fortified to 18 percent alcohol. Within the fino category are the nutty dry amontillado (aged six years after losing its flor); the darker, softer amontillado (aged even longer); and the driest fino manzanilla (uniquely pungent because it ages near the sea, in the town of Sanlúcar de Barrameda). Pale cream sherry is fino that has been sweetened.

Oloroso, fortified with up to 18 percent alcohol, is not protected by flor, and therefore is much darker in color, from gold to brown. There is a very thick, sweet style of oloroso that some consider a separate class unto itself, called Pedro Ximenez (the grape name), that is sometimes used as a flavoring additive in brandy and whiskey. Cream sherries are highly sweetened olorosos of less distinction and less age. Some olorosos are also known as amorosos, Old Brown, and East India. Palo Cortado is sort of a non-category of sherry varying from producer to producer. In Palo Cortado producers often blend the two contrasting styles of dry amontillado and oloroso.

Sherry predated the cocktail as a colonial favorite in drinks like the Sherry Flip, and in a housewives' summer cooler recipe called the Sherry Cobbler in the mid-nineteenth century. Two of my favorite cocktails, the Flame of Love and the Valencia, are both made with fino sherry, which is the driest, in place of vermouth.

The alcohol content for different sherries varies with great subtlety:
* Fino: 15–16 percent alcohol * Amontillado: 16–20 percent alcohol * Oloroso: 18–20 percent alcohol
* Pedro Ximenez: 20–24 percent alcohol

Port

Port is produced in the Douro Valley in Portugal from several varities of grape, including touriga, mourisco, and bastardo and some dark red varieties called the tintas, such as the tinta cao and the tinta francisca. The two basic categories of port are vintage port and wood port. Vintage ports are aged two years in oak barrels and then bottled and aged usually for a minimum of ten years, and often much longer—fifty or sixty years in a good vintage. The decision to produce a vintage port is made by the winemaker late in the season, between mid-September and mid-October, based on weather and the quality of the grapes.

The wood ports, which include the tawny, ruby, and white ports, are aged in the barrel until they are ready to drink and are blended and mixed almost the way sherry is in the solera. Ruby is aged usually for two years and is ready to drink as soon as it is bottled. Tawny ports can be aged for many years in oak barrels and blended from many vintages. The long barrel aging and occasional fining gives the older tawny a light golden color.

Fermentation is short—usually thirty-six to forty-eight hours—and is halted by the addition of brandy when the must reaches the proper level of sweetness. Port-style wines are produced in many countries, including the United States and Australia, but all true port is from Portugal.

Madeira

Madeira from the Portuguese island of the same name is similar to port and sherry in that it is also fortified with brandy. Madeira was popular in colonial America because it was the least expensive of the imported wines. There are four types of Madeira, determined by the degree of sweetness and named after the grapes from which they are produced. Beginning with the driest they are *Sercial,* with a pale golden color and a rich aroma; *Verdelho,* sweeter than the Sercial but still on the dry side; *Bual,* medium brown in color and sweeter than the other two; and *Malmsey* or *Malvasia,* the sweetest and biggest-bodied. Port and Madeira make a wonderful float for some punch and cobbler drinks.

CORDIALS AND LIQUEURS

The historical distinction between cordials, which are fruit-based, and liqueurs, which are herb-based, doesn't really exist anymore, and today the terms are interchangeable. How this happened is unclear, but what we do know is that the origins of liqueurs were developed in the thirteenth century by the Catalan chemist Arnáu de Vilanova, who experimented with distillation and with the extraction of plant essences by steeping in alcohol at the University of Montpellier. Like many intellectual pursuits during the Middle Ages, experiments with herb-infused spirits were conducted in monasteries, and many of the liqueurs created by the monks have survived to the present day, such as Bénédictine and Chartreuse. The Italians, in particular, excelled in the creation of fruit, nut, and herbal liqueurs; many of today's most popular brands of liqueurs are Italian, such as Amaretto, Strega, Tuaca, and Sambuca, to name only a few.

Liqueurs by definition are spirits flavored with between 2.5 percent and 40 percent sweetener whose flavorings may vary widely, including herbs, roots, fruits, nuts, and spices. The alcohol base can be derived from grain, grape, or other fruits or vegetables and may be flavored in four different ways: distillation, infusion, maceration, or percolation (see sidebar). Liqueurs should not be confused with fruit brandies, which are distilled from a mash of the fruit itself and are usually dry and high in proof. Some producers mistakenly label their liqueur products as brandies, like blackberry brandy or apricot brandy, when they are really not. Food colors are permitted in liqueurs, and some lesser brands of liqueurs use artificial flavors. The alcoholic strength of liqueurs is generally between 40 and 60 proof.

FOUR WAYS TO MAKE LIQUEUR

* **DISTILLATION** is the process of blending alcohol and flavoring agents together before distilling them.
* **INFUSION** is the steeping of mashed fruits or herbs in water or alcohol, often with the application of heat, then filtering the liquid and mixing it with neutral grain spirits and sugar.
* **MACERATION** is the steeping of herbs or fruits in alcohol, then filtering the liquid and mixing it with neutral spirits and sugar.
* **PERCOLATION** is like the process inside a coffeepot, circulating the alcohol through a container holding the materials from which the flavor is extracted over and over.

Amaretto

Though there's no doubt it was created in Saronno, Italy, a legend surrounds its creator. It is said that Bernardo Luini, a student of the Da Vinci school, was painting frescos at the Cathedral of Santa Maria della Grazie in Saronno and needed a model, so he used a poor, young woman who worked at the inn where he stayed. She showed her gratitude by making a sweet liqueur from almonds and apricots that is said to be the original recipe for what is surely one of Italy's most famous liqueurs.

Amaro

A category of Italian *digestivo* liqueurs and bitters, very few of which are exported to the United States. They are wonderful and complex and really do aid in digestion after a rich meal. I am glad to see a little movement in the category, no pun intended, with three products that are showing up at bars in many major cities. If you're fortunate enough to find them, try them in this order: Amaro Averna, a sweet and accessible bitter; Branca Menta, which is Fernet Branca blended with crème de menthe; and finally, when you begin to enjoy the complex layers of the flavor of bitters, make the leap to Fernet Branca, which is more bitter than sweet and is definitely an acquired taste.

Anisette

The oldest of the anis-based liqueurs and one of the fist liqueurs produced commercially. The pioneering spirit company Bols in Denmark began production of anisette in 1575.

Bénédictine and B & B

Bénédictine is the oldest of the liqueurs made on the Continent, beginning in 1510 in the Benedictine abbey of fecamp, when Dom Bernardo Vincelli first infused spirit with the secret formula of herbs. The area of Normandy around the abbey was swampy and malaria was prevalent. Later Dom Vincelli's elixir was used to prevent malaria, suggesting that one of the ingredients was bark of cinchona, the source of qui-

nine from the New World. Bénédictine was popular in the nineteenth and twentieth centuries, mixed with brandy or cognac, prompting the company to create B & B—a bottled brandy-and-Bénédictine mixture.

Berentzen's Apple Liqueur

A premium apple liqueur made in Germany that is getting a lot of notice because of the boom in apple drinks, such as the Sour Apple Martini. It mixes well with many other spirits, but it is a match made in heaven when mixed with bourbon (see Apple Martini, page 147).

Crème Liqueurs

A category of liqueurs flavored with fruits, flowers, herbs, and nuts. Despite their names, they don't contain any dairy products, but they are perceived to be creamy because of their heaviness on the palate. Today the most popular of the crèmes are cacao (white and dark), menthe (green and white), and banana.

Drambuie

A scotch-based proprietary liqueur made with heather honey. The actual formula remains a secret of the MacKinnon family, who have produced the spirit since Prince Charles Edward Stuart presented the recipe to them in 1746, in gratitude for their support in his failed bid to defeat the Duke of Cumberland and become the king of England. "Bonnie Prince Charlie," or the Young Pretender as he came to be nicknamed, spent the rest of his life of exile in Italy.

Galliano

A proprietary Italian herb liqueur based on grape eau-de-vie that is infused with a vanilla top note. The Harvey Wallbanger cocktail put Galliano on every American bar in the late 1960s: It consists of vodka and orange juice in a highball glass with a float of Galliano. The companion to Harvey quickly became the Freddie Fudpucker, a tequila version of the same drink.

Maraschino

A sweet, clear liqueur made from Marasca cherries and pits. The Italians have several brands of maraschino, two of which are widely available in the United States: Luxardo and Stock. Maraschino was a popular ingredient in early punches and cocktails, especially paired with Champagne; it is almost never taken straight. The Cuban bartenders added it to Daiquiris, and it is a primary ingredient in the famous Aviation cocktail. The floral nose of maraschino makes it a successful ingredient in cocktails that have a lighter, subtler flavor profile, working well with gin, Champagne, and light rums.

Peter Heering Cherry Heering, from Denmark, is almost entirely opposite in every way from its sister cherry liqueur. Made from local cherries, it is dark red with a bold taste that can stand up to the biggest flavors in cocktails, such as the Blood and Sand, where it is mixed with scotch, sweet vermouth, and orange juice.

Orange Liqueurs

These are for the most part listed under proprietary names. An exception is curaçao, the original orange liqueur made by the Bols company from the curaçao oranges that grow on the islands of the Lesser Antilles, off the coast of Venezuela. In the middle of the nineteenth century, when the cocktail was an emerging phenomenon, many of the first cocktails were a base spirit, such as gin, whiskey, or brandy, dashed with bitters and sweetened with curaçao. In the 1880s vermouth began to become more widely distributed, and it gradually took the place of curaçao as a sweetener in cocktails. By the turn of the century, curaçao was offered in many different colors to jazz up the look of cocktails like the Pousse Café. Cointreau is a proprietary version of orange curaçao that is often promoted to replace curaçao in cocktail recipes. Although the Dutch originally pioneered the orange liqueur, the French have several very successful versions, such as triple sec, a generic name now used by spirit companies around the world, and Grand Marnier, which is considered the aristocrat of the curaçao-based orange liqueurs. The Mexicans have jumped into the premium-orange-liqueur market with a product called Citrónge Orange Liqueur, which they are marketing heavily as *the* liqueur for the margarita. Finally, the Italians, who invented liqueurs and don't want to be left out, have introduced a relatively new product called GranGala Orange Liqueur.

Sambuca

An anise-and-elderberry-flavored herbal liqueur made in Italy. Sambuca Romana, a brand made for export only, rivals Amaretto di Saronno as the most widely enjoyed of all the Italian liqueurs in the United States. Sambuca is popular after dinner, often taken with coffee. Sambuca con Mosca, literally translated "Sambuca with flies," is the popular way of serving sambuca: "up" with three coffee beans floating like flies in the glass. Sambuca Romana Della Notte, a black version, was introduced several years ago, as was Opal Nera, which like the Della Notte is flavored and colored with elderberry. Although Sambuca Romana is by far the most popular version consumed the United States, in Italy the Sambuca Molinari reigns supreme.

Schnapps

A German and Dutch word that translates literally to "a snatch" but came to mean a shot of spirits. There's a whole category of less expensive flavored liqueurs called schnapps, preceded by the individual flavor names. DeKuyper pioneered this category with its wildly successful Peachtree Schnapps, which was embraced by the disco generation in cocktails like the Sex on the Beach (vodka, Peachtree, cranberry juice, and orange or pineapple) and the Fuzzy Navel (Peachtree and orange juice). I counted 118 different Peachtree Schnapps cocktails in a popular cocktail book, most of which I'd call entry level, overly sweet and mostly artificially flavored. Drinks made with schnapps are seldom taken straight, and in cocktails the schnapps needs to be offset by a sour ingredient to work well.

Ricard, Pernod, and Pastis

Their infamous predecessor, absinthe, is a grape-based distillate infused with flavors of anise, licorice, hyssop, melissa (a type of mint), coriander, veronica, chamomile, and other herbs, the most important of which is known as wormwood, or grand absinthe. Absinthe was banned in most countries because the wormwood oil used in its production contains thujone, which is classified as a convulsant poison that attacks the nervous system if taken in large doses. Nineteenth-century absinthe products were produced at a whopping 130 to 140 proof, which could poison anyone who drinks too much of it. The formula for the notorious liqueur was sold by a French national living in Switzerland to Henri-Louis Pernod in 1797, and by the mid-nineteenth century it was the most popular liqueur in the world. By the year 1919, however, absinthe had been outlawed by every nation except Spain and Portugal. Spain continued to make it under the name Absenta until 1985, when it was outlawed to qualify Spain for compliance with other EEC countries.

Enter the absinthe substitutes, Pernod (which tends toward anise in flavor and aroma) and Ricard (which tends toward licorice in flavor and aroma). Both are proprietary brands made in France—without any trace of wormwood oil, *merci*. They are readily available here, as are several brands of pastis, a liqueur flavored with both licorice and anise, from Marseilles. Another new arrival to the United States is Absente, developed by spirits maker Michel Roux, which at 110 proof is being marketed as almost absinthe, complete with the classic slotted spoon used in the nineteenth century to make the Absinthe Drip. Here in the United States, we have our own Absinthe wannabe produced in New Orleans called Herbsaint.

THE COCKTAIL PARTY BAR

DRINK DU JOUR

Feature a special drink or punch for when guests arrive; there's nothing more important than to get a drink in everyone's hand upon arrival. If you hire a bartender and staff, this won't be a problem, but you probably won't. To expedite those crucial arrival moments, feature a simple, special cocktail that you can prepare in bulk in advance—just enough for everyone to have one drink when they walk in. I like to put out a punch so that guests can serve themselves. This will allow me time to enjoy my guests after the initial cocktail has been served. If you're not sure that everyone wants an alcoholic punch, offer a nonalcoholic one to which each guest can add his or her own rum.

THE BAR TABLE

The placement of the bar table will help in the success of your gatherings. Choose a room that has easy flow in more than one direction and is a focal point of the party. In other words, it should be a place where you want everyone to congregate without getting into a traffic jam. Use a table large enough to accommodate the bar and some snacks; a six-foot table is ideal. Place the table so it is accessible from at least three sides; bar setup with plenty of access also invites your guests to help themselves and gives you more freedom to enjoy yourself. To encourage guests to use the bar, create some festive placards with sample cocktails and recipes on them. If you want, choose a cocktail that has a particular theme, history, or story surrounding it.

Cover the table with a festive cloth. Arrange the spirits and cocktail ingredients on trays in the center of the table so they are accessible from all sides. Have a selection of glassware at each end of the table; I typically offer martini glasses, rocks glasses, highball glasses, all-purpose wineglasses, and flutes for Champagne. If you'll be serving after-dinner drinks, put out cordial or snifter-style glasses, too.

Two condiment stations along with serving utensils, cocktail napkins, and stirrers should also be easily accessible. Also place ice buckets (covered) with tongs at each end of the table, and have a couple of cocktail shakers ready for a guest bartender to show off his skills. Finally, offer a soda and juice selection at either end of the table; use large bottles of soda unless you have a staff to replenish the small bottles.

STAFFING

Having a staff to assist you at your party doesn't need to be the privilege of the very wealthy. Hire a neighbor's son or daughter home from college to help with cleanup and replenishment; your helper will be happy to have the spending money, and you will enjoy the party much more. The helper need not handle the beverages, but rather can restock juices, mixes, glasses, and garnishes and remove dirty glassware. This will provide you with the leisure to mingle with your guests and be free of worry.

STOCKING

Spirits

Depending on you budget, choose one or two brands in each of the following spirit categories:

* Rum * Vodka * Gin * Blended scotch
* Triple Sec/Cointreau * Bourbon * Tequila
* Sweet and dry vermouth * Brandy or Cognac (optional) * Single-malt scotch (optional)

Apéritifs and Liqueurs

Choose two: * Dubonnet * Punt e Mes
* Lillet * Cinzano Bianco * Fino sherry * Campari
* Cynar * Amaretto * Sambuca * Grand Marnier
* Kahlúa * Baileys

Staples

* Sweet Vermouth * Dry Vermouth
* Triple Sec or Cointreau

Wine

For a cocktail party, figure one bottle for every seven or eight people. For a dinner party, however, have one bottle of wine for every three people. Consult your wine and spirits merchant for help in choosing a good cocktail-party wine. Provide three bottles of white for each one of red.

Beer

I like to serve a big American favorite like Budweiser and offer two or three micro-brews, such as Sierra Nevada or Anchor Steam. You should also stock a light beer and a nonalcoholic beer.

Flavorings and Condiments

Fee Brothers Orange Bitters * Angostura bitters * Grenadine * Tabasco sauce * Maraschino cherries * Worcestershire sauce * Cocktail olives and onions * Simple Syrup (page 206) * Peychaud's bitters (optional) * Tomolives

Juices

Orange juice * Grapefruit juice * Cranberry juice * Tomato juice * Pineapple juice * Tropical juice blends

Mixers

Club soda * Tonic water * Cola * 7-UP * Diet soda * Ginger ale * Ginger beer (optional, for the Moscow Mule fans; see page 155)

Fruits and Herbs for Garnish

Lemons * Limes * Oranges * Mint * Fresh pineapple for tropical drinks * Berries, tropical fruits, and melons (optional, for specialty cocktails)

Glassware

All-purpose wineglasses * Martini glasses * Rocks glasses * Highball glasses * Brandy snifters

Cocktail Tools

Long cocktail spoon * Two-part Boston shaker set (glass and metal) or a single-unit cobbler shaker with screw top * Cocktail strainer * Paring knife and cutting board * Funnel * Wine opener * Bottle and can openers * Muddler (optional; see page 62).

THE

TOOLS, TECHNIQUES, AND GARNISHES OF THE COCKTAIL

The difference between a gourmet chef and a plain old cook

is the expertise with which he uses his knives. The same

can be said about working behind the bar. But it's

about much more than knives (although they are

pretty important to a bartender). The most impor-

tant thing a bartender needs to know is how to

use the tools of the trade. Here's what I've

learned, and what you need to know.

THE SHAKER AND
OTHER TOOLS

The cocktail shaker evolved slowly with the addition of ice, fruits, and citrus juices to the simple cocktail and punch recipes of the 1860s. The earliest patent for a cocktail shaking apparatus I have been able to find was in 1872, documented in *Vintage Bar Ware,* by Steve Visakay (1997). What a wonderful Rube Goldberg invention it was, with six two-part shakers that fit into a wheel. The wheel was mounted on a spring-loaded plunger that the bartender pushed up and down in the motion of a butter churn, agitating the six shakers and their ingredients. I want one!

Since that first patent in 1872, the cocktail shaker has inspired hundreds of inventors to patent their unusual and unique versions, from penguin-shaped shakers to bell shapes that utilize the handle of the bell for shaking. In the 1870s, the U.S. Patent Office was flooded with shaker designs from hopeful inventors. The designs broke down into two basic styles: the Boston shaker and the cobbler shaker.

The Cobbler Shaker

The glamorous cobbler-style shaker is the one we associate with all those madcap cocktail drinkers in 1930s movies. They are usually all metal (often stainless steel, sometimes silver, rarely glass), with a top that has a smaller cap, which unscrews to reveal a strainer. The shaker is simplicity itself to use: Add ingredients, secure top and cap, shake, unscrew cap, and strain. The cobbler has been executed in hundreds of shapes and designs: Some are battery powered with an automatic mixing mecha-

THE METAL SHAKER

nism similar to contemporary blenders, and some have a divider down the middle walls for chilling without adding water. (Most of the latter have gone the way of the Edsel, since cocktails in fact *require* some water content.)

The Boston Shaker Set

The more mundane Boston shaker set takes a little more practice but offers more versatility than the cobbler style. It's also more fun to use. The choice of professional bartenders these days, it consists of two tumblers: one, about 26 to 30 ounces, is metal; the other, usually around 16 ounces, is glass. When the metal is placed on top of the glass, they fit snugly together to form a sealed container.

You may need to buy the pieces separately. First, find the 16-ounce portion, and look for glass with a "T" on the bottom; this stands for "tempered," which means it can be chilled to freezing then plunged into hot water without cracking. When shopping for the metal half, take your glass with you. Place the glass upright on a table and insert the metal portion upside-down into the glass. Use the heel of your palm to hit the bottom of the upturned metal shaker, creating a seal; you should be able to pick up the two parts as a single unit. If a seal doesn't form, shop around for a different shaker.

When mixing drinks, always assemble the ingredients in the glass part of the Boston shaker, and prepare the drink in front of your guests. The glass half of the shaker also allows you to see and control the amount of each ingredient used, though I recommend actual measuring. Add fresh juice first *before* the ice, because fresh lemon and lime juice are so concentrated that even slight overuse can ruin the drink. Next add the dashes, modifiers, and the base spirit, followed by the ice. Note: With drinks using only spirit ingredients, add the ice first, then the spirits.

Now take the metal half of the Boston shaker and place it over the glass while it is resting on the bar. Hold the glass firmly and make a seal by striking the upturned end of the metal half twice with the heel of your free hand. The shaker should seal so tightly that the whole assembly can be picked up as a single unit. If the metal and glass halves fail to seal properly (try lifting the unit by the metal top about a quarter inch off the bar) then there is a problem with one of the parts and it should be replaced.

After creating the seal, turn the whole assemblage over so that the glass is now on top and the metal half rests on the bar. Strike the upturned glass portion one more time with the heel of your palm to ensure a seal. Now grasp the unit with the metal half resting securely in the palm of one hand and the fingers of the other hand wrapped securely over the top of the glass half, giving you complete control of the unit. Shake hard with the glass half of the set on top; even if the seal were to break, the liquid would be mostly contained within the larger metal half, and there's less danger of splashing cocktail ingredients all over your guests. The shaking should sound like a machine gun; I shake most cocktails vigorously to a slow count of ten. Shake drinks that

ROLLING A DRINK

When making Bloody Marys and other drinks containing tomato juice, always shake them lightly or roll them. Rolling is pouring the drink back and forth between two shaker glasses. Shaking drinks containing tomato juice vigorously creates an unpleasant foamy consistency. I do, however, shake Bloody Bulls (a combination of beef broth and tomato juice), as the beef broth seems to thin the tomato juice enough to cut the cotton consistency that results from shaking tomato juice hard.

contain eggs longer and harder, to emulsify the egg. Hum the tune "Brazil" if you know it; it will give you the natural rhythm for shaking a cocktail. In the end, you want effervescence in a cocktail. A limp shake is a bad show; and shaking style does not come overnight. I've always secretly thought that being a bit of a ham is the secret to making a great cocktail.

After shaking, grasp the unit firmly in one hand with two fingers wrapped around the glass and two fingers wrapped around the metal, along with your thumb. Using the heel of your other hand, hit the top rim of the metal shaker sharply. This will break the seal. Keep in mind that pressure has built up inside the cold shaker, so breaking the seal can be difficult; if it doesn't work the first time, turn the whole unit slightly and try again.

Strainers

The final step in the preparation of a stirred or shaken cocktail is pouring and straining the drink into its proper glass, which should be done with style and flourish. There are two popular types of strainers used for cocktail service: The Hawthorn strainer (the one with the spring) and the julep

Clockwise from top: Waiter-style wine opener, channel knife, nutmeg grater, paring knife, kitchen knife, muddler, ice tong, can and bottle opener, citrus reamer.

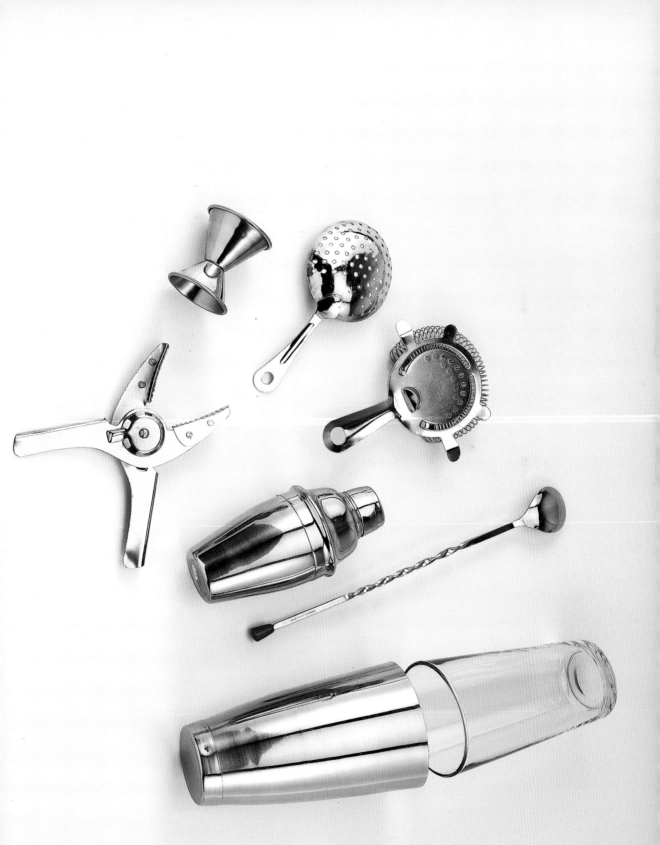

Clockwise from top: Double-sided measuring jigger, julep strainer, Hawthorn strainer, cocktail spoon, Boston shaker, cobbler shaker, hand citrus juicer.

strainer (the one with the holes), both of which are perfect companions for the Boston shaker set. The smaller julep strainer works efficiently with the glass portion of the shaker; and the Hawthorn, with its metal tabs around the edge designed to rest on the rim, works well with the metal part of the shaker. Be sure the Hawthorn strainer you purchase is round and has four tabs, rather than two, because the latter tends to fall into the shaker instead of sitting securely on top. Shaken drinks are usually strained from the metal half, and stirred drinks from the glass half.

Strain using only one hand. To strain from the metal half of the shaker, place the Hawthorn strainer on top, and put your forefinger and middle finger on top of the strainer while grabbing the shaker with your thumb, fourth, and little fingers (see page 52). Hold the metal shaker tightly and strain slowly at first to avoid splashing out of the glass. When straining into a martini or cocktail glass, pour liquid in a circular motion, delicately swirling around the insides of the glass (this will also help avoid spillage). The graceful circular motion slows down as you empty the glass shaker. For the last ounce, draw your hand up high over the middle of the cocktail glass, emptying the last of the liquid. The final motion should be a sharp snap of the wrist to punctuate the ceremony and draw attention to the drink.

To strain from the glass half of the shaker, place the julep strainer over the top of the glass with the concave side up. Grab the glass toward the top with the thumb and three fingers. Curl the forefinger over the handle of the strainer, holding it firmly in place. Strain following the directions above.

Jigger

You should have two, both of which should be stainless steel and feature two different cup sizes. One should have 1-ounce and 2-ounce cups, the other 3/4- and 1½-ounce cups. I still use them myself when I experiment so I can come up with exact recipes.

Long-Handled Cocktail Spoon

This is a standard cocktail spoon with a long, twisted stem that is invaluable for stirring drinks in a shaker. (There are also silver or heavy-duty cocktail spoons that will not bend, but manipulating them requires a different handhold.) For me, stirring a drink is one of those special ceremonies in life. William Powell, the actor and master Martini maker in the *Thin Man* movies, moved the stories forward with dialogue while stirring pitchers of Martinis. When I was stirring Martinis behind the busy bar at the Rainbow Room, I had moments when I would see the whole room in slow motion while I took my time stirring. It simply can't be rushed.

When making stirred drinks like Martinis and Manhattans, add dashes and small amounts first. This allows you to season the ice, as in the In & Out Martini, in which you season the ice with a little vermouth and toss the extra. Then add the base liquor.

Swizzles

The original nineteenth-century swizzle from Jamaica and other islands in the Greater and Lesser Antilles was a much more important tool than the ones we use here in America today. In fact, the swizzle was so distinguished that its name was given to an entire category of drinks. A swizzle is a thin, very

SHAKING VERSUS STIRRING

I have very specific opinions regarding stirring versus shaking: Drinks that contain spirits only—such as Martinis, Manhattans, and Rob Roys—should be stirred. Drinks that also contain fruit or citrus juice should be shaken. The difference between stirring and shaking is most noticeable in the look of the drink and the feel of the texture on your tongue. Shaking adds millions of air bubbles to a cocktail, which is fine for a cocktail like a Daiquiri or a Margarita; those concoctions should be effervescent and alive in the glass when you drink them. As Harry Craddock said in his *Savoy Cocktail Book* (1930), a cocktail should be consumed "quickly while it's laughing at you." Conversely, Martinis and Manhattans should have a cold, heavy, silky texture, not light and frothy. I always stir them. Mind you, shaking doesn't permanently change the flavor of gin or vodka; it temporarily fills the solution with air bubbles that change the texture on the tongue. After a minute, the bubbles will disperse and the drink will taste the same as if you had stirred it. But don't let me dissuade you. Enjoy your Martinis well shaken, if that's your pleasure.

Knives and Cutting Board

I travel with two knives that fulfill all my needs behind the bar: a four-inch paring knife with a wide, spear-point blade; and an eight-inch chef's knife. A paring knife is fine for most garnishes, but for special garnishes like pineapple or any larger fruits, a chef's knife is a must. Cutting boards come in many materials besides wood today, and some might be a better choice than wood. Kitchen-safety studies show the rubber-composition boards made by companies like Rubbermaid and Sani-Tuff are easier to clean and less likely to harbor bacteria. For the bar, there are two board sizes that come in handy: a small eight-by-six-inch for cutting small fruits, and a larger eighteen-by-twelve board for cutting pineapples and melons.

straight hardwood branch about 14 or 15 inches long that ends in a fork of three to five smaller branches that are cut off short. The drink Swizzle is attributed to the Georgetown Club in British Guiana, where the plantation owners gathered at the end of their day to "tell the government what to do next." It was prepared in a pitcher partially filled with crushed ice to which the local rum, fresh lime juice, and bitters were added. (The recipe is very dry and could be sweetened up with sugar syrup or orange curaçao.) The forked end of the swizzle was placed in the pitcher and rotated by rubbing it between the palms. It was very effective, almost like an electric blender, agitating and foaming an admirable drink. Today, the nineteenth-century swizzle is nearly impossible to find in the United States, but they are still sold in the markets in Trinidad and Jamaica.

Cut-Resistant Gloves

These gloves are flexible and thin, and they are a great idea if you're just gaining confidence with kitchen knives. Several companies make them, of which the two prominent are Food Handler (maker of BladeBlockers) and the R. H. Forschner Company (maker of the Shield.)

Corkscrew, Bottle Opener, and Can Opener

A corkscrew, cork extractor, or wine key should be chosen on the basis of ease of handling. Two other types are widely available: the winged corkscrew that you crank from the top, and the waiter's corkscrew that looks sort of like a switchblade knife. Screwpull is one of the leading manufacturers of cork extractors that are simple and easy to use and priced for all budgets. I highly recommend them.

Most beer bottles these days have twist-off tops—but not the ones you should pick up for your party. Have one of those double-sided openers on hand, with a bottle opener on one side and a can opener on the other, which will come in handy when it's time to open cans of pineapple juice to make a big batch of rum punch. Have I mentioned that I have a great rum punch recipe for you? See Planters Punch, page 177.

Top right: Straining a Manhattan from the glass half of the Boston Shaker using the julep strainer. Notice the grip of the hand holding the strainer. *Bottom left:* Creating the "Magic Sea" with a Boston shaker. *Bottom right:* Breaking the seal.

Piano Whip and French Whip or Whisk

The piano whip is a must if you are a fan of the coffee drinks; it has the thinnest-gauge wire of all the whips, and it can whip up a pint of heavy cream to the right consistency for Irish coffee in two minutes. I like to use a thick-wire "French" whip to extract juice from watermelons. The French whip has heavy-gauge wire and is stiff enough to break down the melon and release the juice.

Funnel

Talk about follow-up: You will need a funnel when it comes time to fill that decorative bottle with simple syrup. Bonus points: Try to find a funnel with a built-in strainer to help remove pips and pulp from citrus.

Channel Knife

The channel knife cuts a thin strip of peel from a lemon, lime, or orange to make a wonderfully decorative garnish. This is really an optional tool for the bartender who wants to get creative with spirals of citrus, but it is a must to re-create the Horse's Neck cocktail. Buy one that has a fat, ergonomically designed handle at a good kitchenware store. I recommend OXO brand.

JUICERS AND JUICING

Citrus Juicer

All of my recipes require lots of fresh juices, so if you don't yet have one, I must insist you get a citrus juicer. There are many shapes and sizes on the market, but I recommend one that is large enough to juice a grapefruit. There are several I like made of cast aluminum by two manufacturers, Artimetal and Rachaund, that have a large enough bowl to juice a grapefruit without making a mess. Inexpensive electric citrus juice extractors are not powerful enough, and power juicers like those made by Hamilton Beach and KitchenAid are pricey and really not necessary. A vegetable and fruit juicer is an extra indulgence if you enjoy exotic fruit-based cocktails with mango, papaya, and passion fruit juice that can't be squeezed with a juice extractor. The Bellini, for example, made with peach purée or juice and Champagne, is a good excuse to own a juicer. But expect to spend a minimum of one hundred dollars for a decent one.

Hints for Juicing

The first rule of thumb is always choosing fruit that is intended for juicing. They are fruits with the thinnest skin; if you have doubts, ask a good grocer for help. Also:

* Be sure to remove all agricultural stamps and stickers with the knife, by either pulling them off or scraping them away.

* Never refrigerate lemons, limes, or oranges that are meant for juicing, because cold fruit is stingy with juice. If the fruit is cold, soak it in warm water for fifteen or twenty minutes, then roll it under the palm of your hand across the counter to break the cells and release the juice. Follow these simple steps and you'll almost double the amount of juice you extract.

* Strain fruit juice through a fine strainer to remove seeds as well as pulp. Some people like fruit juice with lots of pulp, but it can present some problems with glassware, especially those washed in a dishwasher. The pulp becomes baked on the inside of the glass and, even though the glass is sterile, it looks dirty and is unusable. The glassware then has to be soaked in a soapy solution, and the pulp has to be removed with a hand brush.

* All juices should be stored in the refrigerator to safeguard against bacteria. Don't save lemon or lime juice overnight, as they become bitter and astringent. Fresh-squeezed orange juice and grapefruit juice, on the other hand, can be saved in the refrigerator for a few days, because they have a higher sugar content to preserve the flavor. However, remember that they are not pasteurized like commercial juice, and they will turn a lot faster.

Fruit for Daiquiris

Fresh-fruit daiquiris are usually prepared as frozen drinks, but they can also be prepared as "up" drinks. Strawberries, bananas, papayas, and mangos make wonderful drinks. They can be prepared ahead of time for a party and stored in simple syrup. Most fresh fruit will hold in the syrup for two or three days, but ideally they should be used the same day.

* STRAWBERRIES: Wash and remove the leaves, then cut into one-inch pieces. For each pint of strawberries, prepare a half-pint of simple syrup, combine, and store them covered in the refrigerator.

* BANANAS: Bananas are easy: They don't need any prepping, just remove the skin and cut them into one-inch slices right into the blender. But bananas need to be used right away; if you prep them and they start to turn, just freeze them.

* PAPAYA: Papayas can be skinned and cut into one-inch chunks right into the blender. They can also be stored in simple syrup, covered, in the refrigerator. Six Hawaiian papayas cut up can be stored in a quart of simple syrup.

* PASSION FRUIT: Fresh passion fruit is very tart and needs a lot of sweetening. It can be stored in simple syrup.

* MANGO: Peel and pit mango and cut into half-inch slices to avoid the stringy texture. Store in simple syrup or lemon juice, but use the same day.

* BERRIES: When buying berries, examine the package. If there are any bad ones on top, there will be twice as many below. At home, open the container and remove any mildewed fruit and refrigerate in an air-tight container (such as Tupperware). Don't wash the berries until just before using to avoid rot.

GARNISHES

I've always been amused by the definition of "garnish" in the dictionary as "something on or around food to add color or flavor." Beverage garnishes, I guess, don't make the cut. That's fine with me, because my definition of a cocktail garnish is something that adds both color *and* flavor. That thin sliver of dried lemon peel or the half wedge of brown lime that bobs to the surface of your drink is not garnish.

For me, there are two words that are paramount to garniture presentation: *bountiful* and *fresh*. A garnish should be chosen for size, beauty, and freshness. And when I say size, I am not implying bigger is better. A juice orange is not acceptable for garnishing because its skin is too thin. Then again, the large, thick-skinned navels that make wonderful garnishes are very stingy in the juice department—not to mention expensive. The orange must be just right. Preparation is important, too. That big beautiful navel can be butchered down to little chunks that retain nothing of the original shape and beauty of the whole fruit.

The first cocktail books, in the mid-nineteenth century, take a simple approach to the question of garnish. In his 1862 book, *The Bon Vivant's Companion, or How to Mix Drinks,* "Professor" Jerry Thomas instructs us to "dress" or "ornament the top with fresh fruits in season." Finding fresh fruit year-round was no easy task back then, so Thomas solved the problem by using dried fruit. He created a novel concoction called Burnt Brandy and Peach, prepared by burning Cognac and sugar together in a saucepan and pouring it over dried peaches. According to Thomas, it was "very popular in the Southern states, where it is sometimes used as a cure for diarrhea." (Thanks, Jerry.) These days, the long and short is: Buy whatever you can, whenever you can, as long as it's absolutely fresh.

Lemon and Lime Wedges

Wedges should be cut in the following way:

* Begin by cutting the ends, or poles, off of the fruit; cut about an eighth-inch nub off each end, being careful not to cut into the fruit.

* Cut in half lengthwise (through the poles) and lay the two halves face down on the cutting board.

* Holding one half at a time, make two cuts lengthwise, at a 45-degree angle, creating three wedges; then do the same with the other half. With larger fruit it's possible to get four wedges (instead of three) out of each half.

* Cut lemons will remain fresh for two days if covered with a damp cloth and refrigerated. Cut limes, however, oxidize quickly, turning the edges brown and unusable for garnishing after one day. (Use the day-old lime wedges for juicing and for muddling in drinks such as the Caipirinha.)

* Depending on the time of year and the source, lemons have more seeds than other times, so one more step is necessary: After the final cut, you'll notice that the seeds are generally gathered along the center line of the wedge. With a quick cut, remove that quarter-inch of seed-filled gutter.

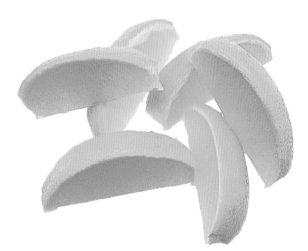

Lemon wedges for garnish.

Lemon quarters for muddling.

Lime wedges for garnish.

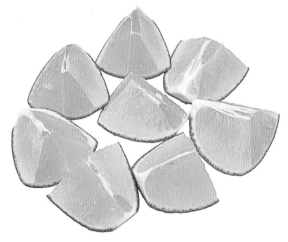

Lime quarters for muddling.

Pineapple wedges for garnish.

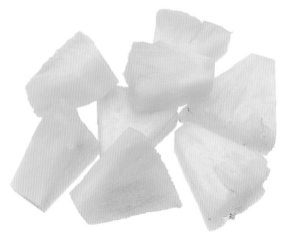

Pineapple chunks for muddling.

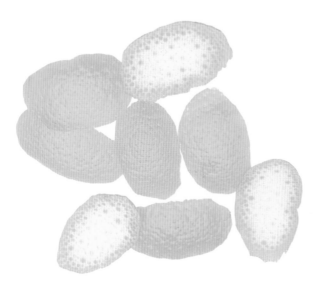

Lemon zest for flaming.

Orange zest for flaming.

Lemon zest spiral for garnish.

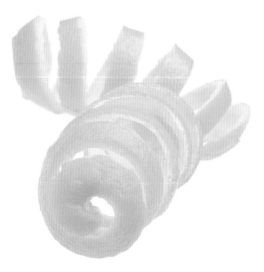

Horse's neck garnish.

Mint sprigs for garnish or muddling.

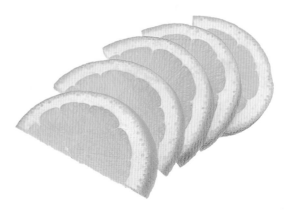

Orange slices for garnish.

Pineapple Wedges

Cut off both ends, then cut one-inch-thick slices crossways (through the equator, not pole to pole). Cut the slices into a wheel of eight wedges for garnishing.

Flaming Lemon and Orange Twists

The aroma and flavor in citrus fruit is concentrated in the oil cells of its peel. Chefs and bartenders often extract this oil along with the juice to add the essence of the fruit to various dishes and drinks. In cocktails, the oil in the citrus peel provides an additional advantage because it can be flamed.

* Always use firm, fresh fruit; the skin will have higher oil content.

* Use large, thick-skinned navel oranges and large lemons; ask your grocer for 95-count lemons (as opposed to juice lemons, which are 165 count).

* Cutting uniformly sized, thin oval peels that flame up well takes control, concentration, and practice. If you are just developing confidence and skill with kitchen knives, begin with this easier technique: First cut a half-inch nub off each end as described on page 55 for the wedges. Place the fruit on the cutting board with one of the poles resting on the board. Hold it firmly down on the cutting board and, using the paring knife, cut thin oval-shaped twists ¾ inch by 1½ inches long. The peel should be thin enough that the yellow shows all around the circumference with just a small amount of white pith visible in the center. This type of peel will maximize the amount of oil expressed into the drink and minimize the amount of bitter white pith on the

twist. Cut twists in a downward motion from the middle of the fruit down to the bottom, following the curve of the fruit and turning the fruit after each cut until you have circled the fruit completely. Then turn the fruit over and perform the same operation on the other half. Navel oranges should yield twelve to fifteen twists and large lemons ten to twelve twists. If the large 95-count lemons are not available, choose the largest lemons available and be sure the skin is fresh and firm; as the fruit dries out, the skin will feel softer and have much less oil.

There's another technique for cutting these types of twists that gives me more control and produces a more uniform twist consistently—the problem is I break a couple of the safety rules for handling knives. The technique is not dangerous—it just requires concentration. (To avoid accidents when practicing, use cut-resistant gloves.) Grasp the lemon or orange firmly in the palm of your hand with your fingers on the lower half so they will be well clear of the top surface, which you will be cutting. Begin at the top of the lemon and slowly and carefully draw the paring knife toward you, cutting a thin oval–shaped peel ¾ inch by 1½ inches long. Continue in this fashion, turning the lemon as you go so that you're always cutting along the top. This should yield ten to fifteen twists.

Now that you have the peels, you can create festive pyrotechnical displays for your guests with the oil present in the skin of lemons and oranges. To flame the oil:

* Hold a lit match in one hand, and pick up the twist in the other very carefully, as if holding an eggshell; if you squeeze the twist prematurely, the oil will be expelled.

* Hold the twist by the side, not the ends, between thumb and forefinger, skin side facing down, about four inches above the drink.

* Don't squeeze or you'll lose all the oil before you flame.

* Hold the match between the drink and the twist, closer to the twist. Snap the twist sharply, propelling the oil through the lit match and onto the surface of the drink. (Be sure to hold the twist far enough from the drink to avoid getting a smoky film on the glass.)

Lemon-Peel Spiral Garnish

Here's a fun and extravagant garnish used for drinks that are served in a tall, chimney-style glass, like the Horse's Neck and Gin Sling. You will need a channel knife, a tool with a flat piece of stainless steel punctured with a sharp hole, through which you can cut a small groove in the skin of the fruit, creating a long spiral length of lemon peel. Begin the same way as you would make peels above:

* Remove the small nubs at each end.

* Grasping the lemon in one hand, tool in the other, begin cutting at the pole farthest from you, in a line toward the other pole, maintaining steady downward pressure so the blade will cut into the maximum skin.

* When the cut is 1/4 inch long, turn the blade sharply to the left and cut in a downward spiral leaving a half-inch strip of peel on the fruit. Cut all the way to the other pole and end the cut as you began.

* The half-inch-wide spiral peel left on the lemon is the garnish for the Horse's Neck cocktail, and it has to be cut from the lemon. Take the paring knife and carefully cut the second spiral peel from the lemon, keeping the knife tilted slightly inward toward the fruit to avoid cutting through the peel.

* Store the peels in ice water and the spiral will tighten up and become springy. The thicker peel is the Horse's Neck garnish. The spiral garnish has to be placed in the glass before the ice and ingredients. Hook the curved end of the peel over the rim of the glass and drape the remaining peel in a spiral down inside the glass until it reaches the bottom. Hold the portion of the peel curled over the rim of the glass so it doesn't fall into the glass. The ice will hold the garnish in place.

The thinner spiral peel can be cut in shorter lengths and used on the rim of a champagne flute as a garnish for champagne cocktails. These same techniques can be applied as well to oranges and limes. The thinner peel will tighten into a spiral when stored in cold water. Curl it around a swizzle or a chopstick—whatever you have handy—in a nice tight spiral, then slide it off into a glass of ice water and let it stand for a half hour; it will tighten, creating another decorative garnish that can be cut in shorter sections and used on the rim of a glass.

Orange Slices for Garnish

* Choose fresh, thick-skinned navel oranges.

* Cut both ends off the orange; note that some oranges have an inch or more of pith before you actually reach the fruit. (Navel oranges at the pole often have skin up to an inch thick that has to be cut away before you reach the meat of the fruit.)

* Next, cut the orange in half lengthwise, through the poles, then place both halves flat-side down

on a cutting board and cut half-inch slices, following the line of the equator, not from pole to pole. (If your glassware is small, halve the slices into quarter-round pieces.) When you combine one of these orange slices with a maraschino cherry, you have the famous "flag," a popular garnish for Collinses and sours.

Mint and Other Herbs

Mint for garnishing has been a part of the American beverage since colonial times, when it appeared in the first brandy and peach-brandy juleps that were a signature early-American drink. When choosing mint for beverage applications, find springy young mint. Some varieties are more suited to garnish and beverage application. Avoid what I call the elephant-ear mint, with large floppy leaves; they look wilted on top of a drink. After muddling or shaking mint in a drink, strain the drink through the julep strainer to remove most of the bits of mint that are floating in the drink. It is not necessary to shred the mint when muddling, only to bruise the leaves to extract flavor. A mint garnish on top of a drink should look generous and bushy. Drinks garnished with mint should be served with straws.

Other useful herbs include pineapple sage, which has a wonderful aroma that would enhance lots of drinks like my Pineapple Julep, or even tropical drinks with pineapple as an ingredient. Black peppermint, besides adding a dramatic visual to a drink with its dark maroon stem veins, packs the most concentrated peppermint aroma of any in the category; try it with whiskey and sweeten with sugar or a liqueur like orange curaçao. Verbena and lemon verbena have dark green leaves that add a refreshing lemony note when muddled into citrus-based vodka, gin, and rum drinks. And borage, used in the famous Pimm's cup, has a cucumber aroma that would be a perfect partner to the quinine-based apéritifs of France and Italy.

For herb-flavored simple syrups, take a quarter cup (tightly packed) of the leaves of the herb you wish to infuse, and bruise them in the bottom of a ceramic bowl. Pour 1 cup of boiling water over the herbs and let steep for 30 minutes. It is fun to throw in some citrus peels for additional flavor. Strain and save the water and use it to make Simple Syrup (page 206). Simple Syrup can also be flavored by macerating different spices like cinnamon or vanilla. Drop two vanilla beans in a quart of Simple Syrup or four cinnamon sticks and refrigerate for a couple of days. Try your own flavored syrup with spices of your choice.

MUDDLE THIS OVER

Muddling is a constant theme running though the recipes in this book. (I even have an icon of a muddler next to the recipes that require muddling or that would be improved by muddling fruit or herbs as part of the preparation.) The standard muddler available at cocktail websites or in retail stores is not the same as the natural, hardwood muddler that I'm accustomed to using behind the bar; mine is made of hard fruitwood. What disturbs me about the new muddlers is that they are coated with a varnish that eventually wears off—right into your drink. Try to find the old-style natural-wood muddlers; or if you have a friend who lives in Brazil, have him send you one, as they are a common tool used to make the national drink, the Caipirinha. If you cannot find one, buy a thick wooden spoon instead.

Clockwise from top left: Cutting lemon zest for flaming, cutting horse's neck garnish, grating fresh nutmeg on a Brandy Alexander, muddling lime for a Caipirinha.

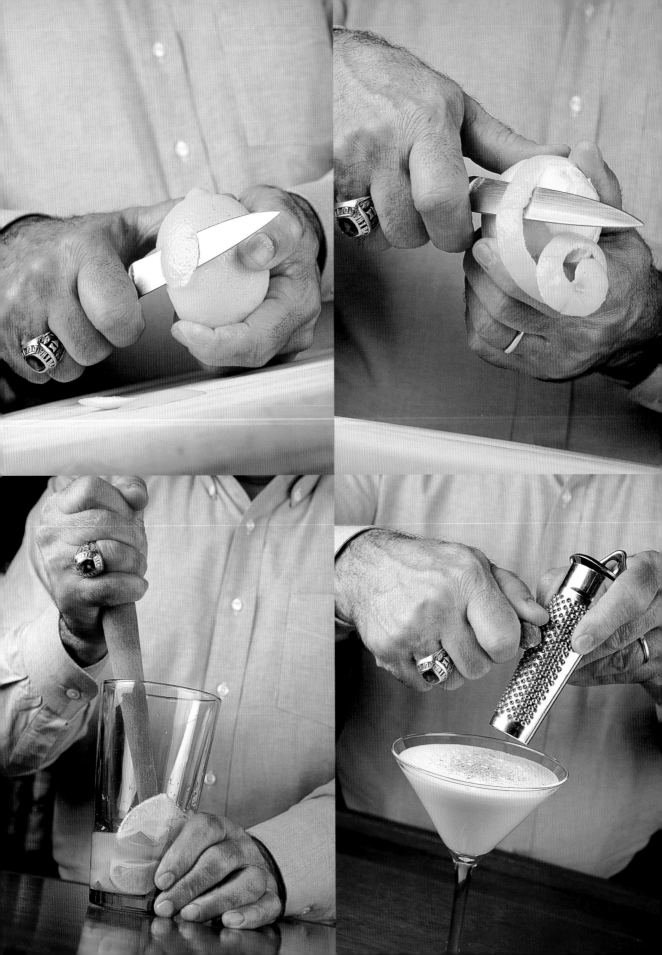

MUDDLING

The muddler, toddy stick, or squeezing stick (as it was called in the nineteenth century) is a mandatory tool for a *real* cocktail bar. I use it for everything— to release the oils in citrus rind into a drink, to open the veins of a mint leaf into a julep—and sometimes I even use the handle to crack ice cubes. A muddler should be at least six inches long to reach to the bottom of the mixing glass, and the flat, or blunt, end of the muddler is always positioned down in the glass. At home, a wooden spoon or the pestle half of a mortar-and-pestle set can do nicely in a pinch.

The style of drink making that I have evolved over the years relies heavily on fresh fruit juices and fresh fruit pieces muddled in the drinks. I have played with many shapes and sizes of fruit pieces for muddling, and have come up with some cuts that work well for the different fruits.

* **LEMONS AND LIMES:** Quarters work better here than the wedges used for garnish. Wash the fruit and cut the nubs from both poles, then cut the fruit in half through the equator. Place both halves face down on the cutting board and cut into four equal quarters. The quarters are more compact than wedges and are easier to muddle and mash in the bottom of a mixing glass.

* **ORANGES:** Because of their size, I muddle oranges in the slice form.

* **PINEAPPLE:** Cut off the rind and both ends. If you have a pineapple corer, remove the core; if not, cut one-inch-thick slices crossways (through the equator, not the pole). Cut the slices into a wheel of eight wedges, and use the pieces for muddling.

* **MANGOS:** Cut away or peel the skin, then cut around the large pit, making slices about one by two inches each.

There are two types of actions I perform with the muddler: muddling and bruising. I will just bruise soft fruits and herbs by muddling gently for a short time; the action of shaking with ice will do the rest of the job. With mint leaves, I don't want to tear them in tiny pieces because then they become difficult to strain out of the drink. Soft fruit, like mangos, I muddle very gently, then shake. And because I don't want a lot of pulp and fiber in my drinks, I strain from the glass portion of my Boston shaker using the julep strainer because it's more thorough.

Muddling can turn everyday drinks into something special. Even a drink as simple as the Rum and Coke can become something a little more interesting if you throw a slice of lemon and a slice of lime in the bottom of the highball glass with the rum. Mash it a couple times with your muddler or wooden spoon, then add the Coke. The oil from the skin of the fruit as well as the juice will add extra flavor to the drink.

GLASSWARE

Glassware needs today are far simpler than they were in the nineteenth century. In his 1888 book, *New and Improved Illustrated Bartender's Manual, or How to Mix Drinks of the Present Style,* Harry Johnson recommends six different wineglasses, five different beer glasses, and thirteen different drink glasses. Patrick Gavin Duffy's 1934 book, *The Official Mixer's Manual,* lists thirty-six vessels in his glassware chart. The advantage to using a great variety of glassware was that the portion of spirit, beer, or wine was often determined by the size and shape of the glass, leaving a smaller margin for error for waste on the part of the bartender. Today, the exact opposite is true: Glasses are often oversize, placing full responsibility for portion on the bartender's skill, precision—and generosity!

With regard to specific glasses for certain cocktails, such as the martini and the Irish coffee glass, I adhere to the old-fashioned idea of closely matching the glass size to portion size. Sure, there are times when an oversize glass is appropriate: An over-size Burgundy or Bordeaux glass adds elegance to wine service, and a scotch on the rocks looks and feels better in a double old-fashioned glass. However, there is no advantage to a 10- or 11-ounce martini glass. Although they may appear to be crowd pleasers, they are a losing proposition. The cocktail is intended to be a door opener at a cocktail party, a before-dinner appetite stimulant, not an evening-ender. Oversize cocktails also inhibit the classic bar etiquette of sending a friend a drink and then accepting one in return. If this happens before a meal, there will be no meal. Period.

The two most important considerations when purchasing a martini or cocktail glass are size and balance. If you keep in mind that many classic cocktail recipes are designed for 3- to 4-ounce cocktail glasses, you'll find that many glasses on the market are simply too big. When I was re-creating the classic bar at Aurora and the Rainbow Room, this was one of the most difficult obstacles I had to overcome. Converting classic recipes to fit an 8-ounce glass proved nearly impossible, especially with recipes containing volatile ingredients like fresh lemon or lime juice. I eventually switched to a 5.5-ounce glass, which at first garnered negative customer reactions. Eventually, though, check averages increased as people felt free to enjoy more than one drink. (Of course, this was not my intention, but the management was indeed happy.) I think a smaller glass is perceived as not only manageable but also elegant and classic, like the drinks I am serving in them. There's no reason why you shouldn't do the same at home.

For your home bar, you certainly don't need to purchase a dozen different glasses; five or six will do.

Dessert Wine and Cordials

* LONDON DOCK GLASS: A port or sauternes glass that will fill the bill for dessert wines as well as for fine spirits "neat" (without ice), and some special cocktails like the straight-up sours. The London docks were the clearing house for wine, sherry, and brandy from Portugal, Spain, France, and Maderia. The products arrived in barrels and in many cases were bottled in England. To determine the quality of the merchandise, the buyers would remove the bung

Red wine "balloon"

Red burgundy

White wine

London dock

Martini

Shot

Highball

Chimney

Rock or Old Fashioned

Brandy snifter

Whiskey tasting

Frappé

Champagne flute

Art Deco champagne flute

Nineteenth-century Absinthe glass

Irish coffee

Specialty glass

Hot Toddy mug

from barrels and taste. And the glasses they used were small stem glasses similar to port glasses called London dock.

* BRANDY SNIFTER: A nice addition to your collection, albeit optional, that can be used for quite a few specialty drinks. Many Cognac producers prefer a London dock–style glass for brandy, believing the snifter collects the strong alcoholic fumes and overpowers the delicate aroma of the brandy. But the snifter is a definite crowd pleaser, and therefore a better choice for your bar.

Pony, Pousse-Café, and Copita Glasses

* The pony looks like a miniature port glass, which is perfect because the classic Pony cocktail is only one ounce.
* The copita, the traditional Spanish sherry glass, is the same shape but slightly larger, 1.5 to 2 ounces. Both of these glasses are hard to find in bars and retail stores today, as they have fallen victim to the big guys.
* The pousse-café glass stands slightly taller, has straighter sides, and flares out at the top instead of inward.

Irish Coffee and Hot Drink Glasses

* If you're a big fan of coffee drinks, a classic Irish coffee glass with a tulip shape and medallion in the stem would be a good investment for esthetic as well as practical reasons. The classic Irish coffee glass is only 7 or 8 ounces, so after the whiskey and the brown-sugar syrup are poured in, there is room left in the glass only for the exact amount of coffee you need, then a nice

generous one-and-a-half-inch float of cream. The glass forces you to make a perfect drink.

Shots

Shot glasses are an extra you could easily do without, unless of course you are a fan of *los tres cuates* (the three chums): salt, lime, and tequila.

Pitchers, Bowls, and Cups

Group drinks served in pitchers, punch bowls, or any large container are a big part of home entertaining. I serve a rum punch at my Super Bowl party in a big plastic cooler, just like the one the winning team dumps over the head of the coach at the end of the game. And a premade cocktail by the pitcher can solve the problem of getting a drink into the hand of each guest upon arrival. I like to keep a couple of nice glass pitchers, between 32 and 46 ounces, on hand for parties.

Prepping Glassware

Always assume that your glassware is at least in need of polishing and probably in need of washing before use. That doesn't mean your day-to-day dinner glassware; we're talking about those special martini glasses and wineglasses that have probably been shelved for some time. Modern dishwashers with no-streak rinse products turn out sparkling glassware, but holding a glass up to the light can reveal streaks and cloudiness that will not enhance the look of a martini or a glass of Champagne. Polish glassware with a lint-free cloth (in a pinch, use paper towels). Chill martini and cocktail glasses by placing them in the freezer before a party, especially if the glasses are on the large side; it will really keep the drink colder. If your freezer can't accommodate several glasses, fill the glasses with ice cubes and water before use and they will chill up nicely.

Rimming a Glass

I sometimes shudder sitting at a bar and watching the bartender take the glass from which I will be drinking, turn it upside down, and dunk the rim into a container with some wet spongy material in it, then dip the rim into salt. The rim of the glass gets coated on the inside and the outside with salt, not to mention the mysterious wet stuff in the sponge. (Who knows if it has been changed recently?) When the drink goes in the glass, a half teaspoon of salt gets dissolved into the drink. Yuck.

Here's the right way to do it: Take a saucer or a small bowl and fill it with kosher salt; never use iodized salt for rimming glasses. Using a fresh lemon or lime wedge, carefully wet only the outside rim of the cocktail glass. Then, holding the glass so the stem is parallel to the bar surface, dab the rim into the salt while turning the glass slowly, until the whole circumference is covered with salt. Hold the glass over the sink or the trash container and tap the bowl of the glass gently to knock off the excess salt. The effect is a delicately salted rim that looks almost frosted. Tommy's Mexican Restaurant, a San Francisco restaurant that is famous for margaritas, has a clever tradition: They salt only half the rim of the glass so the drinker can go back and forth between the salted and the unsalted part of the rim. (Colored and flavored margarita salt is available online—see page 203). Use the same technique for a sugared rim, for drinks like the Sidecar. Do not try to sugar the rim of a frozen glass; as the glass warms, it sweats, and the sugar runs down the glass, making a sticky mess on its bowl and stem.

WHICH GLASS FOR WHICH DRINK?

must-haves

MARTINI: All "up" cocktails.

HIGHBALL: Highballs, soda, and beer.

ROCKS OR OLD FASHIONED GLASS: Spirits over ice, cocktails over ice, specials like the Mai Tai and Old Fashioned.

ALL-PURPOSE WINEGLASS: Red and white wine, frozen drinks.

LONDON DOCK OR PORT GLASS: Port, sauternes, fine spirits, and liqueurs neat.

CHAMPAGNE FLUTE: Champagne and Champagne cocktails.

optional glassware

SPECIALTY GLASS: Frozen drinks and tropical rum drinks.

PILSNER GLASS, PINT GLASS, OR STEIN: A must for the beer-drinking household.

IRISH COFFEE GLASS: All hot drinks.

BRANDY SNIFTER: London dock glass is a fine substitute, but not as good aesthetically.

SHOT GLASSES: For the crowd that enjoys shooters.

COLLINS OR CHIMNEY GLASS: Zombies, Tom Collinses, and Long Island Iced Teas.

BALLOON WINEGLASS: A must if big red wines are served regularly at your table.

SAUCER CHAMPAGNE GLASS: Great for Daiquiris, but not for Champagne.

PUNCH BOWL AND CUPS: A must if you have a holiday punch tradition or want to start one.

PART 2

COCKTAILS AND BAR TALES

EXPLANATORY NOTES

DRINK NAMES, RECIPE SEQUENCE, AND INDEX

Some drinks go by many different names. What one person calls a Bucks Fizz, another calls a Mimosa. It's usually a matter of opinion who's right or wrong, and often they are both right, and it's sometimes impossible to even guess. So I used the name that has the widest use and that's where you'll find the recipe.

In a similar vein, a given drink may make sense in more than one alphabetical order—should the Brandy Alexander be alphabetized as *Brandy* or *Alexander*? Should a Frozen Margarita be alphabetized at *Frozen?* Tough call.

And similarly, should a Dirty Martini, a Blood Orange Martini, and a Knickerbocker Martini be spread out all over the book? Should a Gin Fizz be separated from a Silver Fizz? No, I decided. So I created a number of special features—such as for Martinis, Fizzes, Bloody Mary variations, and Punches—to group together all the members of these tightly knit families.

All of which is to say that organizing and alphabetizing the drink recipes isn't as straightforward as you might think. So if you don't find something you're looking for, consult the index in the back of the book, either for the name or for a special ingredient; chances are that the recipe is in here somewhere, probably in a special feature.

RECIPE SIZES AND GLASSWARE

Straight Up

The "straight-up" recipes are between 3 and 4 ounces before shaking or stirring. Proper shaking or stirring should add 1 to 1½ ounces of water. Water is as important as any other ingredient to the flavor of a proper cocktail. With the water content, the "up" recipes are all designed to be served in a 5½- to 7-ounce cocktail or martini glass; the terms *cocktail glass* and *martini glass* are interchangeable.

Highballs

Highball recipes generally contain between 1½ and 2 ounces total alcohol.

On the Rocks

Drinks on the rocks should contain between 2 and 3 ounces of alcohol, with the Martinis and Manhattans in the upper range and spirits on the rocks in the lower range.

STANDARD GLASS SIZES

* JIGGER: 1½ ounces

* ROCKS/OLD FASHIONED: 6 to 10 ounces

* DOUBLE OLD FASHIONED/BUCKET/
MAI TAI: 10 to 14 ounces

* FIZZ OR DELMONICO: 6 to 8 ounces (note that
fizz drinks with cream and egg were served without ice
in this short highball-style glass)

* HIGHBALL: 10 to 12 ounces

* COLLINS/CHIMNEY: Tall, 12 to 14 ounces

* COCKTAIL/MARTINI: 5 to 7 ounces

* CHAMPAGNE FLUTE: 4 or 5 ounces

* MULTIPURPOSE WINE: 8 to 10 ounces
(note that wineglasses are seldom filled above the
half mark)

* LONDON DOCK/PORT/SAUTERNES:
5 to 7 ounces

* SHOOTER: ¾ to 1 ounce

* IRISH COFFEE: 6 to 8 ounces
(large Irish-coffee glasses promote overpouring of coffee and drowning the drink)

* EXOTIC/FROZEN: 12 to 16 ounces

* POUSSE CAFÉ: 1 to 3 ounces narrow with straight
sides and a flared top

* BRANDY SNIFTER: Snifters come in all sizes; the
standard range is 6 to 10 ounces, but larger 10- and
12-ounce snifters are often used for exotic drinks

FLAMING

Throughout the recipe library, I call for flamed orange and
lemon peels. This is a neat trick that was a regular part of
the drink service at the bar of the Rainbow Room. It
brought a little drama *and* added a wonderful burnt-orange
or -lemon flavor to the drinks. The technique is easy to
master: Just follow the instructions on page 58.

ABBEY COCKTAIL◆

To get this drink where I want it, I have already added the word "fresh" in front of the orange juice and changed the standard orange zest to a flamed orange peel. But for an even bigger flavor impact: Cut an orange slice or two and toss into the shaker before you add the other ingredients. Bruise the meat and the skin of the orange slices with a bar muddler or a wooden spoon, then add the other ingredients and the ice, and shake hard. Strain into a cocktail glass, then taste.

1¹/₂ ounces gin

³/₄ ounce Lillet Blonde

1 ounce fresh orange juice

Dash of Angostura or orange bitters

Flamed orange peel (see page 58), for garnish

Shake all the ingredients with ice and strain into a chilled cocktail glass. Garnish with the flamed orange peel.

Absinthe Drip.

ABC POUSSE CAFÉ

¹/₂ ounce Amaretto

¹/₂ ounce Baileys Irish Cream

¹/₂ ounce Cointreau

Layer in a pousse-café glass, beginning with the Amaretto on the bottom, and continuing in the order listed. You can also try this drink as a coffee drink. See Irish Coffee (page 127) for technique.

ABSINTHE DRIP

Although absinthe is illegal and no longer available, I have included this drink because there was a time in the nineteenth century when absinthe was the most widely used alcoholic beverage in the world. It was bottled between 131 proof and 150 proof. There is a product called Absente available on the market now that uses a type of wormwood called south-wood. Absente is sweeter than the original, and the drip-style preparation might make it too sweet.

2 ounces absinthe or Absente

1 to 2 lumps sugar

Put the absinthe and one large cube of ice into a good-size tumbler. Place an Absinthe spoon across the top of the glass with 1 to 2 lumps of sugar on it (the Absinthe spoon is a flat spoon with small holes). Now pour water drop by drop on the sugar. The water dropping through the spoon melts the sugar, sweetens the drink, and lowers the alcohol content.

ABSINTHE №2

Modified from *The Artistry of Mixing Drinks* (1936), by Frank Meier (of the Ritz Bar in Paris).

2 ounces gin

1 ounce Absente (absinthe substitute)

2 dashes of orange bitters

Stir the ingredients with ice and strain into a chilled martini glass.

ABSINTHE SUISSESSE

Drinks shaken with egg form a great-looking layer of foam on top and don't usually need a garnish, with the exception of a dusting of grated nutmeg or powdered cinnamon. But the flavor of this drink would be greatly enhanced with a little orange peel grated over the top.

1 ounce Absente (absinthe substitute)

1/4 ounce anisette

1/2 ounce green crème de menthe

1 ounce fresh egg white

Dash of orange flower water

Shake all ingredients very well, making sure to completely emulsify the egg white. Strain into a Marie Antoinette–style champagne glass or Cuban daiquiri glass.

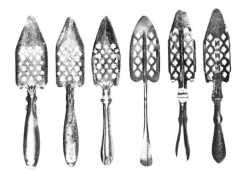

ABSOLUTELY BANANAS

David Thompson of the Capital Hotel in London won first prize with this drink in the first annual London Absolut Vodka Cocktail contest in 1996. Absolut sponsored the contest, so David was required to use vodka in this recipe. But I suspect it would work equally well with your favorite rum and a dash of Angostura bitters.

1 1/2 ounces vodka

1/2 ounce banana liqueur

1 1/2 ounces pineapple juice

Shake well with ice and strain into a chilled martini glass. If this cocktail is shaken very hard to a slow ten count, a handsome layer of foam from the pineapple juice will float on top of the drink and make a great presentation.

ADONIS COCKTAIL 11 * ◆

Named after a Broadway musical in 1884. The recipe for the Adonis as listed in most books is simply sherry, vermouth, and bitters, but this adaptation is far superior, with many more layers of flavor. Try muddling a section of fresh orange in the bar glass with syrup before adding the remaining ingredients; then shake.

1 ounce dry sherry

1 ounce sweet vermouth

1 ounce fresh orange juice

Dash of bitters

Dash of Simple Syrup

Orange peel, for garnish

Shake with ice and strain into a small cocktail glass. Garnish with the orange peel.

AGAVE PUNCH *

This formula will work with many spirits; just omit the tequila and use the spirit of your choice.

1 1/2 ounces 100% blue agave tequila

3/4 ounce fresh lemon juice

1/2 ounce Simple Syrup

2 ounces fresh orange juice

1/2 ounce ruby port

Orange slices, for garnish

2 dark grapes, for garnish

Shake the tequila, lemon juice, syrup, and orange juice with ice and strain into an iced stem glass. Top with the port. Garnish with the orange slice and grapes.

ALABAMA SLAMMER

3/4 ounce Southern Comfort

1 ounce vodka

3/4 ounce sloe gin

4 ounces fresh orange juice

6 dashes of grenadine, for garnish

Shake all ingredients hard with ice, strain into six 1-ounce shot glasses, and dash the top of each with grenadine. Bottoms up!

ALABAZAM ◆

This drink from *The Flowing Bowl,* by William Schmidt (1891), was frequently bottled for picnics in the nineteenth century. This drink also works well as a cocktail: Just shake and strain into a cocktail glass and omit the soda.

2 ounces brandy

³/4 ounce fresh lemon juice

1/2 ounce orange curaçao

1/2 ounce Simple Syrup

2 dashes of Angostura bitters

Soda water

Shake all the ingredients except the soda water with ice and serve in a tall glass with ice. Top with the soda and stir.

ALEXANDER

This may be served as a frappé:

1 ounce gin or brandy

1 ounce dark crème de cacao

2 ounces heavy cream

Pinch of nutmeg, for garnish

Shake the ingredients with ice and strain into a small cocktail glass. Garnish with the nutmeg.

ALGONQUIN

They served this at the famous Algonquin Hotel in New York City at some time in the past, but sadly you would probably get a blank stare from the bartender if you ordered one tonight at the hotel's Blue Bar. I served it with great success at the Rainbow for many years.

2 ounces light rum

1/2 ounce blackberry brandy

1/2 ounce Bénédictine

1/2 ounce fresh lime juice

Cherry, for garnish

Shake the ingredients with ice and strain into a small cocktail glass. Garnish with the cherry.

ALIZÉ COCKTAIL *

This is the classic sour formula with some new ingredients plugged into the three slots of sweet, sour, and strong.

1¹/2 ounces Alizé Red Passion

1 ounce apricot brandy

1 ounce fresh lemon juice

Cherry, for garnish

Shake the ingredients with ice and strain into a chilled cocktail glass. Garnish with the cherry.

ALLEGHENY

I found this in *The Ultimate A-to-Z Bar Guide,* and I include it with a thank you to Sharon Tyler Herbst and Ron Herbst. For extra flavor, muddle in a piece of lemon.

1 ounce bourbon

1 ounce dry vermouth

1/2 ounce blackberry brandy

1/2 ounce fresh lemon juice

Lemon peel, for garnish

Shake the ingredients well with ice and strain into a chilled cocktail glass. Garnish with lemon peel.

ALPHONSO COCKTAIL

This cocktail was served at the Deauville Resort in Normandy around 1920. The original recipe called for Secrestat Bitters, no longer produced.

1 sugar cube soaked with Angostura bitters

1 ounce Red Dubonnet

Champagne

Lemon peel, for garnish

Place the bitters-soaked sugar cube in a white wineglass with a couple of ice cubes. Add Dubonnet and fill with Champagne or other Sparkling wine. Garnish with lemon peel.

ALPHONSO XIII (DALE'S VERSION) ◆

I took this old standard of Dubonnet and sherry and played with it a bit to add some flavor.

1 slice of orange dusted with cinnamon

1¹/₂ ounces dry sherry

1¹/₂ ounces Red Dubonnet

Flamed orange peel (see page 58), for garnish

Muddle the orange slice and the sherry together in the bottom of a mixing glass. Add the Dubonnet and shake well with ice. Strain into chilled martini glass. Garnish with the flamed orange peel.

AMBER DREAM

This recipe is from *BarKeeper's Golden Book,* edited by O. Blunier (1935). When made with sweet vermouth, this is called the Club Cocktail.

2 ounces dry gin

1 ounce French dry vermouth

¹/₄ ounce yellow Chartreuse

Dash of orange bitters

Flamed orange peel (see page 58), for garnish

Place the ingredients in a bar glass with ice and stir. Garnish with the flamed orange peel.

AMERICAN BEAUTY

I don't know which came first, the rose or the cocktail, but they are both perfect.

1 ounce brandy

1 ounce dry vermouth

1 ounce fresh orange juice

2 dashes of grenadine

2 dashes of Simple Syrup (optional, for a sweeter drink)

¹/₂ ounce port

Rose petal (organically grown), for garnish

Shake all the ingredients except the port with ice and strain into a chilled cocktail glass. Float the port on top. Garnish with the rose petal.

AMERICANO HIGHBALL

This cocktail was bottled and sold around the world by Martini & Rossi in the 1890s. Note that most apéritif, sherry, and vermouth drinks should be served in stemware, but the Americano Highball should obviously be in a highball glass.

1¹/₂ ounces sweet vermouth

1¹/₂ ounces Campari

Soda water

Flamed orange peel (see page 58), for garnish

Pour the vermouth and Campari into an ice-filled highball glass and top with soda water. Garnish with the flamed orange peel.

THE AMERICANO AND ME

Soon after arriving in Los Angeles in 1978, I hopped into my 1969 Dodge Dart and drove out to the Hotel Bel-Air. Word was that a bartender position was available. The lounge was a big, almost square room with a baby grand piano slightly off center and a long narrow bar off to one side. A big red-faced Irishman, who appeared to be in his fifties, greeted me from behind the bar: Jim Kitchens, the head bartender. I told him I was interested in working . He asked me where I had worked and for how long; I'd been at Charley O's for a couple of years, which he was familiar with. He asked me to pick up a bottle and pour a shot, then quizzed me: "How do you make an Americano?" I told him, and he asked me if I could start the following day.

"You'll have to join the union, you know…"

"I'm a union man already," I told him.

No lie there; at the time I was a member of everything from Amalgamated Meat Cutters to Local 1 Bar & Restaurant Workers, SAG, AFTRA, and AEA. I couldn't believe my good fortune. My second day in Los Angeles, and I landed a job at the classiest bar in town. No application form, no interview, no résumé—just hired.

AÑEJO HIGHBALL *

I created the Añejo Highball as a tribute to the great bartenders of Cuba, in particular Constante Ribailagua, from Habana's Floridita bar, who created the Papa Doble Daiquiri for Ernest Hemingway. The Añejo evokes the spiciness of the Caribbean rum drinks; curaçao, lime, and rum are the holy trinity of the island-rum drink.

1¹/₂ ounces Añejo rum

¹/₂ ounce orange curaçao

2 ounces ginger beer

¹/₄ ounce fresh lime juice

2 dashes of Angostura bitters

Lime wheel, for garnish

Orange slice, for garnish

Build in a highball glass and fill with ginger beer. Garnish with the lime wheel and orange slice.

APPLE JACK COCKTAIL

Adapted from a recipe served at the Ritz Bar in Paris and published in *The Artistry of Mixing Drinks* by Frank Meier, 1936.

2 ounces Calvados or applejack

³/₄ ounce orange curaçao

¹/₂ ounce fresh lime juice

2 dashes of orange bitters

Apple slices, for garnish

Orange peel, for garnish

Shake all the ingredients with ice and strain into chilled martini glass. Garnish with a thin slice of apple and a strip of orange peel.

APRICOT COCKTAIL * ◆

I started playing with the recipe for a Bermuda Rose (gin, apricot, lime, and grenadine) and came up with my two apricot cocktails. Later I came across the Bermuda Cocktail (gin, dry vermouth, lime, grenadine, and curaçao) and the Bermuda Highball (gin, brandy, dry vermouth, and ginger ale). See also the Douglas Fairbanks for something similar; I guess he got jealous when Mary Pickford got her cocktail, so the Cuban bartenders named one after him, too. These two apricot cocktails are a good match for either sushi or tapas. When ripe mangos are available, muddle two or three pieces in the mixing glass before shaking the drinks. Strain out the muddled fruit.

1 ounce gin

1 ounce apricot brandy

1 ounce fresh orange juice

¹/₂ ounce fresh lemon juice

Cherry, for garnish

Flamed orange peel (see page 58), for garnish

Shake the ingredients well with ice and strain into a chilled martini glass. Garnish with a cherry and flamed orange peel.

APRICOT-MANGO MARTINI * ◆

I created this cocktail to be served with lobster ravioli with leek and red pepper sauce at a cocktail dinner with chef Andre Guerrero, at Linq Restaurant in Los Angeles.

2 pieces of fresh mango

2¹/₂ ounces Tanqueray No. Ten Gin

¹/₂ ounce apricot brandy

¹/₂ ounce Simple Syrup

³/₄ ounce fresh lemon juice

Muddle the fresh mango in the bottom of the mixing glass and add all other ingredients. Shake well with ice and strain into a chilled martini glass. Garnish with the lemon peel.

ANGEL'S KISS

"ANGEL" DRINKS ARE THE ORIGINAL SHOOTERS CREATED DURING THE JAZZ AGE. THE FOLLOWING RECIPES APPEAR AS ORIGINALLY DESIGNED— TO BE SERVED LAYERED IN A 1-OUNCE PONY GLASS. IF YOU WISH TO SERVE THIS DRINK IN A LARGER GLASS, THE RECIPE AMOUNTS NEED TO BE ADJUSTED UPWARD.

angel's kiss

Layering is achieved by pouring slowly over the back of a spoon held against the inside of the glass (see Pousse Café). The cream should be lightly whipped without sugar, as in an Irish coffee, and ladled on top.

1 part crème de cacao

1 part brandy

1 part cream, lightly whipped

Layer the ingredients in the order listed above in a pony glass.

angel's tip

1 part dark crème de cacao

1 part heavy cream

Layer in a pony or cordial glass beginning with the crème de cacao.

angel's tip

1 part crème de cacao

1 part heavy cream

Cherry, for garnish

Layer in a pony glass beginning with the crème de cacao. Spear the cherry with a cocktail pick or toothpick and rest across the mouth of the glass.

COCKTAILS WITH DINNER

Periodically, I team up with a chef friend and present a cocktail dinner of five or six courses paired with cocktails instead of wine. The Balm Cocktail (page 79) and the Bamboo Cocktail are sherry-based, lighter cocktails that I've used as a fine partner to a soup course in my cocktail dinners.

AQUEDUCT

I can't resist a drink named after a racetrack. Harry Johnson has another horsy drink called the Turf Cocktail in the 1888 edition of his *Bartender's Manual* with the following recipe: equal parts dry gin and vermouth with 3 dashes maraschino, 3 dashes orange bitters, and 3 dashed absinthe. Stir and serve up with an olive. Sounds very martini-like to me.

1½ ounces vodka

½ ounce Triple Sec

½ ounce apricot brandy

½ ounce fresh lime juice

Shake all ingredients with ice and strain into a chilled cocktail glass.

AVIATION COCKTAIL

The Internet cocktail crowd has breathed new life into this chestnut.

2 ounces gin

1 ounce maraschino liqueur

²/4 ounce fresh lemon juice

Flamed lemon peel (see page 58), for garnish

Shake all the ingredients with ice and strain into a chilled cocktail glass. Garnish with the flamed lemon peel.

B-52

This was one of the first floaters that came along with disco, and it is still one of the best. See Pousse Café for help with layering.

³/4 ounce Kahlúa

³/4 ounce Baileys Irish Cream

³/4 ounce Grand Marnier

Layer in a cordial glass in the listed order, starting with the Kahlúa.

BACARDI COCKTAIL

This was the Cosmopolitan of the thirties. Add orange juice and you have the Robson; add dry vermouth and you have Frank Meier's version from the Ritz Bar in Paris. My guess is Frank was being patriotic and wanted to get a French product in this popular cocktail. Johnny Brooks created the Cubanola by adding fresh orange juice, pineapple juice, and egg white to the regular Bacardi Cocktail with great success. Brooks worked at the famous Stork Club in New York City until it closed.

1½ ounces Bacardi Light

1 ounce fresh lemon juice

1 ounce Simple Syrup

3 dashes of grenadine

Shake all the ingredients with ice and strain into a small cocktail glass. Garnish with the flamed lemon zest.

BACARDI MARTINI

2 ounces Bacardi Silver

2 dashes of Angostura bitters

2 dashes of Martini & Rossi dry vermouth

Lime peel, for garnish

Stir the ingredients to chill and strain into a chilled martini glass. Garnish with the lime peel.

BAHAMA MAMA

³/4 ounce light rum

³/4 ounce añejo rum

³/4 ounce dark rum

½ ounce coconut liqueur

2 ounces fresh orange juice

3 ounces pineapple juice

¼ teaspoon grenadine

Dash of Angostura bitters

Maraschino cherry, for garnish

Pineapple slice, for garnish

Orange slice, for garnish

Shake all the ingredients with ice and strain into a large goblet or a specialty drink glass. Garnish with the Maraschino cherry, pineapple slice, and orange slice.

BAHÍA BREEZE *

Bahía means "bay" in Spanish. There's a drink called simply Bahía, by Trader Vic that is his version of a Piña Colada. The Bay Breeze, (vodka and pineapple with a float of cranberry) is a descendant, like the Sea Breeze, (vodka and grapefruit with a splash of cranberry) of the Cape Codder, a highball made with vodka and cranberry juice. The Madras, which rounds out the series, is vodka and orange juice with a float of cranberry.

1¹/₂ ounces Cuervo Gold

4 ounces pineapple juice

1¹/₂ ounces cranberry juice

Lime wedges, for garnish

Build in a highball glass over ice as listed above. Garnish with the wedge of lime.

BAKUNIN

Served at Pravda in New York, a beautiful bar with a Russian theme and more than a hundred vodkas and in-house infused vodkas.

1¹/₂ ounces Stolichnaya Ohranj

1 ounce Grand Marnier

2 ounces fresh orange juice

¹/₂ ounce fresh lemon juice

Dash of grenadine

Combine all the ingredients in a shaker. Shake well and serve over crushed ice.

BALM COCKTAIL

If you can find fresh lemon balm, shake a leaf with this cocktail and use as garnish.

2 ounces medium sherry (such as Dry Sack)

³/₄ ounce fresh orange juice

¹/₂ ounce Cointreau

2 dashes of Angostura bitters

2 orange slices

Flamed orange peel (see page 58), for garnish

Mix all the ingredients with the orange slices and shake well with ice. Strain into a chilled martini glass. Garnish with the flamed orange peel.

BANANA DAIQUIRI, FROZEN

I use only a small amount of banana liqueur and get the flavor from the fruit.

1 ounce light rum

1 ounce amber rum

³/₄ ounce fresh lime juice

2 ounces Simple Syrup

¹/₂ ounce banana liqueur

¹/₂ small banana

Blend the ingredients, reserving 1 slice of banana, with crushed ice and serve in a large goblet. Garnish with a slice of banana.

BANSHEE

A Grasshopper made with crème de banane instead of crème de menthe.

BARCELONA, FROZEN *

I created this for the James Beard House in New York City, during the Barcelona Olympics.

³/₄ ounce Spanish brandy

³/₄ ounce Dry Sack sherry

³/₄ ounce Cointreau

³/₄ ounce fresh orange juice

³/₄ ounce heavy cream

1 ounce Simple Syrup

Pinch of cinnamon, for garnish

Freeze in the blender with ³/₄ cup of ice. Serve in a London dock or sherry-style glass. Garnish with a light dusting of cinnamon.

BATIDAS FROZEN

These Brazilian milk shakes are made in many flavors; choose your favorite purée or nectar.

2 ounces cachaça

2 ounces tropical fruit purée or nectar

1 ounce sweetened condensed milk

1 ounce Simple Syrup

Lime wheel, for garnish

Blend all the ingredients with ice and serve in a stem glass, or shake with ice and strain into a rocks glass. Garnish with a lime wheel.

BEE'S KISS

Modified from a recipe from the Ritz Bar in Paris as printed in *The Artistry of Mixing Drinks,* by Frank Meier, 1936.

1¹/₂ ounces Bacardi

1 ounce heavy cream

³/₄ ounce Honey Syrup (page 206)

Shake all the ingredients with ice and strain into a chilled cocktail glass.

BEE'S KNEES

2 ounces gin

³/₄ ounce Honey Syrup (page 206)

¹/₂ ounce fresh lemon juice

Shake all the ingredients with ice and strain into a chilled cocktail glass.

THE BELMONT BREEZE*

When I set out to invent a great whiskey punch, I wanted to use a spirit that had significance to New Yorkers, so I chose rye whiskey, since New York has always been a big rye town. I also wanted a drink that would appeal to a wide audience, so I introduced a flavor to ameliorate the strength and bite of the rye: Harveys Bristol Cream Sherry. Then I finished the mix with a combo that forms the base of the most popular drinks in the last ten years, the Cosmopolitan's cranberry and citrus.

In 1997 I approached the New York Racing Association with this idea, and the Belmont Breeze was born. It has been served at the Triple Crown Race every year since—with, I dare say, great success. For a gallon of Belmont Breeze, combine the following ingredients in a punch bowl, decorate with seasonal fruits, and serve: 25 ounces Seagram's 7, 12 ounces Harveys Bristol Cream Sherry, 16 ounces Sweet and Sour, 24 ounces Fresh Orange Juice, 24 ounces Cranberry Juice, 16 ounces 7-UP, 16 ounces soda water.

THE BELLINI

The Bellini was invented by Giuseppe Cipriani in 1948, at Harry's Bar in Venice. Originally the drink was made only for four months of the year, when the sweet white peaches used for the purée were in season. But when the Cipriani empire spread to New York City, Giuseppe's son, Arrigo, found a flash-frozen peach purée that he could use year-round. Unfortunately, the purées are not widely available to the public, so it's hard to make the original Bellini unless you have a food processor to prepare your own.

BELLINI

1¹/₂ ounces white peach purée

3 ounces Prosecco or some other dry sparkling wine

¹/₂ ounce Marie Brizard peach liqueur

Put the peach purée in the bottom of a mixing glass without ice. Slowly pour in the prosecco while gently pulling the purée up the side of the mixing glass to mix with the prosecco. Don't stir briskly or the prosecco will lose its effervescence. Strain into a champagne flute. Float the peach liqueur on top.

BELMONT BREEZE *

1¹/₂ ounces rye whiskey

³/₄ ounce Harveys Bristol Cream Sherry

³/₄ ounce Simple Syrup

¹/₂ ounce fresh lemon juice

1¹/₂ ounces fresh orange juice

1 ounce cranberry juice

1 ounce 7-Up

1 ounce soda water

1 strawberry, for garnish

Mint sprig, for garnish

Lemon wheel, for garnish

Shake the liqueurs, syrup, and juices with ice and strain into a highball glass filled with ice. Top with the 7-Up and soda. Garnish with the strawberry, mint, and lemon.

BLACKBERRY JULEP *

This was my signature drink at Blackbird Bar and also the most popular. We used this berry sauce over the Baked Alaska for years at the Rainbow Room.

1¹/₂ ounces Marie Brizard blackberry liqueur

1 ounce fresh lemon juice

¹/₂ ounce Simple Syrup

1 tablespoon Mixed-Berry Marinade (see page 90)

Shake all the ingredients with 1 ounce of water and ice, and strain into a highball glass filled with crushed ice. Stir until the glass begins to frost. Garnish with the berries.

BETWEEN THE SHEETS

This drink is a relative of the Sidecar. There are other versions that omit Bénédictine and use rum instead, but two base spirits can confuse the palate; this version is more interesting.

1¹/₂ ounces brandy

¹/₂ ounce Bénédictine

¹/₂ ounce Cointreau

³/₄ ounce fresh lemon juice

Flamed orange peel (see page 58), for garnish

Shake all the ingredients with ice and strain into a chilled cocktail glass. Garnish with the orange peel. Optional: Rim the glass with sugar.

BLACK ROSE

1 dash of grenadine

2 dashes of Peychaud's bitters

2 ounces bourbon

Flamed lemon peel (see page 58), for garnish

Fill an old-fashioned glass three-quarters full with ice. Add the grenadine, bitters, and bourbon. Stir and garnish with the flamed lemon peel.

BLACK RUSSIAN

A classic. For a White Russian, add cream and shake.

1 ounce Kahlúa

1 ounce vodka

Build over ice in an old-fashioned glass. No garnish.

BLACKTHORN

This cocktail was created by the famous barman Harry Johnson.

2 1/2 ounces Irish whiskey

1/2 ounce dry vermouth

2 dashes of Angostura bitters

2 dashes of Pernod Fils

Flamed lemon peel (see page 58), for garnish

Stir all the ingredients with ice and strain into a chilled martini glass. Garnish with the flamed lemon peel.

BLACK VELVET

This unusual drink dates to the death of Queen Victoria's husband Prince Albert in 1861, which set off deep mourning. They even draped the Champagne in black for this recipe.

4 ounces Guinnes Stout

4 ounces Champagne

Slowly pour together equal parts of Guinness Stout and Champagne in a beer glass.

BLACK WIDOW *

This one completes the trilogy of Stinger and White Spider.

2 ounces Myers's rum

1 ounce white Crème de menthe

Shake both ingredients with ice and strain over ice into a rock glass.

BLAZER

Jerry Thomas's famous flaming drink is challenging and can be dangerous. Use large mugs with insulated handles and try pouring back and forth a few times with water to practice. Use mugs that are designed for hot liquids. If they are glass, look for the "T" on the bottom that indicates the glass is tempered. Finally, make a small amount for each batch to avoid spillage. And try it outdoors to avoid a chance of fire. Indoors, make it over a nonflammable surface. *Never attempt it at table.*

1 1/2 ounces scotch (warmed)

Splash of fresh lemon juice

1/4 ounce Simple Syrup

Lemon twist, for garnish

Warm two silver vessels (with insulated handles) with hot water. Leave 1 1/2 ounces of hot water in one and pour the scotch into the other. After warming the scotch, ignite it with a match. Pour the flaming scotch into the other vessel containing the hot water. Pour the flaming liquid back and forth a few times. Have a London dock glass prepared with lemon juice and Simple Syrup, and pour the flaming mixture into the glass. Garnish with the twist of lemon. Note: The scotch will not ignite unless it is sufficiently heated. Try warming it gently for less than a minute in a saucepan over a low flame.

BLOOD AND SAND

At first glance, this unusual cocktail seemed a godawful mix. But over time, I noted that the recipe appeared in some serious cocktail books, so I finally tried it. The taste convinced me never to judge a drink again without tasting it.

³/₄ ounce scotch

³/₄ ounce Cherry Heering

³/₄ ounce sweet vermouth

1 ounce fresh orange juice

Flamed orange peel (see page 58), for garnish

Shake all the ingredients well with ice and strain into a chilled cocktail glass. Garnish with the flamed orange peel.

BLOODHOUND *

*Modified from a recipe from *The Artistry of Mixing Drinks* by Frank Meier, 1936, the Bloodhound appears in many books throughout the twenties and thirties. This cocktail uses a technique I adopted at the Rainbow Room and perfected at Blackbird Bar: shaking different fresh fruits with the other ingredients of a cocktail. I added an additional step of mashing with a muddler and then shaking to extract more flavors. All kinds of seasonal fruits can be used in this manner.

¹/₂ ounce dry vermouth

2 ounce gin

¹/₂ ounce sweet vermouth

8 raspberries

Shake all the ingredients well with ice and strain well into a chilled martini glass.

BLOOD ORANGE COSMO

Created by Julie Reiner in New York City.

1¹/₂ ounces Stolichnaya Ohranj

¹/₂ ounce Triple Sec or Cointreau

¹/₄ ounce fresh lime juice

¹/₄ ounce fresh blood orange juice

Splash of cranberry juice

Orange slice, for garnish

Shake well with ice and serve in a chilled martini glass. Garnish with the orange.

BLOODY MARY

See pages 84–88.

BLUE HAWAIIAN, FROZEN

1 ounce light rum

1 ounce blue curaçao

1 ounce Coco Lopez

2 ounces pineapple juice

Pineapple slices, for garnish

Cherry, for garnish

Blend with 1 cup of cracked ice. Garnish with the fresh pineapple slice and the cherry.

BLUE MONDAY

From Harry Craddock's *Savoy Cocktail Book*, Blue Monday is one of the first vodka drinks to appear in a cocktail book, and that is really the most interesting thing about the drink. It calls for Cointreau and blue vegetable extract. I have taken the liberty of replacing the extract with blue curaçao.

1¹/₂ ounces vodka

¹/₂ ounce Cointreau

¹/₄ ounce blue curaçao

Flamed orange peel (see page 58), for garnish

Shake well with ice and strain into a chilled martini glass. Flame the orange peel over the glass.

BLUE TRAIN

1¹/₂ ounces gin

¹/₂ ounce Cointreau

¹/₄ ounce fresh lemon juice

Dash of blue curaçao

Flames orange peel (see page 58), for garnish

Shake well with ice and strain into a chilled martini glass. Flame the orange peel over the glass.

THE BLOODY MARY

THE BLOODY MARY IS LIKE THE BACKYARD BARBECUE: EVERYONE THINKS HIS IS THE BEST—AND OF COURSE I'M NO DIFFERENT. MY RULE AT THE BAR HAS BEEN TO APPEAL TO THE WIDEST POSSIBLE AUDIENCE WITH MY BLOODY MARY. FIRST, I DON'T DESTROY THE HEART OF THE DRINK, WHICH IS THE SWEETNESS OF THE TOMATO JUICE. TOO MUCH WORCESTERSHIRE OR HOT SAUCE WILL MAKE THE DRINK MUDDY AND TOO SPICY. LEMON JUICE IS A MUST WITH TOMATO JUICE, AND SO THE BLOODY MARY SHOULD ALWAYS HAVE A COUPLE OF SQUEEZES OF LEMON—A QUARTER OUNCE, IF YOU WANT TO BE EXACT. I THEN GARNISH WITH ANOTHER LEMON AND A LIME SLICE ON THE SIDE AND LET THE DRINKER DECIDE WHICH—IF EITHER—TO ADD ON HIS OR HER OWN.

The creation of the Bloody Mary in Paris is said to have coincided with the arrival of the first tins of tomato juice from the United States, right after World War I. Evidently, Frank Meier, head barman at the Ritz Bar, had been mixing his famous Tomato Juice Cocktail for years. But his recipe was missing one fundamental ingredient: booze! At Harry's American Bar in Paris, barman Ferdinand "Pete" Petiot made the Bloody Mary with vodka. The name, according to Duncan McElhone (son of Andy McElhone, the original storyteller and owner of Harry's), came into being because of the continued appearance at the bar of a woman named Mary, who was regularly left waiting for her man, nursing one of Pete's tomato cocktails. A comparison was made between the imprisonment of Mary, Queen of Scots, and young Mary's long, solitary hours at the bar.

Pete worked at Harry's from 1919 to 1936, until the Astor family, loyal customers of his, convinced him to head the bar staff at their St. Regis hotel in New York. When he arrived at the King Cole Bar, he introduced the drink to New Yorkers with gin, since vodka was not yet available in the United States, and changed the name to the Red Snapper at the behest of the Astors.

John Martin, grandson of Heublein founder Andrew Martin, used the drink as a vehicle to promote a new product, Smirnoff vodka in the 1960s. This led to an almost exclusive use of vodka in the drink, and helped to make it the de rigeur morning-after cocktail.

TOMATO JUICE COCKTAIL

In a shaker, crush one large ripe tomato. Add celery salt to taste and $1/2$ teaspoon of Worcestershire sauce. Shake well, strain into a double cocktail glass and serve

bloody mary

There's something about the Bloody Mary that makes people competitive. Every weekend bartender in America has his own, and of course, his is the best recipe in Western civilization. But this is *really* the best recipe. A dash of celery salt is a nice touch, and New Yorkers traditionally add horseradish. The Bloody Mary offers rich ground for improvisation both in garnish and ingredients. Have fun.

$1^{1}/_{2}$ ounces vodka

2 dashes of Worcestershire sauce

4 dashes of Tabasco sauce

Pinch of salt and pepper

$^{1}/_{4}$ ounce fresh lemon juice

4 ounces tomato juice

Combine all the ingredients in a mixing glass and roll back and forth to mix. Strain into a large goblet or pint glass three quarters filled with ice. Garnish with the lemon and lime wedges on a side plate.

bloody caesar

This Canadian import is a wonderful change from the ordinary.

Use the Bloody Mary (above), but omit the salt. Instead of regular tomato juice, use 3 ounces tomato with 2 ounces clam juice. Garnish by placing a fresh clam in an endive-leaf "boat" on a side plate.

bloody bull

$1^{1}/_{2}$ ounces vodka

Dash of fresh orange juice

4 dashes Tabasco

Dash of pepper

3 ounces beef broth

2 ounces tomato juice

Orange peel, for garnish

Combine all the ingredients in a mixing glass and shake well. Strain into a goblet or pint glass over ice. Garnish with the orange peel.

bull shot

$1^{1}/_{2}$ ounces vodka

Dash of orange juice

4 dashes of Tabasco sauce

Dash of pepper

4 ounces beef broth

Combine all the ingredients in a mixing glass and shake well. Strain into a goblet or pint glass over ice. Garnish with the orange peel.

bloody san *

The pickled Japanese vegetables used as a garnish can be found in Asian markets, in jars packed with vinegar.

2 ounces vodka

2 dashes Tabasco sauce

1 dash of Worcestershire sauce

$1/4$ ounce fresh lemon juice

Pinch of Wasabi mustard

4 ounces tomato juice

Dash of rice vinegar

1 ounce pickled Japanese vegetables, for garnish

Roll all the ingredients in a mixing glass with ice and strain into a goblet or pint glass. Garnish with the pickled Japanese vegetables.

bloody butrum

From my buddy Carl's kitchen, served at his infamous "Straight on 'til Morning" parties; prepared right after Chris Gillespie plays "Rhapsody in Blue," just in time for the sunrise.

2 ounces vodka

2 dashes of celery salt

Pinch of dry dill

2 dashes of ground pepper

2 dashes of Tabasco sauce

3 dashes of Worcestershire sauce

4 ounces Clamato juice

2 wedges lime

Build over ice and roll all ingredients in a mixing glass with ice, strain into a goblet or pint glass over ice.

bloody maria

Use the Bloody Mary recipe (page 86) but substitute Sangrita for the spicy tomato juice and tequila for the vodka. Garnish with a lime piece.

danish mary

Substitute Akvavit for vodka in the original Bloody Mary recipe (page 86). Garnish with a lemon piece and a giant caper berry on a side plate.

macho gazpacho

$1^{1}/_{2}$ ounces vodka or tequila

5 ounces puréed Gazpacho (page 89)

Garlic breadstick, for garnish

Red pepper spear, for garnish

Lemon wedge, for garnish

Combine the vodka and the purée ingredients and roll back and forth to mix. Pour into a goblet or pint glass over ice. Garnish with the garlic bread stick, red pepper spears, and lemon on a side plate.

red snapper

Substitute gin for the vodka in the Bloody Mary original recipe (page 86). Garnish with lemon and lime wedges on the side.

THE BLOODY
MARY BUFFET

SPIRITS

Vodka * Gin *
Tequila * Aquavit

SHELLFISH

Clams * Oysters * Shrimp

The shellfish should be presented
on a platter piled with crushed ice
and surrounded with lemon wedges.
Have tongs available for serving.

GLASSWARE: goblets * highballs

CRUDITÉS STATION with all raw and
pickled garnishes. Provide small bread
and butter dishes at this station. *
Radishes * Scallions * Olives * Cocktail
onions * Peppers * Baby fennel * Tomolives * Elephant caper berries * Endive *
daikon * A fresh horseradish root skinned and
cut for grating into the drinks. * Tall crudite
spears that can act as stirrers, celery, carrots,
and cucumber * Fresh potted herb plants—dill,
basil, oregano * Peppermills and salt cellars *
Dried fennel * Citrus wedges in bowls * Silver bowl
with ice to display spirits bottles * Bottled hot
sauces, including Tabasco and Worcestershire sauce.
* Large display basket of peppers, tomatoes, and
other fresh vegetables.

This is a wonderful brunch party featuring a buffet for preparing self-service Bloody Marys, stocked with all kinds of vegetables and shellfish for garnish. The simple tomato juice is augmented with several home-made vegetable juices. A variety of spirits is available for all the many variations on the theme.

You'll need a draped table about six feet by three feet. Build a double-sided display, with the different Bloody Mary juice mixes (see opposite) in carafes or pitchers presented in a bowl of ice in the center of the table. Create two garnish displays radiating to either side, so more guests can garnish at the same time. Also place an ice bucket with tongs or an ice scoop on each end of the table. Provide cocktail mixing sets, in this case the Boston shaker so the drinks can be poured back and forth to mix. Remember to place a trashcan at the table.

The guest takes a goblet and assembles a shot of the spirit of choice and then fills the glass to two thirds with the juice of choice. Now take one of the cocktail shaker sets and add four pieces of ice (more if they are small chips), then pour in the bloody mixture and roll back and forth *slowly and carefully* two or three times to mix. Return the mixture to the original goblet. Use a small bread-and-butter plate for garnish.

Note: All recipes are based on one 46-ounce can of tomato juice.

THE JUICE RECIPES

sangrita

1/4 cup puréed jalapeño

2 1/2 ounces fresh lime juice

5 ounces fresh orange juice

1 ounce grenadine

4 ounces Simple Syrup

46 ounces tomato juice

3/4 tablespoon kosher salt, plus more to taste

3/4 tablespoon ground white pepper, plus more to taste

Combine all the ingredients and mix well. Chill. Adjust seasonings, and serve with shots of tequila or as a Bloody Maria.

spicy tomato juice

2 1/2 ounces fresh lemon juice

2 teaspoons Tabasco sauce

1 teaspoon Worcestershire sauce

46 ounces tomato juice

Salt and pepper, to taste

Combine all the ingredients and mix well. Chill.

clam and tomato juice

For use in the Bloody Caesar Cocktail.

25 ounces fresh chilled clam juice

46 ounces tomato juice

Salt and pepper, to taste

Combine all the ingredients and mix well.

rainbow v-7 juice

Prepare with a juicer.

46 ounces tomato juice

4 ounces celery juice

4 ounces fresh carrot juice

4 ounces fresh green pepper juice

4 ounces fresh red pepper juice

2 ounces fresh onion juice

2 ounces fresh fennel juice

Salt and pepper, to taste

Combine all the ingredients and mix well. Chill.

green gazpacho

Use for the Macho Gazpacho cocktail.

3 large cucumbers, peeled and cut into small pieces

2 red onions, peeled and quartered

1/2 jalapeño pepper

1 bunch of scallions, stems removed

4 green bell peppers, stems removed and quartered

3 celery ribs, washed and cut into 1-inch pieces

1/2 bunch of watercress, washed and stems removed

1/2 small bunch of wheatgrass

1/2 small piece of gingerroot

Salt and pepper, to taste

Lemon juice, to taste

Lime juice, to taste

Combine small batches of vegetables in a food processor and purée until smooth. When all the vegetables are puréed, place in a large container and cover with 3 quarts of water. Let the mix stand refrigerated for 1 hour. In 1-quart batches, purée and strain the mix. Adjust the seasoning with salt and pepper, lemon juice, and lime juice.

BLUE LAGOON

³/₄ ounce white rum

³/₄ ounce dark rum

¹/₂ ounce blue curaçao

3 ounces fresh orange juice

3 ounces pineapple juice

Dash of Angostura bitters

Fresh fruit of choice, for garnish

Shake all the ingredients with ice and strain into a large goblet filled with ice. Garnish with fresh fruit of the season.

BOBBY BURNS

Frank Meier's version in *The Artistry of Mixing Drinks* (1936) calls for one part sweet and one part dry vermouth.

2 ounces scotch

1 ounce sweet vermouth

¹/₄ ounce Bénédictine

Shortbread cookies, for garnish

Stir all the ingredients with ice and strain into a chilled cocktail glass. Garnish with a shortbread cookie on the side.

BOCCI BALL

1¹/₂ ounces Amaretto

4 to 5 ounces fresh orange juice

Orange slice, for garnish

Build in a highball glass over ice. Garnish with the orange slice.

MIXED-BERRY MARINADE

Wash and dry a mixture of blueberries, strawberries, and black and red raspberries. Cut the strawberries into quarters. Marinate them for several hours in brandy, Cointreau, and sugar, stirring occasionally. For each pint of berries, use ¹/₂ ounce brandy, 1 ounce Cointreau, and ¹/₂ cup superfine bar sugar.

BOSOM CARESSER

³/₄ ounce fresh egg yolk

¹/₂ ounce Madeira

¹/₂ ounce brandy

¹/₂ ounce orange curaçao

2 dashes of grenadine

Freshly grated nutmeg, for dusting

Shake very well with ice to completely emulsify the egg. Strain into a chilled London dock glass. Dust with the nutmeg.

BOULEVARD

From G. Selmer Fougner of the *New York Sun*, 1935.

2 ounces rye whiskey

¹/₂ ounce Grand Marnier

¹/₂ ounce dry vermouth

Flamed orange peel (see page 58), for garnish

Stir with ice and strain into a chilled cocktail glass. Garnish with the flamed orange peel.

BOURBON CHERRIES

If you don't like the maraschino cherries called for in the Stone Fence and Stone Sour, try the following recipe from David Page and Barbara Shinn's book, *Recipes from Home*:

1 cup superfine sugar

3 pints black Montmorency cherries, stemmed

2 (1-liter) bottles of Kentucky bourbon

Place 2 tablespoons of the sugar and 3 tablespoons of water into each of 8 sterilized pint mason jars. Fill the mason jars with the cherries, packing them tightly but being careful not to crush them. Fill each jar with bourbon, leaving 1/2 inch of headroom. Seal the jars and shake them to dissolve the sugar. Store them in a dark place for 3 months.

BOURBON STONE SOUR

The expression "stone" or "California sour" has come to mean a sour with orange juice added.

1¹/₂ ounces bourbon

1 ounce Simple Syrup

³/₄ ounce fresh lemon juice

1 ounce fresh orange juice

Orange slice, for garnish

Cherry, for garnish

Shake all the ingredients with ice and strain into a rocks glass filled with ice. Garnish with the orange slice and cherry.

BRAMBLE

Created by the leading bartender in the U.K., Dick Bradsell.

1¹/₂ ounces gin

³/₄ ounce fresh lime juice

³/₄ ounce Simple Syrup

³/₄ ounce crème de mure (raspberry liqueur)

Lime wheel, for garnish

Raspberries, for garnish

Shake the gin, lime juice, and syrup well with ice, and strain into a highball filled with crushed ice. Dribble the crème de mure down through the ice, and garnish with lime wheel and raspberries.

BRANDY COCKTAIL

The original cocktails in Jerry Thomas's *The Bon-Vivant's Companion* or *How to Mix Drinks* (1862) were just called by the main spirit they contained—like this one. The word "fancy" was tacked on if a lemon peel garnish was used.

2 ounces brandy

¹/₂ ounce orange curaçao

2 dashes of Angostura bitters

2 dashes of Peychaud's bitters

Lemon peel, for garnish

Shake with ice and serve in a small cocktail glass. Garnish with the lemon peel.

BRANDY CRUSTA

See page 92.

BRANDY MILK PUNCH

To turn this into quick brandy eggnog by the glass, add a small egg and substitute heavy cream for one of the ounces of milk. I found a delicious version of this in *The Flowing Bowl* by Edward Spencer, called Arctic Regions and made with 4 ounces whole milk, 2 ounces sherry (medium to sweet), and 1 ounce brandy. Shake well with ice and serve over ice that's been dusted with cinnamon.

2 ounces brandy

1 ounce Simple Syrup

4 ounces milk

Shake with ice and serve in a punch glass. Dust with nutmeg.

BRANDY PLUSH

This drink is adapted from the 1862 edition of Jerry Thomas's *How to Mix Drinks*. See also White Tiger's Milk.

1¹/₂ ounces brandy

1 ounce Simple Syrup

4 dashes of Angostura bitters

4 ounces milk or cream

Freshly grated nutmeg, for dusting

Shake well with ice and strain into a chilled wine glass. Dust with the nutmeg.

BRASSY BLOND

Ty Wenzel created this drink while tending bar at Marion's in New York City.

2 ounces Stolichnaya Limonaya

2 ounces pineapple juice

¹/₄ ounce Cointreau

Shake well and strain into a chilled cocktail glass.

BRAVE BULL

1 ounce Kahlúa

1 ounce Tequila

Pour over ice in an old-fashioned glass. No garnish.

BREAKFAST MARTINI

Created at the Lanesborough Hotel in London, where Salvatore Calabrese—one of the true masters behind the bar—keeps the staff on their toes and the guests very happy. *Burke's Complete Cocktail and Drink Book* (1934) by Harman Burney Burke, has a variation called the Miami Cocktail made with gin as the base and sweet vermouth, orange juice, bitters, and marmalade.

1¹/₂ ounces Bombay Sapphire Gin

³/₄ ounce fresh lemon juice

³/₄ ounce Cointreau

1 teaspoon light marmalade
(not much rind)

1 slice toast

Shake all the ingredients with ice and strain into a chilled martini glass. Garnish with the slice of toast.

BRONX COCKTAIL

When the Waldorf-Astoria Hotel was just the Waldorf, and it stood where the Empire State Building stands today, it was the home of the famous Big Brass Rail, *the* watering hole for the robber barons of the late nineteenth and early twentieth centuries. It was also the home of Johnnie Solon, top barman of the day. Shortly after a trip to the newly opened Bronx Zoo, Johnnie invented the Bronx Cocktail for a guest, claiming it was impossible to discern any difference between the zoo and his bar.

1¹/₂ ounces gin

¹/₄ ounce sweet vermouth

¹/₄ ounce dry vermouth

1¹/₂ ounces fresh orange juice

Orange peel, for garnish

Shake all the ingredients with ice and strain into a large cocktail glass. Garnish with the orange peel. Dash of Angostura, optional.

BRANDY CRUSTA

Crustas were extra-fancy cocktails invented by Joseph Santina, who opened the Jewel of the South in 1852 on Gravier Street in New Orleans. (The name refers to the sugar crusted around the rim of the glass.) In a mixing glass combine 1¹/₂ ounces brandy, ¹/₄ ounce maraschino liqueur, ¹/₄ ounce Cointreau, ¹/₄ ounce fresh lemon juice, and lemon-peel spiral (see page 59) for garnish. Strain into a small cocktail glass with a lightly sugared rim (see page 67). Garnish with the spiral of lemon around the rim of the glass.

BROOKLYN COCKTAIL

2 ounces Canadian Club

1 ounce dry vermouth

Dash of maraschino liqueur

Dash of Amer Picon

Lemon peel, for garnish

Shake all the ingredients with ice and strain into a chilled cocktail glass. Garnish with the lemon peel.

BROWN DERBY COCKTAIL

This cocktail is from the Vendome Club, Hollywood, 1930, and is named after the famous hat-shaped restaurant on Wilshire Boulevard that opened in 1926. The restaurant is gone, but the hat still stands.

2 ounces bourbon

1 ounce fresh grapefruit juice

1/2 ounce Honey Syrup (page 206)

Shake well with ice and strain into a cocktail glass.

CAFÉ BRULÔT

Created at Brennan's in New Orleans in the 1920s. Special Sheffield-silver-lined equipment exists to withstand the flaming brandy, but a simple chafing dish and metal ladle will do.

1 cup VS Cognac brandy

4 ounces orange curaçao

12 cloves

2 whole orange peels cut in one piece with very little pith (see spiral-cut peel, page 59)

6 teaspoons granulated sugar

2 cinnamon sticks

1 liter strong French-roast coffee, flavored with chicory if available

1 1/2 ounces overproof rum

Mix the brandy, curaçao, 6 of the cloves, 1 of the orange peels, and sugar in a bowl. Break up the cinnamon sticks and drop them in. Let stand for several hours prior to serving. Prepare the second spiral-cut orange peel by studding it with the remaining 6 cloves.

Pour the prepared mixture into the Café Brulôt bowl or chafing dish. Prepare the coffee and keep it hot. Thread one end of the clove-studded orange-peel spiral through a serving fork and set it aside.

If you are using a chafing dish, light the fuel to warm the mixture. If you are using the brulôt apparatus, pour the rum in the tray below the bowl and light it. CAUTION: Use no more rum than called for, and keep the bottle in another area; it is extremely flammable. When the mixture warms up, ladle a small amount and expose it to the flame, and use it to ignite the rest of the mixture in the bowl. Pick up the fork with the orange peel and position it over the center of the bowl with the spiral dangling into the mixture. Using the ladle, slowly pour the flaming brandy over the peel. The oil in the peel will provide a nice light show. Do this a couple of times, then pour the coffee slowly into the bowl until fire is extinguished. Serve in demitasse cups. If the flame is difficult to extinguish, place a large dinner plate over the bowl briefly.

THE BUD IN THE BUD HERRMANN HIGHBALL

BUD HERRMANN HIGHBALL

2 ounces Metaxa 5-Star Brandy

4 ounces club soda

Build in a highball glass.

When I started working at the Hotel Bel-Air, Bud Herrmann, a very talented piano player, presided over the lounge, where he had played for eighteen years. He was also master of ceremonies and a matchmaker in business as well as affairs of the heart. It is said that a good friend and customer who made a sizable fortune through an introduction made by Bud awarded him with an apartment building in Hollywood.

In the 1940s, Bud met Benny Goodman at Bugsy Siegel's Flamingo Club in Las Vegas. At the time, while Goodman was playing in the main showroom, Bud would stand in the wings to listen to the show. One night Goodman, having just fired his regular piano player, invited Bud to sit in. Later Goodman asked Bud how he liked "the seat"—meaning at the piano—and Bud said he liked it just fine. "Well," said Goodman, "it's yours if you want it." So Bud traveled with the Goodman band for the several months.

Years later, while Bud was visiting New York, he returned a bag that Goodman had left at his house in Los Angeles many years earlier. Inside it was the tape of a 1936 Carnegie Hall concert—the only tape in existence, recorded with a single microphone over the stage at the first jazz concert ever played at Carnegie Hall. Today, it is considered to be one of the greatest jazz recordings in history.

After Bud died, the lounge at the Bel-Air was never the same, and the change prompted my departure. In honor of Bud, I'm listing his favorite and only drink, the Bud Herrmann Highball. I can still see the shots of Metaxa lined up on the piano, sent by guests in the room. Some nights Bud didn't get to half of them, but that didn't matter to people; they just wanted to buy them and see them up there. That's the bar business.

BULL'S BLOOD

3/4 ounce rum

3/4 ounce orange curaçao

3/4 ounce Spanish brandy

1 1/2 ounces fresh orange juice

Flamed orange peel (see page 58), for garnish

Shake all the ingredients with ice and strain into a cocktail glass. Garnish with the flamed orange peel.

CAPE COD

1½ ounces vodka

Cranberry juice

Lime wedge, for garnish

Combine the vodka and cranberry juice in a highball glass with ice. Garnish with the lime wedge.

CARIBBEAN BULLDOG *

1 ounce Kahlúa

1 ounce Caribbean Cream

2 ounces milk or half-and-half

4 ounces Coca-Cola

Build the first three ingredients over ice in a tall glass. Add the Coca-Cola and stir gently. Serve with long straws.

CARIBE COSMOPOLITAN *

1½ ounces Bacardi Limón

1 ounce cranberry juice

1 ounce Cointreau

½ ounce fresh lime juice

Flamed orange peel (see page 58), for garnish

Shake all the ingredients with ice and strain into a chilled martini glass. Garnish with the flamed orange peel.

BROWN DERBY COCKTAIL
½ Whisky
¼ Grapefruit Juice
¼ Honey
Shake well and strain into cocktail glass.

CARICATURE COCKTAIL

Created by Gary and Mardee Regan for my wife, Jill, who loves to capture unsuspecting victims with her caricature pen. Most of the victims are delighted; this cocktail will appease those who are not.

2 ounces gin

½ ounce sweet vermouth

½ ounce Campari

1 ounce fresh grapefruit juice

1 ounce Simple Syrup

Flamed orange peel (see page 58), for garnish

Shake all the ingredients over ice and strain into a very large chilled cocktail glass. Garnish with the flamed orange peel.

CASINO ROYALE *

1 ounce gin

1 ounce fresh orange juice

½ ounce maraschino liqueur

¼ ounce fresh lemon juice

Champagne

Orange peel, for garnish

Shake all the ingredients except the Champagne and strain into a chilled martini glass. Fill with Champagne and garnish with the orange peel.

CHAI TODDY *

1½ ounces spice rum

1 dash of peppermint schnapps

1 teaspoon honey

4 ounces hot tea

Peppermint stick, for garnish

Stir all the inredients in a mug or stem glass. Serve steaming hot, garnished with the peppermint stick.

CAIPIROSCA ◆

A variation on the classic Brazilian Caipirinha.

1/2 lime, quartered

3/4 ounce Brown Sugar Syrup (page 206), or
   1 teaspoon brown sugar

2 ounces vodka

Place the lime quarters in the bottom of mixing glass, add the syrup, and muddle, extracting the juice and the oil in the skin from the lime quarters. Fill a rocks glass three-fourths full of cracked ice and pour it over to the mixing glass along with the vodka. Shake well, pour the entire contents back into the rocks glass, and serve.

CAIPIRINHA ◆

Note that this is one of the only drinks that retain the ice used while shaking the drink.

1/2 lime, quartered.

3/4 ounce Brown Sugar Syrup (page 206), or
   1 teaspoon brown sugar

2 ounces cachaça

Chill a rocks glass with cracked ice. Place the lime quarters in the bottom of a mixing glass, add the syrup, and muddle, extracting the juice and the oil in the skin from the lime quarters. Add the cachaça to the mixture in the mixing glass, dump the ice from the rocks glass into the mixing glass, and shake well. Pour the entire contents of the mixing glass back into the chilled rocks glass and serve.

Variation: For a Caipirissima, make a Caipirinha with regular rum.

CAIPIRINHA, CHERRY ♦*

1/2 lime, quartered

4 pitted sour or sweet cherries

3/4 ounce Brown Sugar Syrup (page 206) or
    1 teaspoon brown sugar

2 ounces cachaça

Chill a rocks glass with cracked ice. Place the lime quarters and cherries in the bottom of a mixing glass, add the syrup, and muddle, extracting the juice and the oil in the skin from the lime quarters. Add the cachaça to the mixture in the mixing glass, dump the ice from the rocks glass into the mixing glass, and shake well. Pour the entire contents of the mixing glass back into the chilled rocks glass and serve.

CAIPIRINHA

The Caipirinha came from the countryside, where it was a favorite drink of farmers. The word *caipira* means "country man," and Caipirinha is a little drink with country brandy.

CAIPIRINHA DE UVA
(OR CAIPIRUVA) ♦

1/2 lime, quartered

4 seedless green grapes

3/4 ounce Brown Sugar Syrup (page 206), or
    1 teaspoon brown sugar

2 ounces cachaça

Chill a rocks glass with cracked ice. Place the lime quarters and grapes in the bottom of a mixing glass, add the syrup, and muddle, extracting the juice and the oil in the skin from the lime quarters. Add the cachaça to the mixture in the mixing glass, dump the ice from the rocks glass into the mixing glass, and shake well. Pour the entire contents of the mixing glass back into the chilled rocks glass and serve.

COCKTAIL TRIVIA

The old-fashioned saucer-shaped "Marie Antoinette" Champagne coup, which was purportedly created by using her breast as a model, is not good for bubbly because it does not show off the beautiful bubbles and lets it go flat faster. However, it is an elegant glass to serve a Daiquiri straight up.

CHAMPAGNE COCKTAIL

This classic recipe can be traced back to 1862, when it first appeared in *How to Mix Drinks* or *The Bon Vivant's Companion* by Jerry Thomas. For a stronger drink, add a float of Cognac or Grand Marnier. And for other Champagne cocktails besides the few listed below, see Le Perroquet and D'Artagnan.

Champagne

Sugar cube soaked with Angostura bitters

Lemon peel, for garnish (optional)

Place the Angostura-soaked sugar cube in the bottom of a champagne glass and fill the glass with Champagne. Pour slowly to avoid spillage. Garnished with the lemon peel, if using.

CHAMPAGNE PASSION *

Passion fruit purée is very tart, so I sweeten it with Simple Syrup to taste. If the purée is unavailable, use passion fruit nectar.

1¹/₂ ounces passion fruit purée

Simple Syrup, to taste

Champagne

¹/₂ ounce Alizé (passion fruit) Liqueur

Pour the passion fruit purée into a mixing glass and stir in the Simple Syrup. Slowly add the Champagne while stirring gently. Float the Alizé on top.

CHAMPAGNE TROPICALE *

1¹/₂ ounces mango purée

4 ounces Champagne

1 ounce maraschino liqueur

Pour the mango purée into a mixing glass, then slowly add the Champagne while stirring gently. Float the maraschino liqueur on top.

CHARLIE CHAPLIN COCKTAIL

1 ounce Marie Brizard Apry or other apricot brandy

1 ounce sloe gin

1 ounce fresh lime juice

Lime peel, for garnish

Shake all the ingredients with ice and strain into a chilled martini glass. Garnish with the lime peel.

CHERRY BLOSSOM ◆

Adapted from Harry Craddock's *Savoy Cocktail Book,* 1930. Make this in the summer, when fresh cherries are availab.e Try different varieties of cherries as they come into season; the sour cherries from upstate New York can add lots of zing to the cocktail.

5 sour cherries, pitted

¹/₂ ounce fresh lemon juice

¹/₂ ounce orange curaçao

¹/₂ ounce Peter Heering Cherry Heering

1¹/₂ ounces brandy

In a mixing glass, muddle 4 or 5 cherries with the lemon juice and liqueurs. Add the brandy and shake well with ice. Strain into a chilled cocktail glass.

CHERRY CRUSH * ◆

5 sweet cherries, pitted

1/2 ounce fresh lemon juice

1 ounce maraschino liqueur

1 1/2 ounces gin

In a mixing glass, muddle 4 of the cherries with the lemon juice and maraschino. Add the gin and shake well with ice. Strain into a chilled cocktail glass. Garnish with the remaining cherry.

CHERRY KISS *

1 1/2 ounces gin

3/4 ounce maraschino liqueur

2 ounces pineapple juice

3 dashes of grenadine

Freshly grated nutmeg, for dusting

Shake all the ingredients well and strain into a chilled martini glass. Dust with a little bit of grated nutmeg.

HARRY'S GIFT

Harry Nilsson was a scotch drinker, and a vodka drinker, and a Cognac drinker, and a beer drinker. He loved a good bottle of wine and often celebrated with Champagne. His generosity was as legendary at the Hotel Bel-Air as his appetites were excessive.

Once while sitting in his favorite corner of the bar, by the window, Harry noticed a bride and groom approaching down the garden path that connected the bungalows. They had just arrived from their wedding and were on their way to their honeymoon suite. Harry grabbed a waiter, who frantically motioned to me to open a bottle of Dom Pérignon. He quickly sent it on a tray with two glasses to the entrance of the bar, where the waiter presented the Champagne to the bride and groom as they walked by.

CHI CHI

Make a Piña Colada (page 162) but substitute vodka for the rums.

CHOCOLATE PUNCH

This is the ultimate dessert drink, and it is so rich that it must be shared. I found the recipe in *The Flowing Bowl* by William Schmidt, 1891.

1 ounce Cognac

1/2 ounce Ruby Port

1/2 ounce dark crème de cacao

1/2 ounce Simple Syrup

1 ounce heavy cream

Whole nutmeg, for grating

Shake all the ingredients very well with ice and strain into a chilled cocktail glass. Grate a little nutmeg on top.

CIGAR LOVER'S MARTINI

Recipe by Andrea Immer, noted wine and spirits authority.

2 1/2 ounces VS cognac

1/2 ounce 5-year tawny port

Flamed orange peel (see page 58), for garnish

Combine the ingredients with ice in a mixing glass and stir to chill. Strain into a chilled martini glass. Garnish with the flamed orange peel.

CITRUS CREAM * +

This was a popular nonalcoholic drink at the Rainbow Room.

2 ounces fresh orange juice

1 ounce fresh grapefruit juice

1/2 ounce Simple Syrup

1/2 ounce grenadine

1 ounce heavy cream

Shake all the ingredients with ice and strain into a London dock glass.

CLAREMONT ◆

Use pitted fresh cherries if available.

3 dashes of Angostura bitters

3/4 ounce orange curaçao

2 orange slices

2 sweet or sour cherries

1 1/2 ounces bourbon

1 ounce soda water

In the bottom of an old-fashioned glass, carefully muddle the bitters, curaçao, 1 of the orange slices, and 1 of the cherries. Remove the orange rind and add the bourbon, ice, and soda. Garnish with the remaining orange slice and cherry.

CLARET LEMONADE

This is basically lemonade, but with the interesting addition of red wine instead of water. Harry Johnson in his book *Bartender Manual*, 1898, called it Claret Lemonade and prepared it by filling a tumbler with crushed ice, filling it three-fourths full with lemonade, and floating the claret on top.

4 ounces red wine

1 ounce Simple Syrup

3/4 ounce fresh lemon juice

Lemon wheel, for garnish

Shake all the ingredients with ice and strain into a goblet over ice. Garnish with the lemon wheel.

CLOVER CLUB ◆

In his *Old Waldorf Bar Days* (1931), Albert Stevens Crockett credits this pre-Prohibition cocktail to the Bellevue-Stratford Hotel in Philadelphia, where an Algonquin Round Table sort of group called the Clover Club lent its name to the drink. When raspberries are in season, omit the raspberry syrup and instead muddle 6 fresh raspberries in the shaker with the Simple Syrup, then add the rest of the ingredients, shake, and strain.

Drinks with egg must be shaken harder and longer to emulsify the egg.

1 1/2 ounces gin

3/4 ounce Simple Syrup

3/4 ounce fresh lemon juice

1/4 ounce raspberry syrup

2 teaspoons of egg white

Shake all the ingredients well with ice and strain into a chilled cocktail glass.

Variation: To make the Clover Leaf, add a sprig of mint to the shaker before shaking.

CLUB COCKTAIL

This is adapted from *Just Cocktails* by W.C. Whitfield, who produced a series of whimsical cocktail books with carved wood covers in the 1930s.

2 ounces brandy

1/2 ounce maraschino liqueur

1/2 ounce pineapple juice

2 dashes of Peychaud's bitters

Lemon peel, for garnish

1 strawberry, for garnish

Shake all the ingredients well with ice and strain into a martini glass. Garnish with the lemon peel and strawberry.

Variation: Add 1/2 ounce of orange curaçao and switch to Angostura bitters, and you have a Rising Sun.

COCO BERRY * ◆

4 fresh raspberries

1/2 ounce raspberry liqueur (Chambord)

2 ounces white rum

1/2 ounce white crème de cacao

In a mixing glass, muddle the berries and Chambord. Add ice, the rum, and the crème de cacao. Stir to chill and strain into a chilled cocktail glass.

COFFEE COCKTAIL

This nineteenth-century specialty drink is from Jerry Thomas's 1887 *The Bar-Tender's Guide or How to Mix All Kinds of Plain and Francy Drinks.*

1 ounce Cognac or brandy

1 ounce ruby port

1 small egg

1/2 teaspoon sugar

Freshly grated nutmeg, for dusting

Shake all the ingredients well with ice and strain into a port glass. Dust with nutmeg.

COFFEE NUDGE

1 ounce brandy

1/2 ounce dark crème de cacao

1/2 ounce coffee liqueur

Hot coffee

Hand-Whipped Irish Coffee Cream (page 207)

Build in an Irish coffee glass and float the cream on top.

COGNAC AND SODA

Hemingway's favorite while perusing the *Herald Tribune* in sidewalk cafés on the West Bank in Paris. Listed in Jerry Thomas's 1862 book, *How to Mix Drinks,* as the StoneWall, and in England called Peg (as in "one peg in your coffin"). A dash of Peychaud's bitters from New Orleans is a great addition.

2 ounces Cognac

5 ounces club soda

Pour the Cognac over ice in a highball glass and fill with the soda.

COCTEL ALGERIA

This is an unusual pisco recipe from the menu of Joe Baum's famous Manhattan restaurant La Fonda Del Sol, circa 1960. Pisco is a grape brandy made in Peru and Chile from the muscat grape.

3/4 ounce pisco

3/4 ounce Cointreau

3/4 ounce apricot brandy

1 ounce fresh orange juice

Flamed orange peel (see page 58), for garnish

Shake all the ingredients with ice and strain into a chilled martini glass. Garnish with the flamed orange peel.

Coffee Cocktail.

COLONY ROOM COCKTAIL [*]

The Colony Room Club in London is known for many things, but cocktails is not one of them. As longtime member Roddy Ashworth once put it: "If a member asks for a Piña Colada, he is likely to be served with little more than raised eyebrows and a large vodka and tonic."

In 1995, while visiting London to judge a bartending contest, I ended up at the Colony Room, where I was surprised to discover that the most complex cocktail available was a screwdriver (although to get one, I had to ask for a large vodka and orange). Faced with the prospect of drinking vodka and orange all night, I convinced proprietor Michael Wojas to allow me to get behind the bar and fashion my own special mix. The available ingredients were limited, but I did manage to invent a drink worthy of the club's name. Here's the recipe.

Dash of Ricard

2 ounces gin

2 dashes of Noilly Prat dry vermouth

1 dash of Angostura bitters

Season a chilled martini glass by dashing it with Ricard and coating the inside, then pour out the excess. Chill the gin, vermouth, and bitters by stirring with ice. Strain into the prepared martini glass. Garnish with wit or sarcasm, whichever comes easier; if these are unavailable, strike a pose and garnish with attitude.

COLORADO BULLDOG

This is your basic adult egg cream.

1½ ounces Kahlúa

3 ounces cold milk

3 ounces Coca-Cola

Build the Kahlúa and milk in a highball glass. Add the Coca-Cola last, and gently stir while pouring. Let the foam recede, pour, and stir again. Repeat until full. No Garnish.

COOPERSTOWN [♦]

Albert Stevens Crockett claims in *Old Waldorf Bar Days* (1931) that this was created in the Big Brass Rail at the Waldorf for some high rollers from Cooperstown, New York.

2 fresh mint sprigs

½ ounce sweet vermouth

½ ounce dry vermouth

2 ounces gin

Muddle one of the mint sprigs and the vermouths in a mixing glass. Add the gin and ice, stir well, and strain into a martini glass. Garnish with the remaining mint sprig.

CORPSE REVIVER

Who cares what is in this cocktail? The name sold me when I read it in Harry Craddock's *The Savoy Cocktail Book* (1930). This is one of many variations.

1 ounce gin

½ ounce Cointreau

½ ounce Lillet Blonde

¾ ounce fresh lemon juice

Dash of Absente

Shake with ice and strain into a chilled cocktail glass.

COSMALIZE *

1½ ounces Alizé Gold

1 ounce citrus vodka

1 ounce cranberry juice

¼ ounce fresh lemon juice

Shake with ice and strain into a chilled cocktail glass.

MORE FROM HARRY NILSSON

Cognac and Soda was one of Harry Nilsson's favorite drinks. I can still remember the day that Harry had been nursing several of these prior to an appointment with the film producer Bob Evans. He was negotiating to do the score for a movie and was scheduled to have an important face-to-face. For some reason, Harry's attorney was not available, so he spent the afternoon as he often did, sitting at the bar, with phone and Cognac, taking care of business. Anticipating the meeting with Bob, Harry felt kind of naked without representation. So he turned to Victor Gonzalez, the day man behind the bar, and asked whether he had a suit with him. Victor replied, yes, he had a sport coat and of course his tie. Harry then asked whether Bob Evans was a customer at the bar and Victor said no, he had never met him. So Harry put forth the following proposition: He wanted Victor to be his "attorney" for the meeting that afternoon, with the following instructions: never answer any direct question with yes or no, just shake your head negatively and glance at me; indicate to Bob or his attorney that it needs to be discussed privately with your client and not at this meeting; appear to be negative about everything they offer, but indicate at the end of the meeting that it was a very useful meeting and that we're "very close."

Based on this meeting, Harry got to do the score for the movie *Popeye*.

CRAWDADDY

1½ ounces Stolichnaya vodka

5 ounces lemonade

Splash of soda water

Lemon slice, for garnish

Build in a highball glass, top with the soda, and garnish with the lemon slice.

CUBA LIBRE

Coca-Cola was only available in bottles for four years when the Rough Riders brought it along with them to Cuba. They mixed it with Cuban rum and lime and named it after their battle cry, "Cuba Libre." "Free Cuba" was the cry heard from the Rough Riders and their Cuban counterparts as they swept the Spanish out of Cuba.

2 ounces Cuban rum (Good luck finding it!)

Coca-Cola

Lime wedge

Pour the rum over ice in the highball glass and fill with Coca-Cola. Squeeze in a lime wedge.

CUPID'S COCKTAIL *

I created this in 1991 at the Rainbow Room for Valentine's Day.

1 ounce Peter Heering Cherry Heering

1 ounce Peachtree Schnapps

4 ounces fresh orange juice

Orange slice, for garnish

Cherry slice, for garnish

Shake all the ingredients and strain into a chilled highball glass. Garnish with the orange slice and cherry.

COBBLERS

COBBLERS COMPRISED A BROAD CATEGORY IN THE NINETEENTH CENTURY, WHEN THEY WERE MADE WITH WINE AND SPIRITS AND FRESH FRUITS. THEY WERE DECORATED WITH FRESH FRUIT OF THE SEASON, SWEETENED WITH SUGAR, AND SERVED OVER ICE IN LARGE GLASSES.

Making a cobbler called for shaking, ushering in the use of the modern-day cocktail shaker. These original shakers were just two bar glasses of different sizes, the larger placed over the smaller in the fashion of today's Boston shaker. In the early 1880s, the United States Patent Office received many applications for styles of cocktail mixing and shaking cups, including the odd contraption designed to mechanically shake several drinks by turning a large crank. Today, most shakers are made in either the two-part Boston shaker style or the single-unit Cobbler shaker style with two caps.

The recipes I found in the older books did not go into detail describing the preparation of cobblers. For instance, in his 1862 edition of *How to Mix Drinks,* Jerry Thomas lists a recipe for the Whiskey Cobbler, which calls for 2 wine glasses of whiskey, 1 tablespoon of sugar, and 2 or 3 slices of orange. The recipe's only instructions are to fill a tumbler with ice and shake all the ingredients well. I took Thomas's idea of shaking the fruit right in the cocktail shaker and used it in many different drinks to great success.

The tradition of shaking a cobbler *with* fresh fruit disappears in later recipe books, most noticeably in the influential *The Savoy Cocktail Book* by Harry Craddock (1930). Instead, cobblers were shaken or stirred first, and *then* garnished with the fruit. When I decided to re-create cobblers at the Blackbird Bar, I wanted to revive the tradition of shaking the drink with the fruit. I took it one step further by first muddling the fruit before shaking, in order to extract the oils and juices. Then I added garnish, using the same fruit.

Muddling or mashing with fruit liqueurs and syrups was a commonplace practice for the nineteenth-century bartender, and in many cases the liqueurs and syrups were manufactured on the premises. It was only in the latter part of the century that fruit brandies, liqueurs, and syrups became widely commercially available. The nineteenth-century cobbler drinks inspired the following recipes, but I have adapted them to the modern palate.

Substituting other sweet ingredients for the sugar was commonplace, and many of the old recipes called for curaçao or maraschino in place of sugar or sugar syrup. *The Gentleman's Table Guide* (London, 1871) instructs, "Sugar candy, capillaire, and fruit syrups can be used when fruit cannot be obtained."

COBBLER MIXER.

brandy cobbler * ♦

This recipe is adapted from Ice Punch served at the Metropolitan Hotel in New York City, 1870.

2 fresh pineapple wedges, one with skin and one without

2 orange slices

2 lemon wedges

3/4 ounce raspberry syrup or raspberry liqueur

2 ounces brandy or Cognac

Muddle the pineapple wedge without skin, one piece of orange, and one piece of lemon with the raspberry syrup and 1 ounce of water in a bar glass. Add ice and the brandy and shake well. Strain into a double old-fashioned glass filled with crushed ice. Garnish with an orange wedge, the remaining pineapple wedge, and a lemon wedge.

champagne cobbler * ♦

1 orange slice

1 lemon wedge

1 fresh pineapple wedge without skin

3/4 ounce maraschino liqueur

4 ounces Champagne

Flamed orange peel (see page 58), for garnish

Muddle the fruit and liqueur in the bottom of a bar glass. Add ice and Champagne. Stir gently to retain the bubbles and strain into a champagne flute. Garnish with the flamed orange peel.

gin cobbler * ♦

2 fresh pineapple wedges, one with skin, one without

2 orange slices

2 lemon wedges

3/4 ounce Peter Heering Cherry Heering

1 1/2 ounces gin

In a mixing glass, muddle the skinless pineapple wedge, 1 piece of the orange, and 1 piece of the lemon with Peter Heering. Add the gin and 1 ounce of water. Shake with ice and strain into a double old-fashioned glass filled with crushed ice. Garnish with the remaining pineapple wedge, an orange wedge, and a lemon wedge.

Japanese cobbler * ♦

2 fresh pineapple wedges, one with skin and one without

2 orange slices

2 lemon wedges

1/2 ounce maraschino liqueur

3 ounces sake

Sweet or dry soda, to taste

Sprig of fresh mint

In the bottom of a bar glass, muddle the skinless pineapple wedge, 1 piece of orange, and 1 piece of lemon with the maraschino liqueur. Add the sake and shake with ice. Strain into a double old-fashioned glass filled with crushed ice and top with a splash of sweet or dry soda. Garnish with a sprig of mint, the remaining pineapple wedge, an orange wedge, and a lemon wedge.

port cobbler * ♦

2 fresh pineapple wedges, one with skin and one without

2 orange slices

2 lemon wedges

½ ounce orange curaçao

4 ounces port (Ruby Port)

In the bottom of a bar glass, muddle the skinless pineapple wedge, 1 piece of orange, and 1 piece of lemon with the curaçao and 1 ounce of water. Add the port, shake with ice, and strain into a double old-fashioned glass filled with crushed ice. Garnish with the remaining pineapple wedge, an orange wedge, and a lemon wedge.

sherry cobbler * ♦

2 fresh pineapple wedges, one with skin and one without

2 orange slices

2 lemon wedges

½ ounce maraschino liqueur

3 ounces medium sherry

½ ounce fresh lemon juice

2 ounces fresh orange juice

In the bottom of a bar glass, muddle the skinless pineapple wedge, 1 piece of orange, and 1 piece of lemon with the maraschino liqueur. Add the sherry and the juices and shake well with ice. Strain into a goblet filled with crushed ice. Garnish with the remaining pineapple wedge, an orange wedge, and a lemon wedge.

whiskey cobbler * ♦

This drink works well when paired with meat or game that is sauced with fruit.

2 fresh pineapple wedges, one with skin and one without

2 orange slices

2 lemon wedges

¾ ounce orange curaçao

2 ounces whiskey

In the bottom of a bar glass, muddle the skinless pineapple wedge, 1 piece of orange, and 1 piece of lemon with the orange curaçao and 1 ounce of water. Add the whiskey and ice and shake well. Strain into a double old-fashioned glass filled with crushed ice. Garnish with the remaining pineapple wedge, an orange wedge, and a lemon wedge.

ME AND THE COSMO

The contemporary recipe for the Cosmopolitan goes back to the test-marketing of Absolut Citron. I've heard an unsubstantiated rumor that a woman named Cheryl Cook invented it in South Beach, Miami, though I was given credit for inventing it by *New York* magazine (and other publications that cited the *New York* article as a source). Well, I didn't. What I did do was popularize a definitive recipe that became widely accepted as the standard.

The drink first appeared on menus in the late 1980s, first in New York City at the Odeon in TriBeCa, and first in San Francisco at the Fog City Diner; of course, both locations claim to have invented the drink. I put it on my menu at the Rainbow Room in 1996. Shortly after that, Madonna was spotted drinking one, and overnight I was getting calls from as far away as Germany and Australia for the recipe. I added the additional touches of Cointreau and the flamed orange peel for garnish and presented it several times on television around the country. Now, it is certainly the most recognized drink in the world, next to the classic Martini.

But to go back even further: Ocean Spray Cranberry Juice has promoted spirits with their products aggressively for years, and from 1956 to 1970 they were featuring a series of cocktails, one of which was made with 1 ounce of vodka, 1 ounce of cranberry juice, and a squeeze of fresh lime, called the Harpoon. Add some Triple Sec or Cointreau and you have a Cosmopolitan.

cosmopolitan

1 1/2 ounces citron vodka

1/2 ounce Cointreau

1/4 ounce fresh lime juice

1 ounce cranberry juice

Flamed orange peel (see page 58), for garnish

Shake all the ingredients with ice. Strain into a chilled cocktail glass. Garnish with the flamed orange peel.

cosmopolitan delight

From *Recipes of American and Other Iced Drinks*, by Charlie Paul (1902). I included this turn-of-the-century Cosmopolitan partly because of the name, but mostly because it tastes great.

1 1/2 ounces brandy

1/2 ounce curaçao

1/2 ounce Simple Syrup

3/4 ounce fresh lemon juice

1/4 ounce orgeat

Splash of red wine

Seasonal fruit, for garnish

Shake all the ingredients with ice and serve over ice in an old-fashioned glass. Top with a splash of red wine. Garnish with fresh seasonal fruits. Don't be shy with the garnish—these early drinks looked like fruit salads.

cosmopolitan, strawberry ♦

2 to 4 fresh, sweet strawberries (depending on size)

1 ounce Cointreau

1/4 ounce fresh lime juice

1 1/2 ounces citrus vodka

Halve one of the strawberries and reserve one half for garnish. In the bottom of a mixing glass, muddle the remaining strawberries with the Cointreau and lime juice. Add the vodka and ice and shake well to a ten count. Strain into a martini glass and garnish with the strawberry half.

DAIQUIRI

This Cuban classic gets its name from the town of the same name in the Oriente province. The recipe was created by an American mining engineer named Jennings Cox and a Cuban engineer named Pagliuchi in the late nineteenth century. The talented barmen in Havana, especially Constantino Ribailagua, further refined it.

The Daiquiri made its first appearance in the United States at the Army Navy Club in Washington, D.C., taken there from Cuba by Admiral Lucius Johnson. Today you can have a Daiquiri in the Army Navy Club's Daiquiri Lounge. Below is the original recipe; for Constante's special Papa Doble, see the Hemingway Daiquiri.

1¹/₂ ounces light rum

1 ounce Simple Syrup

³/₄ ounce fresh lime juice

Shake all the ingredients with ice and strain into a chilled cocktail glass.

DALE'S ABSOLUTELY GUARANTEED APHRODISIAC *

Created for Tony Hendra's "Cocktail Challenge" article in *New York* magazine. The other challengers were chef Anne Rosenzweig, winemaker Alex Hargrave, and *Sex and the City* columnist Candace Bushnell. Anne made the final challenge of the afternoon, asking for an "absolutely guaranteed aphrodisiac" with "no fruit."

1 ounce Grand Marnier

1 ounce cachaça

Stir the Grand Marnier and cachaça and serve over ice in a rocks glass.

DALE'S ORANGESICLE *

³/₄ ounce orange vodka

³/₄ ounce vanilla vodka

³/₄ ounce cointreau

1¹/₂ ounces fresh orange juice

Pinch of cinnamon, for garnish

Shake all the ingredients with ice and strain over ice into a highball. Dust with cinnamon.

DARK AND STORMY

2 ounces Gosling's or Myers's dark rum

5 ounces ginger beer

Lime wedge

Pour the rum over ice in highball and fill with ginger beer. Squeeze in the lime wedge.

DARK AND STORMY II *

I'm always tinkering with drinks to see if a touch here or there could make them better, or at least just as good but different.

1 ounce Myers's rum

1 ounce silver rum

2 ounces ginger beer

2 ounces fresh orange juice

2 ounces pineapple juice

Lime wedge, for garnish

Build all the ingredients in a large glass over ice and stir. Garnish with the lime wedge.

D'ARTAGNAN

1 teaspoon Armagnac

1 teaspoon Grand Marnier

3 teaspoons fresh orange juice

¹/₂ teaspoon Simple Syrup

3 ounces chilled Champagne

Orange peel, cut into thin strips

Chill the first four ingredients in a mixing glass and strain into a flute. Top with the Champagne and add strips of orange peel so they extend the length of the glass.

DEBONAIRE COCKTAIL

Gary and Mardee Regan have supplied me for a couple of years now with orange bitters prepared from a recipe that appeared in the 1862 first edition of Jerry Thomas's *How to Mix Drinks*. Gary and Mardee also spend plenty of time in their bar/laboratory creating recipes of their own. This is their recipe.

2¹/₂ ounces Highland Malt Scotch

³/₄ ounce Canton Ginger Liqueur

Stir both ingredients to chill and strain into a chilled martini glass. No garnish.

DERBY COCKTAIL◆

Peach bitters are available from the Fee Brothers in Rochester, New York (see Resources, page 203).

¹/₂ peach, quartered

Several fresh mint leaves

¹/₄ ounce peach bitters or Marie Brizard peach liqueur

2¹/₂ ounces gin

Sprig of fresh mint, for garnish

In a mixing glass, muddle together the peach, mint, and peach bitters or peach liqueur. Add the gin and ice. Shake all the ingredients well and strain into a small martini glass. Garnish with a sprig of mint.

DESERT HEALER

From the Vendome Club, Hollywood, 1930, when most of what's now Los Angeles was still a desert.

1¹/₂ ounces gin

¹/₂ ounce Peter Heering Cherry Heering

1¹/₂ ounces fresh orange juice

4 ounces ginger ale

Orange peel, for garnish

Cherry, for garnish

Build in a highball glass over ice and fill with ginger ale. Garnish with the orange peel and cherry.

DESHLER COCKTAIL

1¹/₂ ounces Red Dubonnet

1¹/₂ ounces rye

¹/₄ ounce Cointreau

Dash of Angostura bitters

Orange peel, for garnish

Shake and strain into a cocktail glass. Garnish with the orange peel.

DEVIL'S TORCH

This drink is from *1800 and All That—Drinks Ancient and Modern,* by R. de Fleury (1937). It is not a particularly stunning cocktail, but there weren't many vodka cocktails around in the early twentieth century, and I like to document them as I find them. This was from a London cocktail book; in the United States, we didn't drink vodka in 1937.

1¹/₂ ounces vodka

1¹/₂ ounce French vermouth

3 dashes of grenadine

Lemon peel, for garnish

Shake with ice and strain into a chilled cocktail glass. Garnish with the lemon peel.

DIRTY MOTHER

1¹/₂ ounces brandy

1 ounce Kahlúa

Serve over ice in a rocks glass.

DIRTY WHITE MOTHER

1¹/₂ ounces brandy

1 ounce Kahlúa

1¹/₂ ounces heavy cream

Shake all the ingredients with ice and strain over ice in a rocks glass.

DI SARONNO PUNCH *

1¹/₂ ounces Amaretto di Saronna

¹/₄ ounce orange curaçao

2 ounces fresh orange juice

2 ounces pineapple juice

Juice of 1 lime

Dash of Angostura bitters

Club soda

Orange slice, for garnish

Cherry, for garnish

Shake the Amaretto, curaçao, juices, and bitters with ice and strain into a collins glass. Top with a splash of club soda. Garnish with the orange and cherry.

D.O.M. COCKTAIL

Modified from a recipe found in *The Artistry of Mixing Drinks* (1936), by Frank Meier of the Ritz Bar, Paris.

2 ounces gin

1 ounce fresh orange juice

1/2 ounce Bénédictine

Flamed orange peel (see page 58), for garnish

Shake all the ingredients with ice and strain into a chilled martini glass. Garnish with the flamed orange peel.

THE DOROTHY

2 ounces silver rum

1/2 ounce fresh orange juice

1/2 ounce pineapple juice

1/4 ounce Apry (apricot liqueur)

WHIPPING PRAGUE INTO SHAPE

I visited Prague just a few years after the country's liberation from Communism. New businesses were opening everywhere, including an Irish bar called Molly Malone's, which had been disassembled in Dublin and completely rebuilt in a fifteenth-century stone edifice in Prague. The owner explained to me, "We've got a problem: There's something wrong with the cream we get here in the Czech Republic; it doesn't whip up properly." I told him to bring me a pitcher, a whisk, and some heavy cream. I buried the pitcher in ice, poured in the cream, and whipped up a round of Irish coffees. As he looked on, I told him: "There's nothing wrong with the cream—you just have lazy bartenders!"—they never chilled the pitcher. It was two weeks before St. Paddy's Day and the owner asked me to create a special cocktail for the holiday, so I created the Dubliner.

Shake all ingredients with ice, strain into a chilled martini glass, and garnish with a flamed orange peel.

DOUGLAS FAIRBANKS

Drinks like this one from the nineteenth or early twentieth centuries that call for *egg, egg white,* or *egg yolk* are tricky. The eggs were smaller than our small eggs are today. Following the old recipe instructions that call for a whole egg or the white of an egg with the size of today's eggs will throw the drink out of whack. The solution is to beat the whole egg or the whites and to emulsify it to a liquid form and then measure. In old recipes that call for a whole egg, I use 3/4 ounce of a small egg.

1 1/2 ounces gin

1 ounce Marie Brizard Apry or other apricot brandy

1/2 ounce fresh lime juice

3/4 ounce egg white

Shake all the ingredients extra hard to completely emulsify the egg, then strain into a chilled cocktail glass.

DUBLINER *

1 ounce Irish whiskey

1 ounce Irish Mist liqueur

Lightly whipped unsweetened cream

Pour the spirits into a mixing glass with ice and stir to chill. Strain into a London dock glass and top with 1 inch of cream.

DUBONNET COCKTAIL

This cocktail is also known as the Zaza.

1 1/2 ounces Red Dubonnet

1 1/2 ounces gin

Lemon peel, for garnish

Pour the dubonnet and gin together over ice in an old-fashioned glass, or chill and serve up in a cocktail glass. Garnish with the lemon peel.

DUSTY ROSE *

You can make a wonderful frosting for the rim of the glass. Slice several maraschino cherries ¼-inch thick and bake them until dry and crisp. Pulverize them to a powder with a mortar and pestle. Dampen the outside rim of the glass with an orange slice and touch the rim in the powder.

1 ounce cherry brandy

½ ounce white crème de cacao

2 ounces heavy cream

Shake and serve in a small martini glass.

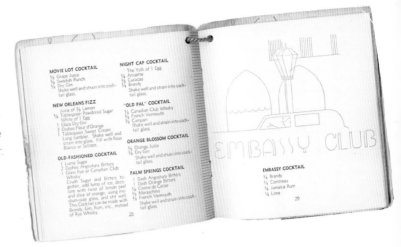

EDITH'S FIZZ *

I created this for Keith McNally's Balthazar Restaurant in Manhattan.

1½ ounces Lillet Blonde

½ ounce maraschino liqueur

4 ounces fresh orange juice

2 ounces soda or seltzer water

Mix all the ingredients in a highball glass.

EGGNOG

See Punch section (page 172).

ELK'S OWN

Modified from a recipe in *The Artistry of Mixing Drinks* by Frank Meier, 1936 (Ritz hotel, Paris). Port was a popular ingredient in punches and cocktails, sometimes as a float and sometimes shaken into the drink. (See the Port Cobbler and the Port Whiskey Punch.) Many of the drinks in the cobbler section, with the exception of the Champagne Cobbler, would be improved with a float of ruby port.

1 ounce Canadian whiskey

1 ounce port

½ ounce fresh lemon juice

¼ ounce Simple Syrup

1 small egg white

Shake all the ingredients with ice and strain into a chilled martini glass.

ELECTRIC ICE TEA

See Long Island Iced Tea.

EMBASSY COCKTAIL

The brandy-and-rum combination was used often in nogs and holiday punches and in an occasional cocktail like this one from the Embassy Club, Hollywood, 1930.

¾ ounce brandy

¾ ounce Cointreau

¾ ounce Appleton Jamaican Rum

½ ounce fresh lime juice

Dash of Angostura bitters

Lime piece, for garnish

Shake well with ice and strain into a chilled martini glass. Garnish with lime piece.

ESPRESSO COCKTAIL

By Dick Bradsell for Jonathan Downey of the Match bars in London. Try this with the addition of 1 ounce of cream for a richer drink.

Brown sugar, for rimming

¾ ounce Kahlúa

¾ ounce vodka

1 ounce espresso

Prepare a martini glass with a brown-sugared rim. Shake all the ingredients with ice and strain into the martini glass. No garnish.

FANCY NANCY *

Created for Nancy, a photographer in Dallas, who found the regular Negroni too bitter.

1 ounce citrus vodka

1/2 ounce sweet vermouth

1/2 ounce Cointreau

1/4 ounce Campari

1 1/2 ounces fresh orange juice

Flamed orange peel (see page 58), for garnish

Shake well and strain into a chilled martini glass. Garnish with the flamed orange peel.

FANCY TEQUILA COCKTAIL *

1 ounce Sauza Hornitos tequila

1 ounce Grand Marnier

1 1/2 ounces fresh orange juice

1/4 ounce fresh lime juice

Flamed orange peel (see page 58), for garnish

Shake all the ingredients with ice and strain into a chilled martini glass. Garnish with the flamed orange peel.

FAUX NOG *

Are you afraid of raw egg? Try this recipe as a substitute for eggnog. It's amazing how authentic it tastes.

1 ounce vodka

1 ounce white crème de cacao

2 ounces heavy cream

3 dashes of Angostura bitters

Freshly grated nutmeg, for dusting

Shake the ingredients well with ice. Strain over crushed ice in a London dock glass. Dust with nutmeg.

FERNET BRANCA COCKTAIL

2 ounces gin

1/2 ounce Fernet Branca

3/4 ounce sweet vermouth

Flamed lemon peel (see page 58) for garnish

Stir with ice to chill and strain into a chilled cocktail glass. Garnish with the flamed lemon peel.

FITZGERALD *

1 1/2 ounces gin

1 ounce Simple Syrup

3/4 ounce fresh lemon juice

2 dashes of Angostura bitters

Lemon piece, for garnish

Shake all the ingredients with ice and strain into a rocks glass. Garnish with the lemon piece.

FIZZ

See pages 116–17.

THAT'S AMORE

In 1936, Dave Chasen and his silent partner, Harold Ross of *New Yorker* fame, opened Chasen's in Beverly Hills. It started out as a chili joint, but it soon turned into a celebrity hangout visited by everyone from presidents and monarchs to the Rat Pack. Dean Martin was at the bar once and asked barman Pepe Ruiz, who had been bartending there for thirty-five years, to create a drink especially for him. The next time Martin came in, Pepe took a whole navel orange and cut the peel into large strips. He poured a little La Ina Fino Sherry into a chilled martini glass, swirled it around, and threw it out. He then squeezed the strips of orange peel, expressing the oil through a lit match, coating the inside of the glass with the caramelized orange oil. He then flamed the peel of the whole orange the same way. Next, he shook a shot of vodka in a shaker, strained it into the martini glass, and garnished the glass with an orange peel. He called it the Flame of Love Martini. When Frank Sinatra saw the drink, he got so excited that he threw a party at Chasen's and ordered two hundred of them.

FLAME OF LOVE

1/2 ounce fino sherry

Several peels of orange

2 1/2 ounces vodka

Coat the inside of a chilled martini glass with fino sherry and toss out the excess. Flame several orange peels into the glass (see page 58). Chill the vodka and strain into the seasoned glass. Garnish with an orange peel.

Variation: The gin version of this drink is called the Valencia or Spanish Martini.

NEVER BEFORE, NEVER AGAIN

While we were living in Hollywood, my wife, Jill, and I had a terrific apartment with a fireplace, high beamed ceilings, and a marble stairway. The place had once belonged to Marge and Gower Champion, and rumor had it that Charlie Chaplin's mistress had also once lived there. Anyway, we used to have great jam sessions with our neighbor Lisa and her father, Tony Romano, a guitar player who traveled with Bob Hope and played in Hollywood studio orchestras for much of his career. Tony made a seminal recording with the jazz violin player Joe Venuti; the story of the making of this record, now a collector's item, is wonderful.

Tony was a big fan of Joe Venuti, so when he found himself doing a gig one day at a sound stage where Joe was one of the musicians, he was ecstatic. After the session ended, Tony secretly sent the engineer out to get sausage and pepper sandwiches as bait for the scheme he had in mind. He arranged for the engineer to stay in the booth while he and Joe shared a bottle of wine and a couple of sandwiches, after which Tony suggested that they jam a little bit. They played for over two hours while the engineer recorded the whole session. When they were finished, Tony gave the tape to Joe to keep, explaining that they had just been recorded. When Joe died, Tony received the tape in the mail with a note that he was free to do what he wanted with it. So Tony took the tape to a studio, sweetened a couple of numbers with the guitar, and cut the album *Never Before, Never Again*.

FLAMINGO

1 1/2 ounces white rum

1 1/2 ounces pineapple juice

1/4 ounce fresh lime juice

1/4 ounce grenadine

Splash of Simple Syrup, optional

Shake all the ingredients well with ice and serve in a martini glass. No garnish.

FLIP

The flip recipes from colonial times were hot drinks, with as many variations as there were inns on the Boston Post Road. Generally they involved a batter made from brown sugar, eggs, and sometimes cream that was added to a large mug of beer, then scalded with a loggerhead (a poker with a ball at the end). The loggerhead was heated in the fire and thrust into the mug; rum, brandy, or applejack was added to fortify the drink.

1 1/2 ounces spirit, sherry, or port

1 teaspoon sugar

1 small whole egg

Freshly grated nutmeg, for dusting

Shake all the ingredients with ice very well to totally emulsify the egg. Strain into a London dock or port glass. Dust with nutmeg.

FLIRTINI * ◆

2 pieces of fresh pineapple

1/2 ounce Cointreau or Triple Sec

1/2 ounce vodka

1 ounce pineapple juice

3 ounces Champagne

Cherry, for garnish

In the bottom of a mixing glass, muddle the pineapple pieces and the Cointreau. Add the vodka and juice and stir with ice. Strain into a chilled martini glass and top with the Champagne. Garnish with the cherry.

THE FIZZ

THE DIFFERENCE BETWEEN A FIZZ AND A COLLINS IS GLASS SIZE AND GARNISH. THE COLLINS GOES IN A TALL, OR COLLINS, GLASS, WITH A CHERRY AND ORANGE SLICE FOR GARNISH. THE FIZZ WAS A SPINOFF OF THE SOUR, MADE POSSIBLE BY THE APPEARANCE OF CHARGED WATER. BOTTLED SODA WATER WAS NOT WIDELY AVAILABLE AND WAS VERY EXPENSIVE IN THE MIDDLE OF THE NINETEENTH CENTURY, SO MANY HOUSEHOLD RECIPES CALLED FOR SODA POWDERS (BICARBONATE OF SODA) TO MAKE EFFERVESCING DRINKS. THE 1860 EDITION OF *THE PRACTICAL HOUSEWIFE* LISTED A RECIPE FOR EFFERVESCING LEMONADE MADE WITH LEMON JUICE, SUGAR SYRUP, WATER, AND 20 GRAINS OF BICARBONATE OF SODA. THE 1862 EDITION OF *HOW TO MIX DRINKS,* BY JERRY THOMAS, HAS ONLY A COUPLE OF RECIPES CALLING FOR BOTTLED SODA WATER. HE DOES CALL FOR EUROPEAN SPARKLING MINERAL WATERS, BUT THESE CAME AT CONSIDERABLE EXPENSE, AND MANY OF THEM HAD A DISTINCTIVE MINERAL FLAVOR. AS FOR THE GIN FIZZ AND THE TOM COLLINS, NEITHER RECIPE APPEARS IN THE 1862 EDITION; BUT THE TOM COLLINS DOES SHOW UP IN THOMAS'S *BARTENDER'S GUIDE* (1887), ALONG WITH SIX FIZZ RECIPES.

A recipe called Gin Punch appears in the 1862 edition and calls for gin, lemon juice, sugar syrup, maraschino liqueur, and seltzer water served well iced. Even with the maraschino, which would give a slight floral note to the drink, it would taste almost exactly like a Gin Fizz or a Tom Collins. A Gin Fizz, after all, is just a short version of a Tom Collins without all the fruit garnish. The New Orleans Fizz—or Ramos Fizz that Henry Ramos brought to New Orleans in 1888—was just a Silver Fizz with a little orange-flower water added.

Over the years, I've cured thousands of hangovers with this famous eye-opener, one of the greats. The old Hotel Roosevelt in New Orleans bought the rights to the trade name Ramos Fizz. Today, the hotel is called the Fairmont, and its bar is a must-stop, where Tony Ortiz carries on the tradition of the Ramos Fizz in grand style. Here are a few recipes that will give you a little insight into the world of the fizz. Remember, the fizz is just a sparkling version of a sour. So the sour formula should be used for the fizz drinks: 3/4 part sour with 1 part sweet and 1 1/2 parts strong.

Alan Lewis, general manager of the Rainbow Room, called me into his office one day to quiz me on how to make a Ramos Fizz. I told him: lime, lemon, egg white, sugar, cream, orange-flower water, and gin. He insisted there was no egg white in a Ramos Fizz. I disagreed, so the crusty old s.o.b. called the Waldorf to quiz those guys—they had all worked as beverage managers for Alan at one time or another. In each case he'd slam down the phone in disgust, evidently hearing the same thing I had told him. Finally he called Brennan's in News Orleans, and got one of the Brennan brothers on the phone, "Ask your oldest bartender how he makes a Ramos Fizz." *Bam,* he slammed down the phone in disgust, exclaiming, "The sonofabitch is drunk!"

Alan must have been thinking of a Gin Fizz, which is simply a Tom Collins on a short plan, with no garnish: lemon and lime juice, sugar, gin, and soda. No milk, no egg white, and served in what used to be called an 8-ounce fizz glass. I continued to make all my Ramos Fizzes with egg white—except for Alan's, since he would never give in.

gin fizz

A fizz, or Delmonico, glass is a highball-style glass but just a little shorter, with an 8- to 10-ounce capacity. Since the fizz-type drinks containing egg are served without ice, this glass is preferable to the standard highball.

1½ ounces gin

¾ ounce fresh lemon juice

1 ounce Simple Syrup, or 1 teaspoon superfine sugar

Club soda

Shake the gin, lemon juice, and syrup and strain into a highball glass (but see headnote) with ice. Fill with club soda. No garnish.

golden fizz

1½ ounces gin

¾ ounce fresh lemon juice

1½ ounces Simple Syrup

1 ounce egg, beaten

Club soda or seltzer

Shake all the ingredients except the soda with ice long and hard to completely emulsify the egg. Strain into a fizz or highball glass without ice, and top with the club soda.

Variation: A Royal Fizz is a Golden Fizz with the whole egg, not just the yolk.

ramos fizz

1½ ounces gin

½ ounce fresh lemon juice

½ ounce fresh lime juice

1¼ ounces Simple Syrup

2 ounces milk

1 small egg white

2 drops of orange-flower water

3 ounces club soda

Shake all the ingredients except the soda with ice and strain into a highball glass without ice. Top with club soda. No garnish.

silver fizz

1½ ounces gin

¾ ounce fresh lemon juice

1½ ounces Simple Syrup

1 egg white (small)

3 ounces club soda or seltzer

Shake all the ingredients except the soda with ice long and hard to completely emulsify the egg. Strain into a fizz or highball glass without ice and top with soda.

whiskey fizz *

1½ ounces American blended whiskey

¾ ounce fresh lemon juice

1 ounce Simple Syrup

3 ounces lemon-lime soda

Shake the first three ingredients and strain into a highball glass filled with ice. Fill with the lemon-lime soda. Variation: The scotch version of the Whiskey Fizz is called the Manhattan Cooler.

FLORADORA

Named after the 1900 Broadway hit that introduced the Floradora Girls, who all were five feet four inches tall and weighed 130 pounds.

1¹/₂ ounces gin

¹/₂ ounce fresh lime juice

³/₄ ounce Framboise liqueur or raspberry syrup

Ginger ale

Lime piece, for garnish

Edible viola flower, for garnish

Build the first three ingredients in a highball glass filled with ice. Top with ginger ale. Garnish with the lime piece and an edible sweet violet or viola.

Note: I like flowers as garnish, but it's hard to find food-grade edible flowers. Everything available in regular markets is covered with pesticide. Check with your local gourmet food shop and see *The Herb Garden Cookbook,* by Lucinda Hutson (1998).

FREDDIE FUDPUCKER

This is Harvey Wallbanger's Mexican cousin.

1¹/₂ ounces tequila

5 ounces fresh orange juice

Float of Galliano

Build in a highball glass over ice and top with Galliano.

FRENCH FLAMINGO

I culled this one from the Sunday *New York Times* "Styles" section: It looked like one of my recipes, and I changed it a bit to suit my taste.

1 ounce Absolut Kurant

1 ounce Cointreau

³/₄ ounce fresh lime juice

³/₄ ounce fresh pomegranate juice

Lime peel, for garnish

Shake all the ingredients well with ice and strain into a chilled Martini glass. Garnish with the lime peel.

FRENCH CONNECTION

Renee's nightcap or eye-opener, and sometimes both.

1¹/₂ ounces Courvoisier

1 ounce Grand Marnier

Serve in a warm brandy snifter.

FRENCH 75

1 ounce brandy

³/₄ ounce Simple Syrup

¹/₂ ounce fresh lemon juice

Champagne

Shake the first three ingredients well with ice and strain into a goblet with ice. Top with Champagne.

FRENCH 95

³/₄ ounce bourbon

³/₄ ounce Simple Syrup

¹/₂ ounce fresh lemon juice

1 ounce fresh orange juice

Champagne

Shake the first four ingredients with ice and strain into an ice-filled goblet. Top with Champagne.

FRENCH KISS

2 ounces sweet vermouth

2 ounces dry vermouth

Lemon peel, for garnish

Mix over ice in a white wine glass. Garnish with the lemon peel.

A MARVELOUS PARTY

We knew the excitement was bound to begin / when Laura got blind on Dubonnet and gin / and scratched her veneer with a Cartier pin: / I couldn't have liked it more.

—FROM THE NOËL COWARD SONG
"I WENT TO A MARVELOUS PARTY"

CAPTAIN TRUMAN THE FRENCH 75

During World War I, Captain Harry S Truman once told his men, just minutes before their French 75 guns rattled 75-millimeter shells at the Germans (at a rate of 30 rounds per minute): "I'd rather be right here than be president of the United States!" This drink is named after that French artillery piece. The recipe originally called for gin, but it became more popular using brandy.

FROZEN DAIQUIRI (PAPA DOBLE STYLE)

Constantino (Constante) Ribailagua at the El Floridita Bar in Havana, Cuba, created the original frozen Daiquiri. I adapted Constante's recipe to accommodate today's larger glassware and to sweeten it slightly. Constante added the juice of the Marsh grapefruit, a very sweet seedless variety from the Isle of Pines near Havana, as well as maraschino liqueur to provide a delicate floral note.

1¹/₂ ounces white rum

¹/₂ ounce maraschino liqueur

1 ounce fresh grapefruit juice

1¹/₂ ounces Simple Syrup

1 ounce fresh lime juice

Blend all the ingredients with a handful of ice and strain into a special frozen-drink glass or into a medium-size wineglass.

FROZEN STRAWBERRY DAIQUIRI

Fresh-fruit versions of the frozen daiquiri are fun to prepare when seasonal fruit is available. Here is one for fresh strawberries.

1¹/₂ ounces white rum

¹/₂ ounce maraschino liqueur

4 to 6 medium-size strawberries, cleaned and cut up, plus one for garnish

1¹/₂ ounces Simple Syrup

1 ounce fresh lime juice

Blend all the ingredients with a handful of ice and strain into a special frozen-drink glass or into a medium-size wineglass. Garnish with the fresh whole strawberry by making a cut on the bottom of the strawberry and perching it on the rim of the glass. See the Hemingway Daiquiri on page 124 and you will note that frozen drinks require a lot more sweetening than shaken drinks because of all the additional water from the ice.

FUZZY NAVEL

Add vodka for the high-test version of this otherwise mild drink.

1¹/₂ ounces Peach Schnapps

5 ounces fresh orange juice

Seasonal fruit, for garnish

Build in a highball glass. Garnish with seasonal fruit.

GIBSON

Prepare a Martini (page 143) but substitute a cocktail onion for the olive. Charles Gibson, who created the Gibson Girls, enlisted the bartender at the Player's Club to create this special cocktail. After several attempts, the bartender came up with a dry Martini with small cocktail onions. That's one story. But not the one Albert Stevens Crockett tells in *Old Waldorf Bar Days,* 1931. According to Crockett, the drink was named for Billie Gibson, a fight promoter.

GIMLET

Be careful about switching fresh lime juice for Rose's lime juice; real Gimlet drinks want the taste of the preserved lime juice. When the drink is made with fresh lime juice and sugar, it is a sweet Gin Rickey, not a Gimlet.

2^1/$_2$ ounces gin

^{1}/$_2$ ounce preserved lime juice (Rose's or Angostura)

Lime wedge, for garnish

Shake the ingredients well with ice and strain into a chilled martini glass or serve over ice in an old-fashioned glass. Garnish with the lime wedge.

GIN AND IT

This cocktail also has a direct line to the Martinez cocktail, minus the bitters and maraschino. The Gin and It was actually ordered in the Hoffman House and other New York bars of the 1880s and '90s, simply as a Sweet Martini, and later as a Gin and Italian. During Prohibition, Gin and Italian was shortened to Gin & It.

1^1/$_2$ ounces gin

1^1/$_2$ ounces sweet vermouth

Dash of Angostura bitters

Orange peel, for garnish

Shake all the ingredients well with ice and strain into a chilled martini glass. Garnish with the orange peel.

GIN AND SIN * ◆

1 orange slice

1 lemon piece

^{1}/$_2$ ounce Simple Syrup

1 ounce fresh orange juice

^{1}/$_2$ ounce fresh lemon juice

^{1}/$_4$ ounce grenadine

2 ounces gin

Muddle the orange slice and lemon piece with the juices. Add the gin and grenadine. Shake all the ingredients well with ice and strain into a chilled martini glass.

THE GIN THING

The Gin and Tonic has always been the traditional cocktail-hour standard for summer gatherings. Several years ago, a customer challenged me to create a new summer drink. I made a gin sour, but I spiced it up by adding Angostura bitters and called it the Gin Thing. It became quite the thing that summer, so I put it on my cocktail menu. One guest who enjoyed the drink was a fiction reader for the *New Yorker* named Valerie, who insisted I give the drink a classier name. Since the Hemingway Daiquiri was on the menu at the time, she thought F. Scott Fitzgerald should get equal representation. I found out much later that what I had made already existed, a drink called the Bennett Cocktail, but I made it with lemon juice instead of lime juice. (See the Fitzgerald.)

GIN GIN HIGHBALL *

1¹/₂ ounces gin

5 ounces ginger ale

2 dashes of Angostura bitters

Lemon peel, to garnish

Build the ingredients in a highball glass over ice. Stir and garnish with a lemon peel.

GIN GIN MULE

Recipe by New York bartender Audrey Saunders.

¹/₂ ounce lime juice

¹/₂ ounce Simple Syrup

6 mint sprigs

³/₄ ounce homemade Ginger Beer (page 207)

1¹/₂ ounces Bombay gin

Splash soda water

Lime wedge, for garnish

Muddle the lime juice, syrup, and mint. Add gin and ginger beer and shake well. Pour over ice in a highball glass. Top with soda and garnish with the lime wedge.

GIN SLING

This is a late-nineteenth-century sling recipe that I served for years at the Rainbow Room with great success. The ladies from the photo-editing department of the Associated Press next door were especially fond of this recipe. The cocktail was first described in print as a bittered sling. Before the addition of bitters, a sling was spirits, sugar water, and sometimes lemon.

1¹/₂ ounces gin

1 ounce sweet vermouth

³/₄ ounce fresh lemon juice

1 ounce Simple Syrup

1 dash Angostura Bitters

Soda water

Lemon-peel spiral garnish (page 58)

Shake all the ingredients except the soda water with ice and strain over ice into a collins glass. Top with soda. Garnish with a spiral of lemon peel as in a Horse's Neck cocktail (page 125).

GODFATHER
(OR GODMOTHER)

1 ounce scotch or vodka

1 ounce Amaretto

Pour over ice in a rocks glass.

GOLDEN CADILLAC

Created at Poor Red's Saloon in Eldorado, California, where everything is golden.

1 ounce Galliano

1 ounce white crème de cacao

2 ounces heavy cream

Cinnamon, for dusting

Shake all the ingredients with ice and strain into a chilled cocktail glass. Dust with cinnamon.

GOLDEN DAWN

Winner of an international cocktail competition in 1930 by bartender Tom Buttery of the Berkeley Hotel in London.

¹/₂ ounce gin

³/₄ ounce fresh orange juice

³/₄ ounce Marie Brizard Apry or other apricot brandy

Dash of grenadine

2 dashes of bitters

Orange slice, for garnish

Cherry, for garnish

Shake all the ingredients well with ice and strain into a chilled martini glass. Garnish with the orange slice and a cherry.

GOLDEN GIRL *

1 ounce Bacardi 8

1/2 ounce Simple Syrup

1 ounce pineapple juice

3/4 ounce Offley Rich tawny port

1/2 small egg

Freshly grated orange zest, for garnish

Shake all the ingredients well with ice and strain into a chilled martini glass. Garnish with grated orange zest.

GRASSHOPPER

1 ounce green crème de menthe

1 ounce white crème de cacao

2 ounces heavy cream

Shake well with ice and strain into a martini glass.

GREEN TEA PUNCH

YIELDS SIX SERVINGS

I haven't found many applications for green tea in the cocktail world, but I did discover a fascinating recipe in an old English book called *The Gentleman's Table Guide* by Edward Ricket, published in 1873. I have adapted the recipe to cut the sweetness.

9 ounces red currant or guava jelly

16 ounces hot green tea

4 ounces brandy

4 ounces rum

2 ounces curaçao

Juice and peel of 2 lemons

Verbena leaf, for garnish

Dissolve the jelly in the hot tea and stir in the rest of the ingredients. Serve piping hot in mugs. Garnish with the verbena leaf.

Note: More tea may be added if the punch is too strong.

GREYHOUND

1 1/2 ounces vodka

4 ounces grapefruit juice

Pour together into an iced highball glass.

TRADITIONAL GROG

Strictly speaking, grog is either a hot or a cold drink of rum, sugar, molasses or honey, lemon juice, and water in the proportions below. In *The Flowing Bowl* by William Schmidt, the author calls for hot tea instead of water.

1 1/2 ounce heavy-bodied rum

1 ounce Honey Syrup (page 206)

3/4 ounce fresh lemon juice

4 ounces water (hot or cold)

1 cinnamon stick or lemon wedge, for garnish

For a hot drink, mix all ingredients in a mug and stir. Garnish with a cinnamon stick. To serve cold, shake the ingredients with ice and serve over ice in a rocks glass. Garnish with a lemon wedge.

NAVY GROG

1 1/2 ounces Dusser's Navy Rum

1 ounce orange curaçao

3/4 ounce fresh lime juice

2 ounces water

2 ounces fresh orange juice

Dash of Angostura bitters

Shake well with ice and serve in a bucket or double old-fashioned glass.

HAPPY HONEY COCKTAIL

2 ounces brandy

1 ounce fresh grapefruit juice

1/2 ounce Honey Syrup (page 206)

Shake all the ingredients with ice and strain into small martini glass.

HARRY'S COCKTAIL ♦

From Harry McElhone's *ABC of Mixing Cocktails*.

3 sprigs of fresh mint

1 ounce sweet vermouth

2 dashes of Absente

2 ounces gin

Stuffed olive, for garnish

In a mixing glass, muddle 2 sprigs of the mint with the vermouth and Absente. Add the gin. Shake with ice and strain into a chilled cocktail glass. Garnish with a stuffed olive and the remaining mint sprig.

OLD GROGRAM

In 1740, Admiral Vernon, the commander of the British naval forces in the West Indies and a hero after capturing Porto Bello from the Spanish, cut the established rum ration for British seamen operating in the Caribbean to a half pint mixed in a half pint of water. Vernon reasoned that with the heat, disease, and dysentery that were unavoidable hazards of operating in the tropical waters of the Caribbean, at least he could keep the men from falling out of the rigging stinking with rum. Vernon cut an imposing figure partly because of his greatcoat, which was made of a blend of silk and wool called grogram. He was soon nicknamed Old Grogram, and his watered-down rum was called grog. Vernon later added lime juice and sugar to the rum barrels to make a more palatable mix—and that sounds remarkably like a Daiquiri, which according to lore wasn't invented until about 150 years later in the town of Daiquiri, Cuba. Vernon was lucky or ahead of his time because in 1753 a Scottish surgeon named James Lind noticed that fresh fruit and fresh vegetables relieved the symptoms of scurvy. In 1793 the British Navy formally adopted the mixture of lime juice and rum begun 53 years earlier by Vernon. From then on British seamen were referred to as "Limeys."

HARRY'S HARVEYS PUNCH *

This cocktail was named after Harry Dwoskin, who into his nineties would throw an elaborate birthday party for himself each year. Harry was fastidious with his money and claimed he had enough to cover the parties through his 104th birthday. I created this drink for his ninetieth at the Rainbow Room. He liked it so much that he served it at every birthday party until his last one at age ninety-six.

2 ounces Harveys Bristol Cream

1 ounce maraschino liqueur

1/2 ounce fresh lemon juice

3 ounces fresh orange juice

Dash of Angostura bitters

Sprig of fresh mint, for garnish

Orange slice, for garnish

Shake all the ingredients with ice and strain into a large goblet. Garnish with a mint sprig and orange slice.

HARVEY WALLBANGER

This 1960s drink is purportedly named after a surfer who drank so much he'd bump into the walls. My all-knowing friend Brian Rea tells me that the reason the surfer drank so many Wallbangers was to get the empty Galliano bottles: women really loved them.

1 1/2 ounces vodka

4 ounces fresh orange juice

Galliano

Pour the vodka and orange juice together in a highball glass and float a little Galliano on top.

HAWAIIAN STONE SOUR *

I created this as a poolside drink for a regular guest and amateur bartender at the Rainbow Room.

1¹/₂ ounces blended whiskey

1 ounce Simple Syrup

³/₄ ounce fresh lemon juice

1¹/₂ ounces pineapple juice

Cherry, for garnish

Pineapple slice, for garnish

Shake all the ingredients with ice and strain into a rocks glass. Garnish with the cherry and pineapple slice.

HEMINGWAY DAIQUIRI (PAPA DOBLE)

In about 1921, the cocktail muse inspired the great Constantino Ribailagua of the El Floridita Bar in Havana when he added fresh grapefruit juice and maraschino liqueur to the Daiquiri. The result is ambrosia. The drink was made as a frozen drink at the famous Floradita and was named Papa Doble, or "Papa's Double," after Ernest Hemingway. The original recipe didn't call for any sugar, just a touch of the maraschino liqueur, and it is always reprinted that way out of respect to Papa; Hemingway had an aversion to sugar. But you can be sure that for the average customer at the Floridita, the Simple Syrup was part of the recipe.

1¹/₂ ounces white rum

¹/₄ ounce maraschino liqueur

¹/₂ ounce fresh grapefruit juice

³/₄ ounce Simple Syrup

³/₄ ounce fresh lime juice

Shake the ingredients with ice and strain into a chilled cocktail glass.

HI HO COCKTAIL

From the Hi Ho Club, Hollywood, circa 1930.

2 ounces gin

1 ounce white port

4 dashes of orange bitters

Lemon peel, for garnish

Shake all the ingredients well with ice and strain into a chilled cocktail glass. Garnish with the lemon peel.

HONEYMOON COCKTAIL

From the Brown Derby, Hollywood, circa 1930.

2 ounces applejack

¹/₂ ounce Bénédictine

¹/₂ ounce orange curaçao

¹/₂ ounce fresh lemon juice

Lemon peel, for garnish

Shake all the ingredients well with ice and strain into a chilled cocktail glass. Garnish with the lemon peel.

HONOLULU COCKTAIL

From the Brown Derby, Hollywood, circa 1930.

2 ounces gin

¹/₂ ounce pineapple juice

¹/₂ ounce fresh orange juice

¹/₄ ounce lemon juice

¹/₄ ounce Simple Syrup

Dash of Angostura bitters

Lemon peel, for garnish

Prepare a chilled martini glass with a sugared rim. Shake all the ingredients well with ice and strain into the prepared glass. Garnish with the lemon peel.

HORSE'S NECK

This drink takes its name from the distinctive garnish that resembles a horse's head and neck peeking over the rim of the glass.

1¹/₂ ounces bourbon

5 ounces ginger ale

1 lemon-peel spiral garnish (see page 59)

Before icing a highball or collins glass, place the lemon-peel spiral in the glass, spiraling up from the bottom with the curled end of the spiral hanging over the rim of the glass. The piece hanging over the edge of the glass should look like a stylized horse's neck and head. Put the ice down through the center of the spiral and then build the drink.

HOT APPLE PIE

Tuaca is an Italian liqueur with honey, vanilla, and butterscotch flavors.

1¹/₂ ounces Tuaca

4 ounces hot apple cider

Sweetened Whipped Cream (see page 207)

Serve in an Irish-coffee glass, and float the cream on top.

Note: Unlike other coffee drinks, this recipe uses sweetened cream.

HOT SHOT

¹/₂ ounce Galliano

¹/₂ ounce hot coffee

Whipped cream

Build in a shot glass. Float whipped cream on top.

THE HI HO COCKTAIL

During the off-season at the Hotel Bel-Air, my schedule would drop down to working only two or three days a week, since I had the least seniority. So I would hustle a few days behind other bars here and there: I'd walk up one side of the street and down the other until I found a place, then I'd just walk in, find the boss, and ask him for a job.

That's how I found the Larsen brothers, who owned the Magic Castle in the Hollywood Hills. Milt and Bill Larsen were the total embodiment of classic show biz—as children, they'd traveled and performed with their vaudevillian parents all across the country. I went to work for them at the Variety Arts Club, a unique institution devoted to the history and preservation of vaudeville. The club served as a museum of show business, featuring the largest selection of radio scripts in the world, a complete archive of the films of Buster Keaton, a vast compilation of joke files, and all sorts of Hollywood memorabilia. The third floor housed W. C. Fields's pool table, complete with bent cue sticks, along with a hat collection from Gene Fowler, the sports writer and author or *Goodnight Sweet Prince,* an affectionate biography of John Barrymore. Gene's collection includes hats from his favorite drinking buddies and Hollywood pals, like John Barrymore, W. C. Fields, John Carradine, George Raft, Jimmy Durante, Douglas Fairbanks, and many others. Gene Fowler's son taught filmmaking and enjoyed taking his students to the club. After touring the museum, they'd have cocktails in the memorabilia-filled lounge.

On any given afternoon, you might see Victoria Jackson (before her *Saturday Night Live* fame) standing upside down on her hands in a Victorian maid costume, singing a drawl-inflected, off-key version of "All of Me" or Nissan the Gypsy swallowing flaming torches or juggling knives. It was on such an afternoon that George S. Drum, a dapper gentleman who appeared as though he had just stepped out of the 1930s, approached the bar. With the look of a mischievous child who could barely contain his excitement, George ordered a Hi Ho Cocktail (named for the Hollywood's Hi Ho Club, a popular thirties hangout), drank it down rather quickly, licked his lips, and happily pronounced, "I feel much more like I do now than I did when I first came in."

HUMMER

1 ounce coffee liqueur

1 ounce spiced rum

1 scoop of vanilla ice cream

2 ounces milk

Blend and serve in a frozen-drink glass.

HURRICANE

Made famous by Pat O'Brien's in New Orleans, where it's served in a 29-ounce hand-blown crested glass (reminiscent of a hurricane lamp)—a real eye-opener for people at Mardi Gras. According to Brian Rea, there are two versions. The first was a drink of the early twentieth century that contained Cognac, absinthe, and Polish vodka. The rum-juice combination appears to have surfaced at the 1939 World's Fair in New York, at the Hurricane Bar. I suspect that Rea is right—neither the drink nor Pat O'Brien's appear in the 1937 *Famous Drinks of New Orleans,* by Stanley Clisby Arthur. Today O'Brien's uses a mix with some juices and artificial flavorings etc…the usual fare. I went back to what the original bartender, Charles Cantrell, might have used to get more natural fruit flavor.

1 ounce dark rum

1 ounce light rum

$^1/_2$ ounce Galliano

$^3/_4$ ounce fresh lime juice

2 ounces passion fruit nectar, or, in a pinch, passion fruit syrup

2 ounces fresh orange juice

2 ounces pineapple juice

1 ounce Simple Syrup

Dash of Angostura bitters

Fresh tropical fruit, for garnish

Shake all the ingredients with ice and strain into a hurricane glass filled with ice. Garnish with fresh tropical fruit.

Variation: Try preparing this drink by muddling a piece of orange, a piece of lime, and a chunk of pineapple in the mixing glass with the lime juice and Galliano. Add the rest of the ingredients and shake.

ICEBERG

2 ounces lemon vodka

3 dashes of Pernod

Shake the three dashes of Pernod into an empty old-fashioned glass and swirl it around to coat the glass. Toss out any excess. Add ice and the vodka, and stir. No garnish.

ICE HOUSE HIGHBALL *

If edible flowers are not available, garnish this drink with fresh mint and lemon piece. I did a series of summer drinks for Absolut Vodka garnished with edible flowers. This is one example. For information on edible flowers, see Lucinda Hutson's book *Herb Garden Cookbook* (1998).

1½ ounce Absolut Citron

5 ounces fresh lemonade

Dash of white crème de menthe (Marie Brizard)

Edible orchid or other edible flower, for garnish

Build the vodka and lemonade in a large pint glass filled with ice and top with a dash of crème de menthe. Garnish with an edible orchid or other edible flower.

INDEPENDENCE DAY PUNCH +◆

The muddled fresh fruit really enhances the flavor of this nonalcoholic cocktail. Just add a shot of citrus vodka for the high-test version.

$^1/_2$ cup watermelon balls

1½ ounces Simple Syrup

$^3/_4$ ounce fresh lemon juice

4 ounces Lipton cold-brew tea

Thin wheel of lemon, for garnish

In the bottom of a mixing glass, muddle the melon with the Simple Syrup until it is watery. Add all the rest of the ingredients and shake well with ice. Strain into a goblet filled with ice and garnish with a thin wheel of lemon.

INTERNATIONAL STINGER

2 ounces Metaxa

³/₄ ounce Galliano

Shake well with ice and serve up or on the rocks.

IRISH COCONUT *

This would make a good name for an Irish bar in Trinidad.

³/₄ ounce Baileys Irish Cream

³/₄ ounce white rum

³/₄ ounce cream

¹/₂ ounce Coco Lopez

2–3 ounces soda water

Shake all the ingredients well with ice. Strain into an iced highball glass, top with soda, and stir.

IRISH COFFEE

1¹/₂ ounces Irish whiskey

Coffee

1 ounce Brown Sugar Syrup (page 206)

Hand-Whipped Irish Coffee Cream (page 207)

Combine the whiskey, coffee, and syrup in an Irish-coffee glass. Ladle 1 inch of cream on top.

Irish Coffee Variations:

Café Amore: Amaretto and brandy

Calypso Coffee: rum and Kahlúa

Jamaican Coffee: rum and Tia Maria

Mexican Coffee: tequila and Kahlúa

Spanish Coffee: Spanish brandy and Kahlúa

Royale: Cognac and sugar

Kioke Coffee: brandy and Kahlúa

President's Coffee: cherry brandy (whip the cream with a teaspoon of grenadine for color)

ISLAND BREEZE *

1¹/₂ ounces light rum

4 ounces pineapple juice

1 ounce cranberry juice

2 dashes of Angostura bitters

Lime piece, for garnish

Build over ice in a highball glass. Garnish with the lime piece.

IRISH COFFEE

Joe Sheridan, a barman at Foynes "Flying Boat Terminal" (now known as Shannon International Airport) in Ireland, originally prepared this drink. Sheridan had a habit of greeting weary travelers sneaking into war-torn Europe on seaplanes from the United States with hot coffee laced with Irish whiskey and topped with lightly whipped Irish cream. Here are some hints to make Irish as good as Joe's:

* Never use canned cream in an Irish Coffee; whip your own cream *without sugar,* by placing a stainless-steel bowl or pitcher in the fridge until it is very cold.

* Start with very cold heavy cream and whisk or whip to just under stiff, so the cream has no bubbles and will still pour slowly.

* Always sweeten the coffee using brown sugar or brown sugar syrup.

* Don't drown the drink in coffee—about 4 ounces is all you need.

* Find the classic stemmed Irish-coffee glasses; because of their size, they will force you to use the right amount of coffee.

ISLAND ROSE

¾ ounce tequila

¾ ounce Kahlúa

½ ounce Chambord

1½ ounces heavy cream

Organic rose petal, for garnish

Shake well with ice and serve straight up or over ice. Float the organic rose petal on the surface of the drink.

JACANA *

Created for Sharen Butrum's birthday party in 1998 on board the *Jacana,* a private yacht that books out for dinner cruises around Manhattan.

1½ ounce good tequila

½ ounce Grand Marnier

½ ounce Cointreau

¾ ounce fresh lime juice

1 ounce fresh grapefruit Juice

Shake all the ingredients with ice and strain into a chilled cocktail glass.

JACK ROSE

Albert Stevens Crockett, author of *Old Waldorf Bar Days* (1931), loved to set the world straight on cocktail names. He assures us that the Jack Rose was not named after an infamous person, but was in fact named for a pink rose called the Jacquemot rose.

1½ ounces applejack

1 ounce Simple Syrup

¾ ounce fresh lemon juice

2 dashes of grenadine

Apple slice, for garnish

Cherry, for garnish

Shake all the ingredients and strain into a small cocktail glass. Garnish with the apple slice and a cherry.

JAPANESE COCKTAIL

The Japanese Cocktail was one of the very few cocktails listed in Jerry Thomas's 1862 edition of *How to Mix Drinks or The Bon-Vivants Companion.* He calls for stirring with a couple of peels of lemon in the bar glass. Later recipes took the citrus note a bit farther by actually adding lime juice. I don't think limes were as available as lemons in 1862, or perhaps Jerry would have used them as well.

2 ounces Cognac

½ ounce orgeat

½ ounce fresh lime juice

Dash of Angostura bitters

Spiral of lime peel, for garnish

Shake all the ingredients well with ice and strain into a chilled cocktail glass. Garnish with a spiral of lime peel.

JAPANESE FIZZ * ♦

2 pineapple wedges

2 lemon wedges

2 orange slices

½ ounce Simple Syrup

¾ ounce fresh lemon juice

¾ ounce ruby port

1½ ounces straight or blended whiskey

Club soda

Muddle one piece each of the fruits in the bottom of the mixing glass with the syrup and lemon juice. Add the port and the whiskey, and shake well with ice. Strain into a highball glass filled with ice and top with soda. Garnish with the remaining fruit.

JULEPS

THE JULEPS WERE THE FIRST AMERICAN DRINKS TO ATTRACT INTERNATIONAL ATTENTION. EVERYONE THINKS BOURBON WHEN THEY THINK JULEP, BUT ACTUALLY THE FIRST JULEPS WERE MADE WITH COGNAC AND PEACH BRANDY. THEY GARNERED QUITE A BIT OF ATTENTION INTERNATIONALLY, ESPECIALLY IN ENGLAND, BUT IT WAS THE HOT AMERICAN SUMMERS THAT MADE THEM SO DESIRABLE, SERVED ICY COLD, FILLED WITH SHAVED ICE, AND CRUSTED OUTSIDE WITH ICE.

Always use tender, young sprigs of mint for juleps. They last longer and look better in the glass. Spearmint has small leaves with good structure that don't wilt quickly.

Pick about five inches off the top of the mint stalk and use the bottom leaves for bruising, saving the well-formed sprigs on top for the garnish.

dale's julep *♦

3 tender sprigs of fresh mint

2 slices of sweet Georgia peach

1/2 ounce Marie Brizard peach liqueur

2 ounces bourbon

In the bottom of a mixing glass, muddle one sprig of the mint and the peach slices with the peach liqueur. Add the bourbon and strain into a highball glass filled with crushed ice. Swirl with a bar spoon until the outside of the glass frosts. Garnish generously with mint sprigs. Top up with crushed ice.

mint julep ♦

2 tender sprigs of fresh mint

1/2 ounce Simple Syrup

2 ounces bourbon

In the bottom of a highball glass or a silver julep cup, muddle one sprig of mint with the sugar syrup. Fill with crushed ice and add the bourbon. Swirl with a bar spoon until the outside of the glass frosts. Top up with more ice and garnish with the remaining sprig of mint.

peach brandy julep * ♦

2 tender sprigs of fresh mint

1/2 ounce peach brandy (preferably Marie Brizard Peach Liqueur)

2 wedges of sweet ripe peach

2 ounces VS Cognac

Strip the leaves from one sprig of mint and muddle them together with the peach brandy and peach wedges. Add the Cognac and shake. Strain into a highball glass filled with crushed ice and stir until the outside of the glass frosts, adding more crushed ice if necessary. Garnish with the second sprig of mint.

Variation: Of course, you can substitute bourbon in place of Cognac.

pineapple julep * ♦

Leaves from 2 tender sprigs of fresh mint

3 wedges of ripe pineapple

1 ounce Simple Syrup

2 ounces bourbon

2 tender sprigs of fresh mint, for garnish

In a mixing glass, muddle the mint leaves, pineapple wedges, and Simple Syrup. Add the bourbon and ice and shake well. Strain into a highball glass filled with crushed ice and stir well until the glass frosts. Garnish with the mint sprigs.

Variation: There's another recipe for the Pineapple Julep with gin, a slice of pineapple, 2 ounces of orange juice, and a couple dashes of raspberry syrup; shake all those up, strain into an iced goblet, and top off with Champagne. I like the sound of it. This recipe from the 1890s shows there's more to the julep than just mint and bourbon.

rainbow julep * ♦

2 tender sprigs of mint

1/2 ounce Marie Brizard Apry or other apricot brandy

2 ounces bourbon

In the bottom of a mixing glass, muddle one sprig of mint with the Apry. Add the bourbon and strain into a highball glass filled with crushed ice. Swirl with a bar spoon until the outside of the glass frosts. Garnish with the remaining sprig of mint.

JUMP SHOT *

MAKES 4 SHOTS

This drink was created at the Rainbow Room's Promenade Bar for basketball players Rebecca Lobo and Sue Wicks of the New York Liberty, who joined me behind the bar as guest bartenders for charity.

1½ ounces white rum

½ ounce orange curaçao

1 ounce pineapple juice

2 dashes of Angostura bitters

Shake all the ingredients well with ice; strain into four 1-ounce shot glasses.

KAMIKAZI (SHOOTER)

SERVES 4

2 lime pieces

2 ounces vodka

½ ounce Cointreau

½ ounce Rose's lime juice

Squeeze the lime pieces into a mixing glass and drop them in. Add the remaining ingredients and ice. Shake well and serve in four 1-ounce shot glasses. Or serve as a cocktail in a chilled martini glass.

KENTUCKY COLONEL

This is kind of a Southern Stinger. It was the house drink for years at the Hotel Bel-Air in L.A.

2 ounces bourbon

1 ounce Bénédictine

Shake with ice; strain into a rocks glass filled with crushed ice.

KING ALFONSE

1½ ounces dark crème de cacao

1 ounce heavy cream

Layer in a pousse-café or cordial glass.

KIR

Dijon is the official home of the black-currant liqueur Cassis, and the drink Kir is named after a former mayor of Dijon, Canon Delix Kir.

¼ ounce Cassis

White wine

Lemon peel, for garnish (optional)

Pour the Cassis into a white-wine glass and fill with white wine. Garnish with the lemon peel, if using

KIR ROYALE (OR KIR IMPERIAL)

Champagne

¼ ounce Cassis or Framboise liqueur

Lemon peel, for garnish (optional)

Pour the Cassis or Framboise liqueur into the bottom of a champagne glass and fill with champagne. Garnish with the lemon peel, if using.

KNICKERBEIN COCKTAIL

This is an unusual name for a rich cocktail that will take the place of dessert.

¾ ounce orange curaçao

¾ ounce maraschino liqueur

¾ ounce VS Cognac

1 ounce whole egg

Freshly grated nutmeg, for garnish

Freshly grated orange zest, for garnish

Add all the ingredients to a cocktail shaker glass with ice and shake very well to completely emulsify the egg. Serve in a frosted London dock glass and dust with the nutmeg and orange zest.

KNICKERBOCKER

Adapted from Jerry Thomas's *How to Mix Drinks,* 1862. This can also be served over crushed ice with berries as a garnish.

2 ounces Appleton rum

1/2 ounce orange curaçao

1/2 ounce raspberry syrup

3/4 ounce fresh lemon juice

1 lemon wedge

Assemble all the ingredients in a mixing glass with ice, squeeze the lemon wedge and drop it in, shake well, and strain into a chilled cocktail glass.

Variation: When raspberries are in season, omit the raspberry syrup and muddle 6 to 8 raspberries with the lemon juice and curaçao in the bottom of a mixing glass. Add remaining ingredients and shake well with ice.

LATIN LOVE

Just surrender to this drink—but only drink one if you want to keep that hard body that attracts your Latin love. This drink by Aldo Zegarelli won the first annual Most Sensual Cocktail contest sponsored by *Penthouse* magazine.

1 ounce Cruzan Coconut Rum

1 ounce Cruzan Banana Rum

3 ounces pineapple juice

1 ounce Coco Lopez

1 ounce raspberry juice

1 ounce cream

1 scoop of ice

Combine all the ingredients. Blend to a smooth consistency. Rim a hurricane glass with grenadine and coconut shavings. Pour the mixture into the hurricane glass.

LEMONADE IN BULK

MAKES 1 GALLON

24 ounces fresh lemon juice

36 ounces Simple Syrup

68 ounces water

Lemon wedges, for garnish

Combine all the ingredients in a large container and stir well with ice for 3 minutes. Strain off the ice and refrigerate. Serve over ice with a lemon wedge.

LEMONADE [+]

3/4 ounce fresh lemon juice

1 1/2 ounces Simple Syrup

5 ounces water

Lemon wedge, for garnish

Shake with ice and serve over ice with the lemon wedge

LEMON DAISY [*] [+]

3/4 ounce fresh lemon juice

1/2 ounce grenadine

1/2 ounce Simple Syrup

7-Up

Soda water

In a white-wine glass, stir the lemon juice, Grenadine, and Simple Syrup together and add ice. Top with half 7-Up and half soda.

LEMON DROP

1/4 ounce fresh lemon juice

1/2 ounce Cointreau or Triple Sec

2 ounce citrus vodka

1 lemon wheel, for garnish

Shake all the ingredients well with ice and strain into a chilled martini glass with a sugared rim. Float a thin wheel of lemon on top of the drink. To serve as a shooter, use the recipe above and strain into three 1-ounce shot glasses. Cover the mouth of the shot glass with a wheel of lemon that has been dusted with sugar.

LEMON MERINGUE *

If you want to get fancy, beat up some egg whites and sugar until stiff and float it on top of the cocktail.

1¹/₂ ounces citrus vodka

³/₄ ounce lemoncello (Italian lemon liqueur)

¹/₂ ounce white crème de cacao

Shake the three ingredients well with ice and strain into a chilled martini glass.

LEPRECHAUN'S DELIGHT *

2 ounces vodka

¹/₂ ounce white crème de cocao

¹/₄ ounce green crème de menthe

Green maraschino cherry, for garnish

Stir all the ingredients and strain into a martini glass. Garnish with the green cherry.

LE PERROQUET

Generous dash of Campari

Dash of gin

2 ounces fresh orange juice

4 ounces chilled Champagne

Twist of lemon peel

Twist of orange peel

Pour the Campari, gin, and orange juice into a champagne flute. Top with Champagne. Garnish with the lemon and orange twists.

THE PERFECT GENTLEMAN

One day at the Hotel Bel-Air an elderly couple came in and sat at a corner table for lunch. They were alone in the lounge, seated at the one table that was out of view of the bar. In the middle of the lounge was a Steinway piano, which Bud Herrmann played in the evenings. The lock was broken on the piano, and while it was being fixed Bud had asked me to keep an eye out to make sure that nobody played it. So naturally, right after lunch, this slightly built, elderly man began to motor toward the piano. By the time I noticed, he was seated and raising the top. I got to the piano just before his fingers hit the keys and said, "Excuse me sir, I'm sorry, but the regular piano player, Bud Herrmann, would prefer that people not play piano during the day when he's not here."

The gentleman was very understanding and went back to his table. He paid his check with a credit card, and as I was processing it, I noticed his name: Vladimir Horowitz. I called the desk, hoping against hope that this was a different Vladimir Horowitz. But this was the Hotel Bel-Air, and of course it was *the* Vladimir Horowitz. I went back to Mr. Horowitz's table to apologize and to rescind my edict, commenting that I was probably the only person in the world who had ever asked him *not* to play piano. Horowitz completely understood, commenting that he actually had his own instrument shipped to wherever he was appearing. He was a perfect gentleman and bowing to Bud's wish did not touch the piano.

LONG ISLAND ICED TEA

CREDIT FOR THIS INCREDIBLY SUCCESSFUL FRAT-HOUSE DRINK IS ATTRIBUTED TO ROBERT C. BUTT. WHEN MADE PROPERLY, THE DRINK TASTES GREAT AND DOESN'T HAVE TO BE AN EVENING ENDER. THE KEY IS TO HAVE ALL THE SPIRITS PRESENT BUT IN SMALL AMOUNTS. IN THE RECIPE HERE, THE TOTAL ALCOHOL CONTENT IS 2½ OUNCES. IT IS A WELL-BALANCED, GOOD-TASTING DRINK, IN LARGE PART BECAUSE OF THE FRESH LEMON JUICE AND SIMPLE SYRUP. BESIDES THE "LONG ISLAND" VERSION, THERE ARE A FEW OTHER REGIONAL VARIATIONS.

long island iced tea

½ ounce vodka

½ ounce gin

½ ounce rum

½ ounce tequila

½ ounce Triple Sec

¾ ounce fresh lemon juice

½ ounce Simple Syrup

3–4 ounces Coca-Cola

Lemon wedge, for garnish

Shake all ingredients except the Coca-Cola with ice and strain into an iced tea or collins glass three-quarters filled with ice. Top with 3 or 4 ounces of Coca-Cola and stir. Garnish with the lemon wedge.

electric iced tea

½ ounce bourbon

½ ounce vodka

½ ounce gin

½ ounce Triple Sec

3–4 ounces Coca-Cola

2 lemon wedges

Build over ice in a highball glass and squeeze in the lemon wedges and stir.

miami iced tea

½ ounce vodka

½ ounce gin

½ ounce rum

½ ounce Peach Schnapps

1 ounce cranberry juice

7-Up

Lemon wedge, for garnish

Build over ice in a tall glass. Fill with 7-Up. Garnish with the lemon wedge.

london iced tea *

¾ ounce gin

¾ ounce rum

½ ounce Amaretto

½ ounce Simple Syrup

¾ ounce fresh lemon juice

3–4 ounces Coca-Cola

Lemon piece, for garnish

Shake all ingredients except the Coca-Cola with ice and strain into an ice tea or collins glass three-quarters filled with ice. Top with 3 or 4 ounces of Coca-Cola and stir. Garnish with the lemon wedge.

texas tea

½ ounce tequila

¼ ounce vodka

¼ ounce white rum

½ ounce Triple Sec

1 ounce fresh lemon juice

3–4 ounces Coca-Cola

Lemon wedge, for garnish

Shake all ingredients except the Coca-Cola with ice and strain into an ice tea or collins glass three-quarter filled with ice. Top with 3 or 4 ounces of Coca-Cola and stir. Garnish with the lemon wedge.

Variation: For a sweeter drink, add ½ ounce Simple Syrup. For a Dirty Texas Tea, use orange juice instead of lemon juice.

LEO SPECIAL

1 1/2 ounces gin

1 ounce Cointreau

3/4 ounce fresh lime juice

Dash of Pernod

Dash of green crème de menthe

Shake well with ice and strain into a chilled cocktail glass.

LIZZY SOUR *

1 ounce Alizé

1 1/2 ounces apricot liqueur

1 ounce fresh lemon juice

Lemon wheel, for garnish

Shake well with ice and strain into a martini glass. Garnish with the lemon wheel.

LOS ANGELES COCKTAIL

From the Hi Ho Club, Hollywood, circa 1930.

1 1/2 ounces bourbon whiskey

1/4 ounce sweet vermouth

1 ounce Simple Syrup

1 ounce whole egg, whipped to emulsify

1/2 ounce fresh lemon juice

Freshly grated nutmeg, for garnish

Combine all the ingredients in a shaker with ice and shake extra well to emulsify the egg. Strain into a chilled port glass. Dust with the nutmeg.

LUCKY DOUBLE * ◆

The Saucy Sisters cocktail created for the release of *Best Places to Eat in Nashville* by Barbara Nowak and Beverly Wichman.

1/2 lemon, quartered.

1/2 ounce Triple Sec

2 ounces Absolut Mandrin

Drop the lemon quarters into a bar mixing glass. Add the Triple Sec and muddle well. Add the Mandrin and ice. Shake well and pour the entire contents of the mixing glass into a rocks glass. Serve.

LUST FOR LIFE

Jeff Becker worked with me at the Rainbow Room for many years. This recipe is his.

1 1/2 ounces Galliano

1/2 ounce Marie Brizard peach liqueur

1 ounce fresh orange juice

1/2 ounce heavy cream

Freshly grated nutmeg, for garnish

Shake all the ingredients with ice and strain into a chilled martini glass. Dust with the nutmeg.

LYNCHBURG LEMONADE
(DALE'S VERSION)

1 1/2 ounces Jack Daniel's

1 ounce Cointreau

3/4 ounce fresh lemon juice

7-Up

Lemon wedge, for garnish

Orange slice, for garnish

Shake the first three ingredients with ice and strain into an ice-filled highball glass. Top with 7-Up and garnish with the lemon wedge and orange slice.

MACARENA MIST

Thanks to bartender Brian Smith, who worked with me at the Rainbow Room for many years, for this cocktail.

1 ounce Kahlúa

1/2 ounce Malibu rum

1/2 ounce white crème de menthe

1 1/2 ounces heavy cream

Shake all the ingredients with ice and strain into a rocks glass over crushed ice.

MADISON AVENUE COCKTAIL

Created by Eddie Woeke of the Weylin Bar, New York City, in 1936.

1 1/2 ounces white rum

3/4 ounce Cointreau

1/2 ounce fresh lime juice

Dash of orange bitters

3 mint leaves

Sprig of fresh mint, for garnish

Lime slice, for garnish

Shake all the ingredients except the garnishes with ice and strain into a rocks glass filled with ice. Garnish with the mint sprig and lime slice.

MADRAS

1 1/2 ounces vodka

4 ounces fresh orange juice

1 1/2 ounces cranberry juice cocktail

Orange slice, for garnish

Build over ice in a highball glass, floating the cranberry juice on top. Garnish with the orange slice.

MAI TAI

2 ounces aged rum

3/4 ounce orange curaçao

3/4 ounce fresh lime juice

1/4 ounce orgeat

2 mint sprigs, for garnish

Lime wedge, for garnish

Shake the ingredients well with ice and strain into an old-fashioned glass filled with ice. Garnish with the mint sprigs and wedge of lime.

MALIBU BAY BREEZE

1 1/2 ounces Malibu rum

4 ounces pineapple juice

1 1/2 ounces cranberry juice

Lime wedge, for garnish

Freshly grated nutmeg, for garnish

Build in a highball glass and garnish with the lime wedge.

Variation: Try this: Pour 1 1/2 ounces of Malibu rum in a mixing glass. Add 1 ounce each of pineapple and cranberry juices. Shake it very hard until the pineapple juice makes nice foam on top, then strain it into a chilled martini glass. Grate fresh nutmeg on top.

NAMING THE MAI TAI

The Mai Tai was created in 1944 by Victor Bergeron at his famed bar Trader Vic's in Emeryville, California, to take advantage of some good sixteen-year-old Jamaican rum he had around. Victor often said it was one of the finest drinks he'd ever concocted. When he made the drink the first time, he served it to his friends from Tahiti, Ham and Carrie Guild. After tasting the drink, Carrie raised her glass and said, "Mai tai roa ae," which means "out of this world" or "the best" in Tahitian. "That's the name of the drink," replied Bergeron.

This is another sour-formula drink, and in this case the sweet ingredients are orange curaçao and orgeat or orzata syrup. Don't over-use the strong flavor of orgeat, which should be subtle.

MANDRIN CHERRY SMASH *◆

$^1/_2$ lemon, quartered

$^3/_4$ ounce cherry brandy

$1^1/_2$ ounces Absolut Mandrin

In the bottom of a mixing glass, muddle the lemon wedges and cherry brandy. Add the vodka and ice and shake well. Pour all the ingredients into a rocks glass.

MARK TWAIN COCKTAIL

As described to his wife in a letter from London, 1874.

$1^1/_2$ ounces scotch whiskey

$^3/_4$ ounce fresh lemon juice

1 ounce Simple Syrup

2 dashes of Angostura bitters

Shake all the ingredients with ice and strain into a chilled cocktail glass.

MARLENE DIETRICH ◆

From the Hi Ho Club, Hollywood, circa 1930. The fruit could be muddled into this drink and then shaken for added flavor. Strain out the muddled fruit and add fresh fruit as the garnish.

2 ounces Canadian whiskey

$^1/_2$ ounce orange curaçao

3 dashes of Angostura bitters

1 piece of lemon

1 piece of orange

Shake all the ingredients well with ice and strain into a rocks glass filled with ice. Squeeze the lemon and orange.

Mandarin Cherry Smash.

THE MARY PICKFORD

Created at the Hotel Nacîonal de Cuba in Havana during Prohibition for the film star.

2 ounces white rum

$1^1/_2$ ounces pineapple juice

1 teaspoon grenadine

$^1/_4$ ounce maraschino liqueur

Shake with ice and strain into a chilled martini glass.

THE MANHATTAN

THE MANHATTAN IS THE QUINTESSENTIAL RYE COCKTAIL—EXCEPT IN MINNESOTA AND WISCONSIN, WHERE THEY PREFER BRANDY MANHATTANS; OR DOWN SOUTH, WHERE BOURBON MANHATTANS ARE THE CHOICE. LEGEND HAS IT THAT IN 1874, A BARTENDER AT THE MANHATTAN CLUB CREATED THE MANHATTAN WHEN JENNIE CHURCHILL (MOTHER OF WINSTON) THREW A PARTY FOR HER FATHER'S FRIEND, THE NEWLY ELECTED GOVERNOR OF NEW YORK, SAMUEL JAMES TILDEN. (TILDEN LAYS CLAIM TO ANOTHER FOOTNOTE IN HISTORY: LIKE VICE PRESIDENT AL GORE, HE WAS DEFEATED IN HIS 1876 BID FOR THE PRESIDENCY EVEN THOUGH HE WON THE POPULAR VOTE, JUST AFTER HE WAS ELECTED GOVERNOR OF NEW YORK.) THE FORMULA FOR THE MANHATTAN-STYLE DRINK IS TWO OR THREE PARTS OF WHISKEY TO ONE PART SWEET VERMOUTH. FOR THE PERFECT MANHATTAN, BOTH SWEET AND DRY VERMOUTH ARE USED. SINCE NEW YORK WAS A RYE TOWN IN THOSE DAYS, THE ORIGINAL MANHATTAN WAS MADE WITH RYE WHISKEY. ONE OF THE MOST FAMOUS SPIN-OFFS IS THE ROB ROY (PAGE 180).

manhattan

2 ounces blended or straight whiskey

1 ounce Italian sweet vermouth

2 dashes of Angostura bitters

Cherry, for garnish

Pour all the ingredients over ice in a mixing glass and stir as you would a Martini. Strain into a chilled cocktail glass. Garnish with the cherry.

Variation: If you prefer a dry Manhattan, use dry vermouth and garnish with a lemon peel. A Manhattan made with brandy is called a Harvard, and with applejack it's called a Star Cocktail.

apple manhattan

This is one of the best new cocktails I've tasted in twenty years, created by master bartender David Marsden when he worked in a classy little spot called First on First in New York City. Don't try this without the Berentzen's.

2 ounces Maker's Mark bourbon

1 ounce Berentzen's apple liqueur (made in Germany)

Thin slice of Granny Smith apple, for garnish

Stir the two ingredients in a mixing glass with ice and strain into a chilled cocktail glass. Garnish with the apple slice.

eastern manhattan *

Created for the Inagiku Japanese restaurant in the Waldorf Astoria.

2^1/$_2$ ounces Suntory Royal Whiskey

^{1}/$_4$ ounce Ricard or Pernod

^{1}/$_2$ ounce sweet vermouth

Cherry, for garnish

Stir with ice to chill and strain into a chilled cocktail glass. Garnish with the cherry.

red manhattan

2^1/$_2$ ounces Absolut Kurant

^{3}/$_4$ ounce Saint Raphael Apértif de France

2 dashes of Angostura bitters

Cherry, for garnish

Stir with ice to chill and strain into a chilled martini glass. Garnish with the cherry.

Variation: If you can't find St. Raphael, Carpano Punt e Mes makes a wonderfully spicy Manhattan.

man o' war

1^1/$_2$ ounces Wild Turkey 101

1 ounce orange curaçao

^{1}/$_2$ ounce sweet vermouth

^{1}/$_2$ ounce fresh lemon juice

Orange slice, for garnish

Cherry, for garnish

Shake all the ingredients well with ice and serve on the rocks. Garnish with the orange slice and cherry.

Variation: Try shaking the cocktail with a small piece of orange and lemon in the shaker to add to the flavor.

maragato

This was an early recipe from the famous El Floridita Bar in Havana, Cuba.

1 ounce silver rum

^{1}/$_2$ ounce sweet vermouth

^{1}/$_2$ ounce dry vermouth

1 ounce fresh orange juice

^{1}/$_2$ ounce fresh lime juice

Dash maraschino liqueur

Flamed orange peel (see page 58), for garnish

Shake all ingredients well with ice and strain into a chilled cocktail glass. Garnish with the flamed orange peel.

THE MARGARITA

JOE BAUM LIKED MANY DIFFERENT DRINKS: THE MARGARITA, WHISKEY SOUR, BLOODY MARY, BLUE BLAZER, CAIPIRINHA, PISCO SOUR, AND THEN SOME. IN FACT, HE WAS ESPECIALLY PLEASED WHEN I ADDED BOTH THE PISCO SOUR AND THE CAIPIRINHA TO THE RAINBOW ROOM REPERTOIRE. BOTH DRINKS HAD BEEN ON HIS MENU AT HIS FAMOUS LA FONDA DEL SOL, A GREAT SOUTH AMERICAN RESTAURANT THAT WAS WAY AHEAD OF ITS TIME. WHEN CONSIDERING DRINKS TO PUT ON HIS MENU, JOE WOULD ORDER THE SAME DRINK THREE TIMES IN A ROW AND THEN MOVE ON TO ANOTHER DRINK UNTIL HE TASTED ONE THAT PLEASED HIM. IT WASN'T AN EASY PROCESS—THEN AGAIN, NOTHING WAS EASY WITH JOE. WHEN HE DIDN'T LIKE A DRINK, THERE WAS NO EXPLANATION: IT WAS SIMPLY WRONG AND NEEDED FIXING. I WOULD TASTE IT AND TRY TO IMPROVE IT.

One day Joe came in with Gerard Pangaud, who announced that he had just won the Margarita contest in Paris and challenged me to make one. They began to sip several versions of my Margarita, trying to determine the perfect proportions of lime juice, Cointreau, and Cuervo Gold down to the milliliter.

While they were drinking all those Margaritas, I tried to cut them off because Joe was getting drunk. But he just snarled at me that he owned the joint and ordered another one—and another. Later, Joe slipped and fell in front of his home and suffered a cut to his head. I hate to say it, but unfortunately it took twenty-six stitches to prove that I had finally won him over with my Margaritas.

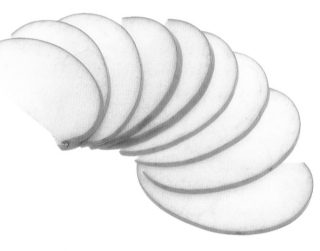

margarita

1¹/₂ ounces tequila

1 ounce Cointreau

³/₄ ounce fresh lime juice

Combine the ingredients in a mixing glass with ice. Shake well and strain into a chilled cocktail glass with a salted rim. Salting the rim: Rim the edge of the cocktail glass by rubbing a lime piece on the *outside rim* of the glass, then dipping the outside rim into a saucer of coarse salt.

big apple margarita

2 ounces tequila

1 ounce Berentzen's Apple Liqueur

³/₄ ounce fresh lemon or lime juice

Green apple slice, for garnish

Shake with ice and strain into a chilled cocktail glass with a salted rim. Garnish with the slice of green apple.

bloody margarita

1¹/₂ ounces tequila

1 ounce blood orange juice

¹/₂ ounce fresh lime juice

³/₄ ounce Cointreau

Shake with ice and strain into a chilled cocktail glass.

cadillac margarita

1¹/₂ ounces 100% blue agave tequila

1 ounce Grand Marnier

³/₄ ounce fresh lime juice

Shake all the ingredients with ice and strain into a chilled martini glass with a salted rim.

dale's ultimate mango-rita * ◆

2 slices of fresh sweet mango

¹/₂ ounce Triple Sec

¹/₂ ounce Simple Syrup

1¹/₂ ounces 100% blue agave tequila

³/₄ ounce fresh lime Juice

Thin lime wheel, for garnish

In a mixing glass, muddle the mango with the Triple Sec and Simple Syrup. Add the rest of the ingredients and shake well with ice. Strain into a chilled martini glass and garnish with lime.

frozen margarita

2 ounces tequila

1 ounce triple sec

1 ounce fresh lime juice

2 ounces Simple Syrup

³/₄ cup cracked ice

Combine all the ingredients in a blender. Blend and pour into a large goblet rimmed with coarse salt.

frozen passion margarita *

³/₄ ounce Alizé Gold

³/₄ ounce tequila

³/₄ ounce Triple Sec

1 ounce fresh lime juice

1¹/₂ ounces Simple Syrup

³/₄ cup cracked ice

Thin lime wheel, for garnish

Pour all the ingredients into a blender and blend. Serve in a margarita glass rimmed with coarse salt. Garnish with the lime wheel.

passion margarita *

³/₄ ounce Alizé Gold

³/₄ ounce tequila

1 ounce Cointreau

³/₄ ounce fresh lime juice

Thin lime wheel, for garnish

Shake all the ingredients well with ice and strain into a chilled cocktail glass rimmed with coarse salt. Garnish with the lime wheel.

tangerine margarita

Created by Fred McKibbon, owner of Grace Bar in New York City.

2 ounces Sauza Conmemorativo

1 ounce Cointreau

¹/₂ ounce fresh lime juice

¹/₂ ounce fresh tangerine juice

Shake all the ingredients with ice and strain into a chilled cocktail glass with a salted rim.

THE MARTINI

LIKE ALL ROYALTY, THE KING OF COCKTAILS HAS LINEAGE. THE BRITISH CLAIM THE MARTINI WAS NAMED AFTER A LATE-NINETEENTH-CENTURY FIREARM OF THE SAME NAME, FAMOUS FOR ITS KICK. THE MARTINI & ROSSI VERMOUTH COMPANY TAKES CREDIT FOR ITS NAME, SINCE VERMOUTH IS THE DEFINING INGREDIENT IN THE MARTINI, AND THEY DID MARKET A BOTTLED DRY MARTINI AROUND THE WORLD IN THE 1890S.

Martini di Arma di Taggia, the principal bartender at the Knickerbocker Hotel in New York City at the turn of the century, is also given credit for the Martini. Mr. Di Taggia played an important role in the evolution of the drink when he married dry gin with dry vermouth (and orange bitters) for the first time, but there is more to the story. There was a cocktail in the 1850s called the Fancy Gin Cocktail (opposite) that paired Old Tom Gin and orange curaçao. At the time the Fancy Gin became popular, Martini & Rossi Vermouth was not readily available in this country, the Martini and Henry rifle was still on the drawing board, and Martini di Arma di Taggia was just a small boy.

When vermouth became widely available by the 1870s, the use of curaçao as a sweetener in cocktails waned, and vermouth became the sweetener of choice, used in almost the same applications married with a base liquor and bitters. Vermouth wasn't even produced commercially until the late eighteenth century in Europe, and it was a relatively new product for the United States; the first shipments arrived in the 1850s. In his 1887 *Bartender's Guide*, Jerry Thomas refers to vermouth several times without designating Italian or French (sweet or dry). This wasn't an omission: French vermouth didn't become widely available until the late 1890s.

martinez cocktail, original

Gum syrup (Simple Syrup) can be added for a sweeter drink.

1 dash Bokers Bitters (substitute Angostura bitters)
2 dashes of maraschino liqueur
1 pony of Old Tom gin (gin with syrup)
1 wineglass of Italian vermouth

Shake well and strain into a large cocktail glass. Put a quarter slice of lemon in the glass and serve.

martini cocktail

This is Harry Johnson's Martini recipe from his 1888 *Bartender's Manual.*
Johnson and Jerry Thomas were the reigning kings of the original cocktail era, 1850 through 1900. Johnson always believed he held the upper
hand, claiming to have published a bar-recipe book prior to
Thomas's 1862 volume. If this is true, no copy has ever turned up in
my research. Johnson did win the first bartender competition in
the history of the modern profession, in New Orleans in 1869,
against five top contenders. Unfortunately, Thomas wasn't
part of the competition, so the debate over who really was
the greatest will never be settled. (The gum syrup Johnson
calls for is Simple Syrup, page 206).

Fill a large bar glass with ice.

2 to 3 dashes of gum syrup (careful—not too much)

2 to 3 dashes of Bokers Bitters (no longer available;
    substitute Angostura bitters)

1 dash of curaçao or absinthe if required

Half a wineglass of Old Tom gin

Half a wineglass of vermouth

Stir well with a spoon. Strain into a fancy
cocktail glass; put in a cherry or medium-
size olive (if required) and squeeze a
lemon peel on top.

extra-dry martini

1 dash dry French vermouth

3 ounces gin and/or vodka

Pitted olive (no pimiento) or lemon peel, for
garnish

Stir with ice in a mixing glass (50 times if using
large cubes, 30 if using small ones). Strain into a
chilled martini glass, and garnish with olive or
lemon peel or both.

fancy gin cocktail

3 or 4 dashes of Simple Syrup

2 dashes of Bokers Bitters

1 wineglass of gin

1 or 2 dashes of orange curaçao

1 small piece of lemon peel

Fill a shaker one-third full of fine ice, add the ingredients, and
shake well. Moisten the edge of a fancy wineglass with lemon
and strain the cocktail into the glass. Toss the lemon peel on top.

martinez cocktail, update

Noilly Prat, the French company that pioneered dry vermouth, didn't begin shipping to the United States until 1896. All Martinis prior to that were made with Italian sweet vermouth.

2 dashes of Angostura bitters

2 dashes of maraschino liqueur (or Cointreau, in a pinch)

1¹/₂ ounces gin

1 ounce dry vermouth

Lemon piece, for garnish

Shake all the ingredients with ice and strain into a chilled martini glass. Garnish with the lemon piece.

nick and nora martini

During Prohibition, the gin tasted so bad that everything imaginable was added to it to mask the flavor. The martini waned in popularity. After Prohibition, Nick and Nora Charles of the *Thin Man* movies and President Franklin Roosevelt put the Martini back on the map. Good gin was back, and people once more embraced the simplicity of the Martini. America got wetter and the Martini got drier: The Nick and Nora recipe calls for 3 parts gin to 1 part dry vermouth. This ratio reigned through the thirties and forties.

1¹/₂ ounces gin

¹/₂ ounce dry vermouth

Olive, for garnish

Fill a mixing glass with ice, add spirit, and stir well. Strain into a chilled martini glass and garnish with an olive.

knickerbocker martini

The modern-style martini of London Dry gin with dry vermouth wasn't offered until the turn of the century. I call it the Knickerbocker Martini. Colonel John Jacob Astor's Knickerbocker Hotel, built in in 1906, housed one of the grandest bars in New York. The bar was also the original home of the Maxfield Parrish triptych of Old King Cole that now hangs above the bar at the St. Regis Hotel. The principal bartender, Martini di Arma di Taggia, made his famous "dry" martini there.

And although his recipe of equal parts of dry gin and dry vermouth was a long way off from our modern dry Martini, it was the first combination of dry vermouth and dry gin. He mixed half Plymouth gin and half-dry or French vermouth with a dash of orange bitters. Sweet Martinis were also still very popular, and eventually they evolved into the Gin and Italian, or Gin and It as the drink was called during Prohibition. Here is a recipe for a "dry" martini similar to the Knickerbocker Martini, from Louis Muckensturm's *Louis Mixed Drinks* (1906). Notice that Muckensturm's version calls for 2 to 1 gin to vermouth, a step forward: but he had that dash of curaçao to cater to America's sweet tooth.

2 dashes of orange bitters

1 dash of orange curaçao

1 liqueur glass of French vermouth

2 liqueur glasses of gin

Lemon peel, for garnish

Fill a mixing glass with ice; add the spirits, stir well, and strain into a chilled martini glass. Squeeze some lemon peel on top.

dirty martini

Franklin D. Roosevelt was the first to popularize this odd drink. After working behind bars, I don't think many bartenders would drink the Dirty Martini—the brine in the olive jar can get pretty funky after sitting around for a while. If you want to try this one at home, get a jar of gourmet martini olives like the Tipsy Olives sold by Sable and Rosenfeld, which are packed in vermouth and spirit vinegar. Another idea is to remove half of the brine from regular store-bought olives and refill the jar with dry vermouth. If the drink is made on the rocks, stir in the glass.

Dash of dry French vermouth

3 ounces gin or vodka

¼ ounce olive brine

Pitted cocktail olive (no pimento), for garnish

Stir all the ingredients with ice in a mixing glass. Strain into a chilled martini glass. Garnish with the olive.

dry martini, cold-war era

After the Second World War, gin was still king, but the amount of vermouth in a Martini began to diminish dramatically. By 1960, the Martini was a lethal 11 parts gin to 1 part vermouth.

3 dashes of dry French vermouth

2 ounces gin

Pitted cocktail olive (no pimento), for garnish

Stir the ingredients with ice in a mixing glass (50 times if using large ice cubes, 30 times if using small cubes). Strain into a chilled martini glass. Garnish with the pitted olive.

EXTRA DRY

It was March 8, 1971, the much-hyped "Fight of the Century": Muhammad Ali's first fight after a three-year, government-imposed lay-off. Ali was fighting Joe Frazier for the world heavyweight championship at Madison Square Garden. Tickets to the Garden were out of the question, but the advertising agency I worked for bought a block of tickets to the Waldorf Astoria's closed-circuit broadcast. It was close, but everyone thought Ali was easily ahead on points. After Frazier won, they took him to the hospital because Ali had done a pretty good job rearranging his face. Famous ad man George Lois said later in the suite, "Where I grew up in the Bronx, the guy who went to the hospital was the loser!" Before the fight, playwright Marc Connelly, one of the original members of the Algonquin Round Table, came to the bar and ordered a Dry Martini. I grabbed a bottle of vermouth and started to make what I have since dubbed an "Irish Martini." With a pained look on his face, Marc's surprisingly steely hand (he was an octogenarian at the time) closed around my wrist and he forced the vermouth bottle back down to the bar, saying, "It is only necessary to grip the Vermouth bottle tightly, and quietly enunciate the word 'vermouth' while looking at the glass."

the vodkatini (THE SILVER BULLET)

In the late 1960s and early 1970s, the Cold War got colder and the Martini got stronger, with barely a hint of vermouth. John Martin succeeded in putting his Smirnoff Vodka bottle in front of all the right people, and vodka actually passed gin as the white spirit of choice.

Hold an open bottle of vermouth in front of a fan across the room.

3 ounces vodka

Pitted cocktail olive (no pimento), for garnish

Stir the vodka with ice in a mixing glass (50 times if using large ice cubes, 30 times if using small cubes). Strain into a chilled martini glass. Garnish with the olive.

apple martini

From the Waterfront Ale House in New York City.

1 pear, cored and cut into pieces

1 green apple, cored and cut into pieces

2 red apples, cored and cut into pieces

2 cloves

1 stick of cinnamon

1 liter vodka

2 ounces marinated vodka

1¹/₂ ounces cranberry juice

Thin slice of Granny Smith apple, for garnish

Marinate the fruit and spices in the vodka overnight. The next day, strain and discard fruit and spices. Assemble the marinated vodka and cranberry juice in a mixing glass and stir with ice. Strain into a martini glass and garnish with the apple slice.

sour apple martini *

I made this for Natalie Cole and her manager, on the occasion of Rupert Murdoch's seventieth birthday party. I had the cocktail gig, and she was the surprise entertainment. Rupert loved her, and she loved my Sour Apple Martinis.

2 ounces citrus vodka

¹/₂ ounce Sour Apple Pucker

¹/₂ ounce Cointreau

³/₄ ounce fresh lemon juice

Thin slice of Granny Smith apple, for garnish

Assemble all the ingredients in a cocktail shaker and shake well with ice. Strain into a chilled martini glass and garnish with the apple slice.

apples and oranges martini

SERVES 10

The German producer Berentzen makes a wonderful apple-flavored liqueur. You should find it in any good liquor store.

10 ounces Berentzen's Apple Liqueur

10 ounces cranberry juice

12 ounces Stolichnaya Ohranj vodka

Orange peel, for garnish

Thin slice of Granny Smith apple, for garnish

Mix all the ingredients together in a large pitcher with ice. Stir about 50 times to properly dilute the drink and remove the ice. Cover and refrigerate until ready to use. If you have the equipment it would be better if you gave each serving a shake at the time of service. Serve in a chilled martini glass. To garnish, express the oil from the orange peel over the top of the drink, discard the peel, and drop in the apple slice

broken heart martini *

Created for Zoe's Restaurant in SoHo, New York City.
My version of the Chocolate Martini.

Sugar

1 tablespoon Hershey's unsweetened cocoa powder

Orange piece

2½ ounces Absolut Kurant

½ ounce Godiva liqueur (dark)

In a saucer, mix together the sugar and cocoa powder. Dampen the outside rim of a chilled martini glass by rubbing an orange piece around it, and rim the glass with the cocoa powder. In a mixing glass, stir the Kurant and the Godiva with ice, and strain into the rimmed glass.

french martini

One of the sparks that got the cocktail-as-martini craze started.

2 ounces premium vodka

½ ounce Chambord

1½ ounces pineapple juice

Shake all the ingredients with ice and strain into a chilled martini glass. No garnish.

melon martini * ◆

½ cup chopped yellow and honeydew melon

1 ounce Honey Syrup (page 206)

1 ounce maraschino liqueur

1 ounce fresh lime juice

1½ ounces Absolut Citron

Sprigs of fresh mint, for garnish

Muddle the melon, Honey Syrup, maraschino liqueur, and lime juice together in a container. Add the vodka and ice. Shake and strain into a chilled martini glass. Garnish with the fresh mint.

pineau martini

2 ounces De Fussigny Pineau des Charentes

1 ounce gin

Flamed orange peel (see page 58), for garnish

Assemble the ingredients in a mixing glass with ice and stir. Strain into a chilled martini glass and garnish with the flamed orange peel.

pomegranate martini

2 ounces citrus vodka

½ ounce fresh lemon juice

¼ ounce fresh pomegranate juice (page 206)

1 ounce Simple Syrup

Dash of rose water, if available

Flamed orange peel (see page 58), for garnish

Shake all the ingredients well with ice and strain into a chilled martini glass. Garnish with the flamed orange peel.

rosy martini

2 ounces citrus vodka

½ ounce Cointreau or Triple Sec

½ ounce Red Dubonnet

Flamed orange peel (see page 58), for garnish

Stir all the ingredients with ice and strain into a chilled martini glass. Garnish with the flamed orange peel.

smoky martini

2 1/2 ounces gin

Splash of blended scotch

Lemon twist, for garnish

Stir both ingredients with ice to chill and garnish with the lemon twist.

Variation: Audrey Saunders makes a version of the Smoky Martini called the Dreamy Dorini Smoky Martini, for Dori, a whiskey-drinking woman. The recipe calls for vodka and a splash of Laphroaig scotch, the smokiest of the Islay scotches, and here is the secret: Season the ice with Pernod.

Broken Heart Martini (left) and the Valencia (below).

sake-tini *

Garnish with an exotic, round, small fruit or nut, such as a litchi.

2 1/2 ounces gin

1/4 ounce dry sake

1/4 ounce orange curaçao

Assemble the three ingredients in a mixing glass, fill with ice. Stir and strain into a chilled martini glass.

salt-and-pepper martini

1 1/2 ounces gin

3/4 ounce fresh lemon juice

3/4 ounce fresh grapefruit juice

1 ounce Simple Syrup

2 dashes of Angostura bitters

Shake all the ingredients with ice and strain into a chilled martini glass rimmed with coarse salt.

IN SEARCH OF THE PERFECT MARTINI GLASS

What constitutes the *perfect* cocktail glass? Let's start with size: A 5- to 6-ounce glass is perfect. It is large enough to feel like a generous drink, but still feel manageable. Through the 1960s, cocktails were served in 3- to 4-ounce glasses that were perfect for keeping drinks icy cold from beginning to end, allowing you to sip, not gulp. They were lovely little appetite teasers that could be enjoyed without making you lose all interest in food. The new 5.5-ounce glass accommodates 3.5 ounces of ingredients. Add ice, stir or shake, and the final drink hits the fill line at about $1/4$ inch below the rim of the glass. Next is shape. The glass should stand between 6 and 7 inches tall. The base should be between 3 and $3^1/2$ inches in diameter. The mouth of the bowl should be slightly larger than the base, but no more than 2 inches larger or the glass will feel top-heavy and tippy.

Finally comes style, which is much more personal. I prefer a clear glass without color and without optics. The Martini is nicknamed "the see-through," and quite frankly, I want to see through it. The stem should flow to the top of the bowl without interruption; if there's a seam, it should be where the stem intersects with the base, not with the bowl. The martini glasses pictured on page 149 illustrate this style.

soho martini*

Created for Zoe's restaurant in SoHo in Manhattan. I never mixed vodkas together in a drink as I have done with rums for years until all the flavored vodkas arrived. Now I'm finding some wonderful combinations using flavored vodkas together in the same drink or paired with regular vodka.

2 ounces vodka

$1/2$ ounce Stolichnaya Vanil

$1/2$ ounce orange curaçao

Dash of orange bitters

Flamed orange peel (see page 58), for garnish

Shake all the ingredients with ice and strain into a chilled martini glass. Garnish with the flamed orange peel.

upside-down martini

$2^1/2$ ounces French dry vermouth

1 ounce gin

Lemon peel, for garnish

Assemble gin and vermouth in a mixing glass filled with ice and stir. Strain into a chilled martini glass and garnish with the lemon peel.

valencia

$1/2$ ounce fino sherry

$2^1/2$ ounces vodka

3 orange peels for flaming (see page 58)

Coat the inside of a martini glass with fino sherry and toss out the excess. Flame two of the orange peels into the glass and discard. Chill the vodka and strain into the seasoned glass. Garnish with the last flamed orange peel.

vesper

The original James Bond Martini. The recipe was created by London-based bartender Gilberto Preti for Ian Fleming at the publication of the first Bond book, *Casino Royale*. The Bond Martini was later streamlined to "Vodka, very cold…very large…shaken, not stirred" to accommodate the Smirnoff brand, which paid well to display their bottle in the movie.

3 parts vodka

1 part gin

¼ ounce Lillet Blonde

Orange peel, for garnish

Shake with ice and strain into a martini glass. Garnish with the orange peel.

watermelon martini

½ ounce fresh lemon juice

1 ounce Midori

1 ounce citrus vodka

1½ ounces fresh watermelon juice

Sprigs of fresh mint, for garnish

Shake all the ingredients with ice and strain into a chilled martini glass. Garnish with the mint.

winston martini

Created by Marie Maher, former head bartender of the Greatest Bar on Earth in the Windows of the World complex, which occupied the 106th and 107th floors of Tower One of the World Trade Center in New York City, destroyed in the terrorist attacks of September 11, 2001. Maher was no longer on staff when the tragedy occurred.

Dash of Frangelico

1 ounce spiced rum

1 ounce gin

Scant dash of Rose's Lime Juice

Lemon twist, for garnish

Season a chilled mixing glass with the Frangelico. Stir the remaining ingredients in the glass and strain into a martini glass. Garnish with the lemon twist.

yin martini *

I created the Yin and Yang Martinis for a wonderful Japanese restaurant in the Waldorf Astoria called Inagiku.

3 ounces sake

½ ounce gin

Oriental fruit or litchi nut, for garnish

Pour both ingredients into a mixing glass with ice and stir to chill. Strain into a chilled martini glass. Garnish with an oriental fruit or litchi nut.

yang martini *

3 ounces gin

½ ounce sake

Olives, for garnish

Prepare the same as the Yin. Garnish with olives.

MILLENNIUM COCKTAIL *
(A.K.A. EAST INDIA COCKTAIL)

I was commissioned to create a cocktail with the Millennium bottling from Courvoisier and it turned out better than I ever expected. But now I guess I need to change the name: It's too good to be relegated to the trash heap of millennium merchandise. But in the couple of years since I thought I invented the drink, I acquired an out-of-print book called *The Roving Bartender,* by Bill Kelly (1946). Much to my surprise, it includes a drink called the East India Cocktail with brandy, curaçao, pineapple, and bitters. I don't know if it was Bill's original or if it predates his book. My version has a couple of subtle additions that translate to a lot of additional flavor—the grated nutmeg and the flamed orange peel.

1½ ounces Courvoisier Millennium Cognac

1½ ounces pineapple juice

1 ounce orange curaçao

1 dash of Angostura bitters

Flamed orange twist, for garnish (see page 58)

Freshly grated nutmeg, for garnish

Shake all the ingredients with ice and strain into a chilled martini glass. Garnish with the flamed orange twist and dust with the nutmeg.

MELON BALL

¾ ounce Midori

¾ ounce vodka

5 ounces fresh orange juice

Orange slice, for garnish

Melon slice, for garnish (in season)

Shake and strain into an ice-filled highball glass. Garnish with the slice of orange and, if seasonal, a small slice of melon.

MELONCHOLY BABY *

One of my most memorable experiences as a bartender was in the Rainbow Room: I created a special drink, on the spot, for a woman who had just ended a love affair and was really, *really* down in the dumps. It had flaming lemon peels and ended up becoming the drink of the night.

1½ ounces Absolut Citron

¾ ounce fresh lemon juice

2 ounces Simple Syrup

½ cup chopped cantaloupe (or similar)

3 ounces water

Flamed lemon peel (see page 58), for garnish

Blend all the ingredients with crushed ice and serve in a tall glass. Garnish with the flamed lemon peel.

MELON DAIQUIRI *

2 ounces sake

¾ cup chopped yellow and honeydew melon

2 ounces Simple Syrup

1 ounce fresh lime juice

Melon balls, for garnish

Blend all the ingredients with a handful of ice and serve in a large goblet. Garnish with melon balls.

The Millennium.

MELON LIME DAIQUIRI * ◆

I invented this drink to go with chef Andre Guerrero's chilean sea bass at Linq Restaurant in Los Angeles, California.

½ cup chopped yellow and honeydew melon

1 ounce Brown Sugar Syrup (page 206)

1 ounce maraschino liqueur

1 ounce fresh lime juice

2 ounces white rum

Sprigs of fresh mint, for garnish

Muddle the melon, Brown Sugar Syrup, maraschino liqueur, and lime juice together in a container. Add the rum and ice. Shake and strain into a chilled martini glass. Garnish with the fresh mint.

MERRY WIDOW

Adapted from *The Savoy Cocktail Book*, by Harry Craddock (1930).

Dash of Absente

2 ounces gin

½ ounce dry vermouth

Dash of Angostura bitters

Dash of Bénédictine

Flamed lemon peel (see page 58), for garnish

Season a chilled martini glass with the Absente and set it aside. Stir the remaining ingredients with ice in a bar glass and strain into the chilled martini glass. Garnish with the flamed lemon peel.

METROPOLITAN

Created by Mike Hewett at Marion's Bar in New York City.

1½ ounces Absolut Kurant

1½ ounces cranberry juice

½ ounce Rose's lime juice

⅛ ounce fresh lime juice

Lime wedge, for garnish

Shake with ice and pour into a chilled martini glass. Garnish with a lime wedge.

MEXICAN BLONDE *

This can also be served as a frozen drink, but double the amount of Kahlúa and orange curaçao.

1½ ounces light rum

½ ounce Kahlúa

½ ounce orange curaçao

1 ounce cream

Shake all the ingredients with ice and strain into a chilled cocktail glass.

MICHELADA

1 ounce fresh lime juice

3 dashes of Tabasco sauce

¼ ounce soy sauce

2 dashes of Worcestershire sauce

Pinch of black pepper

1 ounce Maggi seasoning or habanero sauce

One 12-ounce beer of choice

Mix the first six ingredients in the bottom of a beer glass. Fill the glass with ice and add your favorite beer.

MILLION-DOLLAR COCKTAIL

Created by Ngiam Tong Boon of Raffles Hotel in Singapore, circa 1910.

1½ ounces gin

½ ounce sweet vermouth

½ ounce pineapple juice

½ small egg white

2 dashes of grenadine

Shake all the ingredients with ice and strain into a martini glass.

MIMOSA

This drink was also known as a Bucks Fizz. Frank Meier of the Ritz Bar in Paris had an alternate recipe called the Valencia, with orange juice, apricot liqueur, and Champagne. (Valencia is also a Martini variation, with fino sherry in place of the vermouth.) A float of Cointreau is an appealing extra for a special drink.

2 ounces fresh orange juice

4 ounces Champagne

Pour the orange juice into a champagne glass and fill with the Champagne.

MOJITO ◆

In Havana, Hemingway liked to have his Daiquiris at La Floridita and his Mojitos at La Bodeguita del Medio. Although La Bodeguita is credited with popularizing the Mojito, there's a lot of controversy about the drink's origin. Some believe Constante Ribailagua of the Floridita made the first Mojito. The Mint Julep made in the southern United States beginning in the late eighteenth century from brandy, peach brandy, and eventually from bourbon was one of the first American cocktails to get international recognition, and some believe it sparked the creation of the rum version called Mojito in Cuba. The Mojito was a farmer's drink, sort of the Budweiser of Cuba, with its origins sometime between 1850, when the rum industry in Cuba modernized, in 1920. Those years brought important elements of the drink to Cuba for the first time, like ice and charged water. (The first shipments of ice arrived from New England in the 1850s, but you can bet only the wealthy had access until the turn of the century, when the first artificial ice plants began operation in Cuba.) A spicy sauce of the same name is used in the islands to marinate meat, but it seems to be unrelated to the drink.

2 tender sprigs of fresh mint

1 ounce Simple Syrup

³/₄ ounce fresh lime juice

1¹/₂ ounces Bacardi Silver rum

2 dashes of Angostura bitters (optional)

Soda water

Muddle one mint sprig with the Simple Syrup and the lime juice in the bottom of a mixing glass. Add the rest of the ingredients and shake with ice. Strain over cracked ice into a highball glass, top with soda, and garnish with the remaining sprig of mint.

MONKEY GLAND

Harry McElhone takes credit for this cocktail in his *ABC of Mixing Cocktails* and claims he named it after Dr. Serge Voronoff's experiments in rejuvenation.

Splash of Ricard

2 ounces Beefeater gin

1¹/₂ ounces fresh orange juice

1 teaspoon grenadine

Flamed orange peel (see page 58), for garnish

Splash the Ricard in a mixing glass and follow with the rest of the ingredients. Shake with ice and strain into a small cocktail glass. Garnish with the flamed orange peel.

MOSCOW MULE

John Martin used this drink to promote his new product, Smirnoff Vodka, after the Second World War. He did promotions with the owner of the Cock and Bull, a big star hangout on Sunset Boulevard in Los Angeles. It was served in a copper mug engraved with two mules kicking up their heels. Many of the stars had mugs with their names inscribed hanging over the bar. Smirnoff thus became the first real commercial brand of vodka in this country, built on Hollywood star power.

1¹/₂ ounces vodka

4 to 5 ounces ginger beer

Lime wedge, for garnish

Combine the vodka and ginger beer in an iced glass. Garnish with the lime wedge.

OLD FASHIONED◆

The Old Fashioned was created at the Pendennis Club in Louisville, Kentucky. There are two warring camps of Old Fashioned drinkers: those who muddle the fruit and those who don't. I belong to the first camp, as the muddling adds so much flavor. Those other guys just want some sweetened whiskey, not an Old Fashioned. The 1862 Whiskey Cobbler—the granddaddy of this drink—was shaken with two pieces of orange in the bar glass, so we have history on the muddling side. Shaking the fruit with ice will have the same effect as muddling. Or you can do both.

1 teaspoon sugar

2 dashes of Angostura bitters

2 orange slices

2 maraschino cherries

Water or soda water

2 ounces bourbon

In the bottom of an old-fashioned glass, carefully muddle the sugar, Angostura, one orange slice, one cherry, and a splash of water or soda. Remove the orange rind and add the bourbon, ice, and water or soda. Garnish with the remaining orange slice and cherry.

MUD AND BLOOD *

This is another of the *New York* magazine "challenge drinks" from Tony Hendra's feature in 1996. I had to create a drink *à la minute* from the least favorite liquid of each of several guests, and Alex Hargrave of Hargrave Vineyards chose carrot juice.

2 ounces carrot juice

2 ounces beef broth

2 ounces fresh orange juice

Dash of Tabasco sauce

Dash of Worcestershire sauce

2 ounces pepper vodka

Shake with ice and strain into a glass.

MUD SLIDE

1 ounce vodka

1 ounce Kahlúa

1 ounce Baileys Irish Cream

1 ounce cream

Shake all the ingredients with ice and serve over ice in a rocks glass. The Mud Slide can also be served as a frozen drink. Blend the four ingredients with three-quarters cup of ice and serve in a large goblet.

Variation: Switch Amaretto for the vodka and it is an Orgasm. Add vodka to an Orgasm and it becomes a Screaming Orgasm.

MUSK WE * +

1/2 cup chilled cantaloupe

1/4 cup chilled honeydew melon

3 ounces Sutter Home Fré White Zinfandel (nonalcoholic wine)

1 ounce Simple Syrup

1/2 ounce fresh lemon juice

1/2 ounce fresh lime juice

Blend the ingredients with 1/2 cup of ice and serve in a specialty glass or large goblet.

Old Fashioned.

NEGRITA *

The name means "pretty little dark one" in Spanish. The recipe below is for a shooter.

¹/₂ ounce pisco brandy

¹/₂ ounce coffee liqueur

¹/₂ ounce cold espresso

Combine all the ingredients in a shot glass.

NEGRONI

Created in Florence, Italy, in the 1920s, at the Casoni Bar, when customer Count Camillo Negroni asked the barman to add gin to his Americano. This drink can be made with vodka in place of gin.

1 ounce Campari

1 ounce sweet vermouth

1 ounce gin

Flamed orange peel (see page 58), for garnish

Combine all the ingredients in an iced old-fashioned glass and stir. Garnish with the flamed orange peel.

NEW ORLEANS COCKTAIL *

Peychaud's bitters mix well in most whiskey and brandy drinks.

2 ounces bourbon

3 dashes of Peychaud's bitters

2 dashes of orange curaçao

Flamed lemon peel (see page 58), for garnish

Stir all the ingredients with ice as you would a Martini and strain into a chilled martini glass. Garnish with the flamed lemon peel.

NEWMAN'S OWN STONE SOUR *

SERVES 15 TO 20

Developed by Paul Newman and his staff, Newman's Own products are high quality and all profits (after taxes) are donated to educational and charitable organizations, thus far raising over $100 million.

¹/₂ gallon Newman's Own Lemonade

¹/₂ gallon fresh orange juice

24 ounces Seagram's 7

Oranges slices, for garnish

Cherries, for garnish

Mix the ingredients in a large container and pour into pitchers. (To prepare individual servings, shake well with ice like a whiskey sour and strain into rocks glasses.) Garnish with orange slices and cherries.

NUTTY ANGEL

1 ounce vodka

1 ounce Frangelico

1 ounce Baileys Irish Cream

¹/₂ ounce dark crème de cacao

Freshly grated nutmeg, for garnish

Shake all the ingredients with ice and strain into a chilled martini glass. Dust with the nutmeg.

NUTTY IRISHMAN

1 ounce Baileys Irish Cream

1 ounce Frangelico

Shake and strain over ice in a rocks glass.

OLD FASHIONED ◆

See page 157.

OLD FLAME *

I won first prize in the Fancy Cocktail category at the 2001 Martini & Rossi Grand Prix in Malaga, Spain, with a version of this cocktail.

1 ounce Bombay gin

¹/₂ ounce Martini & Rossi sweet vermouth

¹/₄ ounce Campari

¹/₂ ounce Cointreau

1¹/₂ ounces fresh orange juice

Flamed orange peel (see page 58), for garnish

Shake all the ingredients well to chill and strain into a chilled 5¹/₂- to 6-ounce martini glass. Garnish with the flamed orange peel.

OP SMASH ◆

Recipe by Audrey Saunders, a talented career bartender. "OP" is an aquavit (flavored vodka) from Sweden flavored with peach, orange, ginger, and other spices.

3 lemon pieces, halved
³/₄ ounce Simple Syrup
¹/₄ ounce maraschino liqueur
1¹/₂ ounces OP flavored vodka

Place the lemon pieces in the bottom of a mixing glass along with the simple syrup and maraschino liqueur; muddle well. Fill a rocks glass with ice, and add that ice to the mixing glass along with the vodka. Shake well for 10 seconds, and then pour the entire contents of mixing glass back into the rocks glass, lemon pieces and all. Top with additional cracked ice.

ORANGE BLOSSOM

One of my favorite cocktail authors, David A. Embury, refers to this cocktail as the spawn of the Prohibition toad. But he does reluctantly offer his recipe: 2 parts gin to 1 part orange to ¹/₂ part Simple Syrup. Modern tastes lean toward a lighter drink, so I altered the recipe and added Cointreau instead of Simple Syrup to bring a bit of flavor along with sweetness.

1¹/₂ ounces gin
1¹/₂ ounces fresh orange juice
¹/₂ ounce Cointreau
Flamed orange peel (see page 58), for garnish

Shake all the ingredients with ice and strain into a chilled cocktail glass. Garnish with the flamed orange peel.

ORANGE BREEZE *

1¹/₂ ounces Stolichnaya Ohranj
1¹/₂ ounces Cointreau
3 ounces fresh orange juice
3 ounces cranberry juice
Orange slice, for garnish

Build in a large goblet with ice and stir. Garnish with an orange slice.

PARADISE COCKTAIL

This recipe has been on the back of the Marie Brizard Apry bottle for years. I just touched it up a bit.

2 ounces gin
³/₄ ounce Marie Brizard Apry
³/₄ ounce fresh orange juice
2 dashes of orange bitters
Flamed orange peel (see page 58), for garnish

Shake with ice and strain into a chilled cocktail glass. Garnish with the flamed orange peel.

PARIS

From the celebrated bartender Colin Field at the Hemingway Bar in the Ritz hotel, Paris. While you're there, don't forget to try Colin's legendary Bloody Mary.

1 ounce gin
1 ounce dry vermouth (French, of course)
1 ounce crème de cassis
Flamed lemon peel (see page 58), for garnish

Shake all the ingredients well with ice and garnish with the flamed lemon peel.

PARISIAN BLOND COCKTAIL

This is a vintage cocktail in the tradition of the classic Alexander, but here the liquor is rum and the cordial is orange curaçao. The name remains a mystery to me.

1 ounce rum
1 ounce orange curaçao
1 ounce heavy cream
Vanilla extract, for garnish (optional)

Shake all the ingredients with ice and strain into a chilled cocktail glass. A drop or two of vanilla extract on the cream is an interesting garnish.

OYSTER SHOOTER *

I created this one out of pure selfishness in 1999 at Blackbird Restaurant, and ordered it almost daily for lunch.

3 oysters (small variety like Olympia)

1 1/2 ounces pepper or lemon vodka

3 ounces Oyster Shooter Tomato Mix (see below)

3 oyster shells

3 lemon wedges

3 giant capers, with stem

Drop one oyster in each of the three shot glasses, add 1/2 ounce flavored vodka, and fill with 1 ounce of the tomato mix. Bury the shot glasses in a plate of crushed ice and garnish the ice next to each shot glass with an oyster shell, a lemon wedge, and a giant caper with the stem. The procedure is to suck on the lemon wedge, then take the shooter bottoms up, then bite into the caper.

OYSTER SHOOTER TOMATO MIX

Recipe for 1 quart of Oyster Shooter Tomato Mix (yields 10 oyster shooter plates).

2 leaves pineapple sage

26 ounces tomato juice

2 ounces balsamic vinegar

2 ounces fresh lemon juice

1/4 teaspoon each ground pepper and salt

2 teaspoons Tabasco sauce

1 tablespoon freshly grated horseradish root

Bruise the sage leaves in the bottom of a pitcher and add the rest of the ingredients. Stir and let stand for a couple of hours covered in the refrigerator.

PEACH MELISSA

From Fred McKibbon, owner of Grace Bar in New York City.

1 1/2 ounces Gosling's rum

1/2 ounce Simple Syrup

1 ounce fresh orange juice

1/4 ounce fresh lemon juice

1 ounce peach purée

1 peach slice, for garnish

Shake all the ingredients with ice and strain into a cocktail glass. Garnish with a peach slice.

PEGU COCKTAIL ♦

This was created at the Pegu Club in Burma when the sun didn't set on the British Empire. The Pegu goes very well with a fish course.

4 lime wedges

3/4 ounce curaçao

2 dashes of Angostura bitters

2 ounces gin

Lime peel, for garnish

Muddle the lime pieces, curaçao, and bitters in the bottom of a mixing glass. Add the gin and ice and shake. Strain into a chilled cocktail glass. Garnish with a lime peel.

PICA COCKTAIL *

This was my second-place prize in the Cardenal Mendoza cocktail contest. (My former employee at the Rainbow Room, Jeff Becker, won first. That didn't hurt so bad; I trained him.)

1 1/2 ounces Cardenal Mendoza brandy

1/4 ounce Galliano

1 1/2 ounces pineapple juice

2 dashes of grenadine

Orange peel, for flaming (see page 58)

Pour all the ingredients in the glass section of a Boston shaker. Fill with cubed ice and shake hard to a slow count of ten (or to the count of the first line of "Girl from Ipanema"). Strain into a chilled martini glass. Flame an orange peel over the surface of the drink and drop it into the glass.

PICON PUNCH

2 ounces Amer Picon

1/2 ounce fresh lemon juice

1/2 ounce grenadine

Soda water or ginger ale

Fresh seasonal fruits, for garnish

Shake the first three ingredients well with ice and strain into a highball glass filled with ice. Top with soda, or if you prefer a sweeter drink, top with ginger ale. Garnish generously with fresh seasonal fruits.

PICON PUNCH II

1 ounce Amer Picon

1/2 ounce grenadine

1/2 ounce brandy

4 to 5 ounces soda water

Twist of lemon, for garnish

Shake the first three ingredients with ice and strain into an ice-filled highball glass. Top with soda and garnish with a lemon twist.

PILGRIM COCKTAIL *

This recipe serves 1. For a recipe that serves 6, see the Punch section, page 169.

1/2 ounce dark rum

1/2 ounce light rum

1/2 ounce orange curaçao

2 ounces fresh orange juice

Juice of 1/2 lime

1/4 ounce Pimento liqueur

Dash of Angostura bitters

Shake all the ingredients and strain into a cocktail glass. Can be served hot or cold.

PIMM'S CUP

The traditional recipe is Pimm's mixed with English lemonade—our lemon-lime soda—but I prefer fresh lemonade with soda water.

1 1/2 ounces Pimm's No. 1

3 ounces fresh lemonade

Club soda or sweet soda

English cucumber spear, for garnish

Apple slice, for garnish

Combine all the ingredients in a highball glass and garnish with the English cucumber and apple.

PIÑA COLADA

In the 1950s in Puerto Rico, a man named Don Ramón Lopez-Irizarry came up with a delicious homogenized cream made from coconut. The product became known as Coco Lopez cream of coconut, and it was used for tropical dishes and desserts. But the best was yet to come: In 1957 Ramón Marrero, a bartender at Puerto Rico's Caribe Hilton, combined coconut cream with rum, pineapple juice, and ice in a blender to create this famous drink. Victor Bergeron (Trader Vic) borrowed Marrero's recipe in his later cocktail books and called it the Bahia. The trick to making a great Piña Colada is to use both light rum and dark rum, a dash of bitters, and a little heavy cream, which creates a drink with a much more complex flavor.

1 1/2 ounces light rum

1 ounce Myers's or Gosling's rum

2 ounces Coco Lopez

1 ounce heavy cream

4 ounces pineapple juice

Dash of Angostura bitters

1 cup crushed ice

Pineapple wedge, for garnish

Maraschino cherry, for garnish

Pour all the ingredients into a blender and blend for 15 seconds. Pour into a specialty glass like a poco-grande glass and garnish with the pineapple and cherry.

THE PIMM'S CUP

While working at the Hotel Bel-Air in the late 1970s, my interest was piqued by an odd drink that had a slice of cucumber and a slice of apple as the garnish. I learned more about the drink from some of my British customers, who described how it was served in a mug and garnished extravagantly with borage (a cucumber-tasting herb) or fresh mint sprigs and any or all of the following: orange, lemon, lime, and strawberries. Yes, when served British style, the drink is a real fruit salad.

The drink was Pimm's Cup, the base of which is an apéritif called Pimm's Cup No. 1, which gets its name from James Pimm, who operated an oyster bar in London in the 1840s. He mixed his digestive tonic with gin, herbs, quinine, and other never revealed ingredients. (I suspect that it contains some of the aromatic ingredients found in bitters like Angostura, which would have just arrived on the English market around the time that Pimm was concocting.) Pimm's drink was classified as a gin sling and could have been the first English cocktail, although it was probably served without ice—the early definition of the cocktail was a "bittered sling." Iced cocktails didn't make their appearance in proper British society until the end of the nineteenth century and weren't popular until the First World War, with the invasion of all the American servicemen and their penchant for iced drinks.

James Pimm, with the help of some well-heeled investors from among his clientele, produced Pimm's Cup No. 1 commercially until he died. Eventually the brand name was extended to include Pimm's No. 2, based on whiskey; No. 3, based on brandy; No. 4, based on rum; No. 5, based on rye; and No. 6, based on vodka. Pimm's No. 1 is available in the United States, and numbers 1 and 2 are still available in England. In England, Pimm's Cup is served with lemonade—that is, the British style of lemonade, comparable to our lemon-lime soda. I've made my Pimm's Cup for years with real lemonade topped with a splash of soda or 7-Up; I find the fresh-lemonade version much more refreshing and probably closer to the original 1840s drink, when lemon-lime soda didn't exist. Pimm's is the signature drink of the Wimbledon Tennis Tournament, and according to Nigel Watson's Tennis School (keepers of the "Wimblers Stats"), 40,000 pints of Pimm's Cup No. 1 on average are served at Wimbledon each year. The true way to serve Pimm's Cup No. 1, according to the traditionalists, is topped with Champagne.

PINEAPPLE CHAMPAGNE COCKTAIL

SERVES 6 TO 8

Adapted from a recipe served at the Embassy Club in Hollywood in the 1930s.

1 bottle (750 milliliters) dry Champagne

12 ounces maraschino liqueur

1 cup fresh ripe pineapple cubes

1 cup fresh ripe cherries

2 ounces fresh lemon juice

6 to 8 flamed lemon peels

Bruise the pineapple chunks and cherries and marinate them in the maraschino liqueur and lemon juice for 2 hours. Chill overnight. Strain the marinade. Add 2 ounces of the marinade to each of 6 to 8 chilled martini glasses and top with Champagne. Garnish each with a flamed lemon peel.

Pina Colada.

PINEAPPLE COCKTAIL◆

SERVES 6 TO 8

Adapted from a 1930s recipe from the Embassy Club in Hollywood. For a dryer version, use a fino sherry.

¹/₂ pineapple, cut into chunks

1 bottle dry white wine (without oak character)

12 ounces medium sherry (Dry Sack recommended)

8 ounces pineapple juice

2 ounces fresh lemon juice

Thin slice of pineapple, for garnish

Bruise the pineapple chunks and marinate them in the white wine for 2 hours. Add the remaining ingredients and chill overnight. The following day strain the liquid off the pineapple chunks. For an individual serving pour 3¹/₂ to 4 ounces of the miture into a cocktail shaker and shake with ice. Strain into a chilled martini glass and garnish with a slice from the marinated pineapple.

PINK CORAL

Passoa is a passion-fruit liqueur from the French, who love the flavor and make wonderful liqueurs with it. Passoa is a terrific mixer, especially in rum drinks, but it will mix with many different spirits. Try to find special ceramic pineapple glasses to serve this, or if you're really ambitious, go to the gourmet grocery and get miniature pineapples, hollow them out, and serve in them. Be very careful when scraping out the fruit that you don't puncture the skin.

1¹/₂ ounces vodka

1 ounce Passoa passion-fruit liqueur

3 ounces pineapple juice

1 ounce passion-fruit juice or nectar

1 ounce guava juice or nectar

1 tablespoon grenadine

1 dash of Angostura bitters

Fresh tropical fruit, for garnish

Shake all the ingredients with ice and serve in a large goblet. Decorate with tropical fruit if it is available.

PINK GIN

One of the classic drinks I used to serve at the Hotel Bel-Air was Pink Gin, which called for orange bitters. After going through two or three bottles of DeKuyper Orange Bitters, I spoke to the steward about ordering more. He informed me that it was no longer produced, and had not been available for over twenty years. There are now a few compatible products available: The Fee Brothers in Rochester, New York, produce an orange bitters, but it lacks the flavor and punch of the original. A better one is produced in Europe by the Bols Company, but sadly it is not available here.

2 ounces gin

3 dashes of Angostura or orange bitters

Lemon peel, for garnish

Combine in an old-fashioned glass over ice. Garnish with the lemon peel. Originally this drink was served without ice, but these days you won't find many takers for warm gin.

PINK LADY

1¹/₂ ounces gin

¹/₄ ounce grenadine

³/₄ ounce Simple Syrup

1 ounce heavy cream

Shake all the ingredients with ice and strain into a small cocktail glass.

PINK SQUIRREL

Crème de noyaux is an almond-flavored liqueur.

³/₄ ounce crème de noyaux

³/₄ ounce white crème de cacao

1¹/₂ ounces heavy cream

Shake all the ingredients with ice and strain into a small cocktail glass.

PISCO SOUR

Pisco is a very unusual tasting grape brandy made from the muscat grape in Peru and Chile. The Pisco Sour is the leading cocktail in both countries, and like the Bloody Mary in this country, everyone thinks his or her recipe is the best, including me....

1¹/₂ ounces pisco

³/₄ ounce fresh lemon juice

1 ounce Simple Syrup

1 small egg white

Several drops of Angostura bitters

Shake all the ingredients with ice and strain into a small cocktail glass. Garnish with several drops of Angostura bitters on top of the foam.

PLANTER'S PUNCH *

Planter's Punch is a wonderful opportunity to make your own creative concoction because there are hundreds of recipes. Here's mine, from my days at the Rainbow Plantation. For a batch that serves 6, see the Punch section, page 177.

1 ounce dark rum

1 ounce light rum

¹/₂ ounce orange curaçao

2 ounces fresh orange juice

2 ounces pineapple juice

¹/₂ ounce Simple Syrup

¹/₄ ounce fresh lime juice

Dash of grenadine

Dash of Angostura bitters

2 ounces soda water, optional

Orange slice, for garnish

Cherry, for garnish

Shake all the ingredients except the soda with ice, strain into a collins glass three-quarters filled with ice, and top with soda, if using. Garnish with the orange slice and cherry.

POUSSE CAFÉ

There is a section in *Jerry Thomas's* 1862 edition of *How to Mix Drinks* called "Fancy Drinks" that begins with three Pousse Café recipes. The first is from an early-nineteenth-century saloon owner from New Orleans named Joseph Santina, whom Thomas credits with improving the whole category of cocktail with his Crustas. Santina's Pousse Café is made with Cognac, maraschino, and curaçao. Thomas's instructions say to "mix well"—not what I expected to find in what I have always assumed was a layered drink. Although Santina's may not be layered, mine is. (For a variation, see ABC Pousse Café, page 72). This grouping will really test your skill and the steadiness of your hand.

¹⁄₄ ounce grenadine

¹⁄₄ ounce dark crème de cacao

¹⁄₄ ounce maraschino liqueur

¹⁄₄ ounce orange curaçao

¹⁄₄ ounce green crème de menthe

¹⁄₄ ounce parfait amour (available from Marie Brizard, this is an orange curaçao–based liqueur flavored with violets and spices)

¹⁄₂ ounce Cognac

Pour each liqueur in the order they are listed, beginning with the grenadine, carefully down the inside of a Pousse café glass over the back of a teaspoon positioned down at an angle against the inside of the glass so that each layer floats on top of the previous layer.

POUSSE I AMOUR.

POINSETTIA

This is a great idea for a holiday cocktail party. As an alternative to Champagne, a demi-sec or dessert sparkling wine would be ideal.

2 ounces cranberry juice

4 ounces Champagne

¹⁄₂ ounce Cointreau

Pour cranberry juice into a champagne flute and fill with Champagne. Top with a float of Cointreau.

LAYERING A DRINK

The technique for layering drinks I have used for years simply requires a steady hand, a pousse-café glass, and a bar spoon. The perfect pousse-café glass is hard to find, since the drink has been out of fashion for some time, but it should look somewhat like an oversized pony glass except the top flares out. After pouring the first layer of ingredient, insert the bowl of the spoon into the glass as far as it will go, with the concave part of the bowl facing up. Adjust the tip of the spoon's bowl so it is very near or touching the side of the glass. Pour the liquid layers over the bowl of the spoon so they flow down the side of the glass and gently float on top of the previous layer. Pour in a steady but very slow stream to avoid agitating the previous layer. The sweeter liqueurs are heavier, but sometimes the same liqueur from different producers will have more or less sugar content, so my advice is to practice—experiment with the liqueurs before showing off your skill. Brandy and cream will always be the final layers; brandy is completely dry, and cream will float on top of most spirits.

PORT WHISKEY PUNCH *

1½ ounces Jack Daniel's

¾ ounce fresh lemon juice

1½ ounces fresh orange juice

1½ ounces cranberry juice

1 ounce Simple Syrup

1 ounce ruby port

Orange slice, for garnish

Shake the whiskey, juices, and syrup with ice and pour into a highball glass filled with ice. Top with the ruby port. Garnish with the orange slice.

PRAIRIE OYSTER

No cocktail book would be complete without this frontier chestnut. The idea was to get some vitamins back in the body as soon as possible after a "busy" night. These days, of course, you can pop a multivitamin and an aspirin before bed and avoid gulping whole raw eggs the next day. But for traditionalists…

Dash of malt vinegar

Whole yolk of a small egg

½ teaspoon Worcestershire sauce

½ teaspoon tomato catsup

2 dashes of Tabasco sauce

Place all the ingredients in a small glass in the order listed. Take it down in one gulp and have a Bloody Mary!

PRESBYTERIAN

My mom's favorite drink.

1½ ounces bourbon or blended whiskey

2½ ounces club soda

2½ ounces 7-Up

Lemon peel, for garnish

Build in a highball glass. Garnish with the lemon peel.

PRESIDENTE

Created in the 1920s at the Vista Alegre in Havana and named for General Carmen Menocal, the president of Cuba before Batista.

1½ ounces white rum

¾ ounce orange curaçao

¾ ounce dry vermouth

Dash of grenadine

Shake with ice and strain into a small cocktail glass.

PUNCH AND PLAIN * +

To make this a Punch and Sweet, omit the fruit wedges and replace with soda water and sweet citrus soda, such as 7-Up.

3 ounces fresh orange juice

3 ounces pineapple juice

¼ ounce grenadine

¼ ounce Simple Syrup

Lime wedge

Lemon wedge

Soda water

Orange slice, for garnish

Cherry, for garnish

Shake the first four ingredients and strain into an ice-filled goblet. Squeeze in the lime wedge and lemon wedge and top with soda. Garnish with the orange slice and cherry.

PUNCHES

IN THE LATE SEVENTEENTH CENTURY, THE ENGLISH INTRODUCED PUNCH TO AMERICA FROM THE EAST INDIES. THE WORD *PUNCH* IS FROM THE HINDI *PANCH,* MEANING "FIVE." THE TRADITIONAL EAST INDIAN PUNCH WAS BASED ON A RICE-AND-SUGARCANE DISTILLATE CALLED ARRACK AND FOUR OTHER INGREDIENTS: SPICE, LEMON JUICE, WATER OR TEA, AND SUGAR. BEFORE LONG, PUNCH RECIPES CREATED WITH THE NEW AMERICAN SPIRIT, RUM, BECAME THE RAGE OF HIGH SOCIETY. EVEN MOZART RELAXED WITH SEVERAL BOWLS OF PUNCH THE NIGHT HE COMPLETED *DON GIOVANNI.* THIS EARLY AMERICAN RHYME DESCRIBING A RUM PUNCH RECIPE IS MY FAVORITE WAY TO ILLUSTRATE THE IDEA OF SWEET-AND-SOUR COCKTAILS: "ONE OF SOUR, TWO OF SWEET, THREE OF STRONG, FOUR OF WEAK."

NOTE: THE BEST WAY TO CHILL PUNCH IS TO MAKE AN ICE RING THAT FITS IN YOUR PUNCH BOWL. USE A SAVARIN RING MOLD TO MAKE ICE RINGS. THEY COME IN MANY SIZES (SEE RESOURCE GUIDE, PAGE 204).

FALL AND WINTER PUNCHES

HOLIDAYS AT THE RAINBOW ROOM WERE VERY SPECIAL. SINCE WE DID SO WELL THE REST OF THE YEAR, JOE BELIEVED THAT THE HOLIDAYS WERE A TIME TO SHOW OUR APPRECIATION TO OUR CUSTOMERS AND GIVE SOMETHING BACK. HE HIRED MUSICIANS, ACTORS, AND DANCERS TO ENHANCE THE EXPERIENCE. THE DECORATIONS WERE MARVELOUS—DESIGNER CARRIE ROBBINS AND HER CREW CREATED SEASONAL DIORAMAS WITH LIVE ACTORS PERFORMING OR SIMULATING ACTIVITIES LIKE BAKING BREAD OR PRESSING

APPLES FOR CIDER. AT CHRISTMASTIME, THERE WOULD BE SANTA AND DANCING ELVES, AND THE MAYOR AND OTHER DIGNITARIES WOULD READ EXCERPTS FROM CHRISTMAS TALES. POLITICIANS WERE DELIGHTED TO ASSOCIATE THEMSELVES WITH THESE HOLIDAY CELEBRATIONS; JOE WAS A TIRELESS PROMOTER OF TOURISM IN THE CITY. EVERY HOLIDAY, THE FIRST SEATING IN THE RAINBOW ROOM WAS PARTLY RESERVED FOR NEEDY CHILDREN AND CHILDREN FROM BROKEN FAMILIES. AT THANKSGIVING, THERE WERE PILGRIMS AND INDIANS AND AN AUTUMN DIORAMA WITH CORNSTALKS, PUMPKINS, BUSHELS OF APPLES, AND AN ANTIQUE APPLE PRESS. NATURALLY, ALL THIS FESTIVITY AND HOSPITALITY WERE ACCOMPANIED BY A DELICIOUS WELCOMING PUNCH OR DRINK OF SOME SORT THAT COULD BE SERVED WITH OR WITHOUT ALCOHOL.

the pilgrim cocktail

The Pilgrim Cocktail triggers an especially fond memory for me. When I worked at the Promenade Bar at the Rainbow Room, our neighbor building to the north of Rockefeller Center was the Associated Press. The second-shift A.P. photo editors made a habit of taking their lunch break at my bar, and they were especially fond of my pisco sours. One Thanksgiving, I decided to surprise the A.P. guys by preparing a batch of Pilgrim Cocktails especially for them. It was a bitter day, so rather than serve them cold, I heated the concoction on the range and then poured it into two insulated coffeepots. I put the drink in an insulated pot on a silver tray with twelve stemmed crystal glasses. With tray in hand, dressed in my red Rainbow Room jacket, I rode down the public elevators, fought my way through the throngs of people gathered in Rockefeller Center, wove my way across the street to the A.P. building, grabbed an elevator to the fourth floor, and personally delivered twelve Pilgrim Cocktails to a very happy holiday staff.

If Pimento is not available in your market, steep a cinnamon stick, two cloves, and two cracked whole allspice berries in the rum for a couple of hours.

3 ounces dark rum

3 ounces light rum

3^1/$_2$ ounces orange curaçao

12 ounces fresh orange juice

2^1/$_2$ ounces fresh lime juice

1^1/$_2$ ounces Pimento liqueur

6 dashes of Angostura bitters

To serve cold: Assemble all the ingredients in a large pitcher and stir. For individual servings, pour into a cocktail shaker and shake well with ice. Strain into a London dock glass with an orange slice and a dusting of freshly grated nutmeg.

To serve hot: Assemble all the ingredients in a saucepan with 6 ounces of sweetened orange pekoe tea. Heat the drink to just under a boil, and serve in a punch cup dusted with freshly grated nutmeg.

harvest moon punch*

SERVES 20

For a nonalcoholic version of the drink, simply omit the bourbon.

1 gallon fresh apple cider

6 star anise

6 cinnamon sticks, plus more for garnish

6 cloves

1 orange peel (remove zest of one navel orange, retaining very little pith)

32 ounces bourbon

Combine the apple cider, anise, cinnamon sticks, cloves, and an orange peel in a stainless steel pot and let simmer for 30 or 40 minutes. Do not boil. Strain and add bourbon.

For a party, you can serve the punch in a hollowed-out pumpkin: Prepare the pumpkin by cutting a lid as you would for a jack-o'-lantern. Clean the lid piece by cutting away the pumpkin strands and seeds. Save all the seeds. Using a long-handled spoon, clean the inside of the pumpkin, being careful not to puncture the skin or the bottom. When the pumpkin is clean, rinse the inside with cool water, checking for leaks in the skin. Fill the pumpkin with the hot punch and replace the lid to retain the heat. Serve with a ladle in ceramic mugs and garnish with cinnamon sticks.

Roast the pumpkin seeds on a buttered cookie sheet in a 300° oven for about 8 or 10 minutes, salt, and serve with the punch.

hot spiced cider

1 gallon fresh apple cider

8 cinnamon sticks, plus more for garnish

6 star anise

12 cloves

12 allspice berries, cracked

Simmer but do not boil the cider and spices in a large saucepan for a couple hours. Strain and serve hot with a cinnamon stick garnish.

Variation: To make an alcoholic version of spiced cider, add 1 ounce of Calvados or applejack and 1/2 ounce of Berentzen's Apple Liqueur to each serving.

cider nectar◆

From *How to Mix Drinks* by Jerry Thomas (1862).

1 sprig of lemon verbena

1 lemon, cut into quarters

2 ounces Simple Syrup

2 ounces pineapple syrup

1 quart apple cider

4 ounces medium sherry

2 ounces applejack or Calvados

8 ounces soda water

Freshly grated nutmeg, for garnish

Muddle the lemon verbena, cut-up lemon, Simple Syrup, and pineapple syrup together. Add the remaining ingredients except the soda and chill. Add the soda and ice, and serve as a punch. Dust with the nutmeg.

philadelphia fish house punch

This recipe is from *How to Mix Drinks,* 1862, by Jerry Thomas, with credit given to Charles G. Leland, esquire, the nineteenth-century writer. Thomas was generous in his credit because Fish House Punch goes back over one hundred years before Leland. It originated at the State of Schuylkill Fish House on the Schuylkill River, an eating and drinking club for sportsmen founded in 1732. This recipe is one of many, and most are not very interesting, so I took some liberties.

6 sweet Georgia peaches, washed, pitted, and sliced (or out of season, one 16-ounce can of peach slices in heavy syrup)

1 pound sugar

12 ounces fresh lemon juice

1 pint VS Cognac

1 pint peach brandy or liqueur (I prefer Marie Brizard)

1 liter gold Jamaican rum

If using fresh peaches, cover them with the pound of sugar and stir in 4 ounces each of water and lemon juice. Set aside for 4 hours, stirring occasionally. Mix the spirits and set them aside for the same time.

After 4 hours, mix the remaining 8 ounces of lemon juice and 28 ounces of water with the peaches, stir until all the sugar is dissolved, and add the spirits. Put the entire contents in a punch bowl with an ice ring.

To prepare with the canned peaches, just mix all the lemon juice, 1 quart water, and all the sugar together until the sugar is dissolved. Add the peaches and spirits to the mixture and refrigerate for 4 hours. Serve in a punch bowl with an ice ring.

To make an ice ring, use a savarin ring mold (see page 204), fill it three quarters with water, and cover with plastic wrap; freeze until solid and remove carefully by turning upside down on a clean surface and tapping the bottom of the mold. If the ice will not dislodge easily, run a small amount of warm water on the outside.

HOLIDAY PUNCHES

uncle angelo's egg nog

This was my Uncle Angelo Gencarelli's recipe, which he submitted to the Four Roses whiskey people in a contest—and which won. Uncle Angelo always had two bowls of eggnog at Christmas, one for the kids and one for the grown-ups. What made the recipe special was its lightness: twice as much milk as cream, and the white of the egg whipped stiff and folded into the mix, so it was almost like clouds on top of the eggnog.

Eggs are safe for beverage use if they are handled properly: Mix the egg with the spirit before adding the other ingredients, and if you handle the eggshells, wash your hands before handling the other ingredients. If you're nervous about using raw eggs, see Faux Nog (page 114).

6 eggs, separated

³/₄ cup sugar

1 quart milk

1 pint cream

6 ounces bourbon

6 ounces spiced rum

1 whole nutmeg, for grating

Beat the egg yolks well until they turn light in color, adding ¹/₂ cup of the sugar as you beat. Add the milk, cream, and liquor. Then beat the egg whites with the remaining sugar until they peak. Fold the whites into the mixture. Grate the fresh nutmeg over the drink.

tom and jerry

This was on the bar at every establishment in New York City during the holidays in the Gay Nineties.

For the batter:

12 fresh eggs, separated

3 pounds granulated white sugar

1¹/₂ teaspoons ground cinnamon

¹/₂ teaspoon ground cloves

¹/₂ teaspoon ground allspice

2 ounces añejo rum

In a large bowl, beat egg yolks until they are thin as water, adding the sugar while beating. In a separate bowl, beat the egg whites until stiff. Add the spices and rum to the yolks. Mix in the stiff whites and stir until the mixture is the consistency of a light batter. (1 teaspoon of cream of tartar or ¹/₄ teaspoon of bicarbonate of soda will prevent the sugar from settling to the bottom of the batter.)

For the drink:

2 tablespoons of batter

1¹/₂ ounces brandy

¹/₂ ounce añejo rum

3 or 4 ounces boiling water

Freshly grated nutmeg, for dusting

Put the batter in the bottom of a ceramic mug, add the spirits and the boiling water and stir. Dust with nutmeg and serve.

glogg

In 1946, Kenneth Hansen began a club in Los Angeles called The Vikings of Scandia, which later became the restaurant Scandia. Members included stars like Rita Hayworth, Cornell Wilde, Marilyn Monroe, Gary Cooper, and Marlene Dietrich. Scandia's Glogg, a traditional holiday drink, was a favorite at holiday time. I picked up the tradition and gave it away at the bar of the Rainbow Room in small tastes during the two weeks around Christmas.

1 bottle full-bodied red wine

$^1/_3$ cup raisins, plus more for garnish

$^1/_3$ cup blanched almond slices, plus more for garnish

5 crushed cardamom pods

5 whole cloves

1 cinnamon stick

1 peel of a small orange (without pith)

4 ounces vodka (some recipes use Cognac)

Sugar, to taste

In a container, combine the wine, raisins, almonds, orange peel, and spices. Cover and let the mixture stand at room temperature for 24 hours. Before serving, heat the mixture and add the vodka and sugar. Strain and serve hot with a few raisins and blanched almonds in each cup.

COMPOUND BUTTER

Soften 1 pound of butter in a stainless-steel mixing bowl and mix in 1 teaspoon each of ground cinnamon, nutmeg, and allspice and $^1/_2$ teaspoon of ground cloves. Add $^1/_4$ cup of dark brown sugar and mix well. Prepare a cookie sheet with wax paper and spoon out heaping teaspoons onto the wax paper. Cool in the refrigerator and remove 30 minutes before use.

hot buttered rum

Have fun and experiment with different variations of this recipe. Try using spiced rums or sweetening it with maple syrup or brown sugar. Hot tea can be used instead of hot water and applejack instead of rum.

1 ounce dark rum or spiced rum

1 ounce light rum

Pat of Compound Butter (see sidebar, above)

$^1/_2$ ounce Simple Syrup

Hot water or hot cider

Cinnamon stick, for garnish

Mix all the ingredients in a goblet glass and stir a few times to melt the butter. Garnish with the cinnamon stick.

bishop, american

Bishops have been made since the Middle Ages in England and Holland, with many recipes, some with sweet wine and some with dry wine. A well-made bishop is a warming cold-weather treat with a bit of spice that would go nicely with a piece of mince pie.

1/2 ounce fresh lemon juice

1 ounce fresh orange juice

1/4 ounce medium rum

4 ounces dry red wine

1 ounce Simple Syrup

Soda water

Seasonal fruits, for garnish

Stir all the ingredients together in a large goblet. Top with soda and garnish with seasonal fruits.

bishop, english

If using port, use lemons instead of oranges.

4 whole juice oranges (or lemons)

1/2 cup sugar

1 cinnamon stick

3 whole cloves

1 bottle of dry red wine (or ruby port)

Roast the oranges and lemons in a 350° oven until brown, about 20 minutes for the oranges and 15 minutes for the lemons. Remove to a crockery pot. Add the sugar, spices, and half of the wine or port. Let stand for several hours. Crush the fruit to express the juice and add the remainder of the wine. Heat to just under a boil and strain. Serve steaming in punch cups.

champagne punch ◆

1 whole ripe pineapple, peeled and cubed

3 sweet oranges, peeled and cut up

2 sweet grapefruit, peeled and cut up

1 cup pitted fresh or frozen cherries (if cherries are not available use 1/2 cup of fresh pomegrante separated from husk)

1/2 cup sugar

12 ounces maraschino liqueur

24 ounces VS Cognac

Champagne

Orange peel, for garnish

Fresh fruit, for garnish

Muddle or mash the fruit and sugar together in a large bowl until the sugar is dissolved. Pour the maraschino liqueur and Cognac over the crushed fruit. Cover and leave in the refrigerator for several hours. Remove and stir the mixture. Strain the liquid off the fruit, squeezing to get all the liquid into a pitcher.

To serve, pour 2 ounces of the mixture into a white-wine glass with a couple of ice cubes and top with Champagne. Garnish with the orange peel dropped into the punch. Garnish additionally with fresh fruit to suit your taste.

SUMMER PUNCHES
AND PITCHER DRINKS

pushcart punch cocktail * ◆

SERVES 6

Punches are an adventure and can be made with a wonderful array of seasonal fruits. When my friends Joe and Lauren moved down to Eldridge Street in Manhattan's Chinatown, we had a series of parties to warm up their loft. Joe and I went exploring the fruit and vegetable stands on pushcarts in Chinatown and the Lower East Side. Along with the lemons, limes, and pineapples that I was buying for my fresh-fruit cocktail, I found several varieties of miniature melons. They were very inexpensive, so I bought a couple dozen. I cut them into little cubes and muddled them along with the lemon, orange, lime, and pineapple chunks to create a fruity base to which I added different spirits. I experimented with different recipes, one of which became this.

$\frac{1}{4}$ cup mixed melon cubes (1-inch squares)

$\frac{1}{4}$ cup fresh pineapple cubes

1 orange, halved and quartered

2 lemons, halved and cubed

3 ounces fresh lemon juice

4 ounces Simple Syrup

4 ounces fresh orange juice

4 ounces pineapple juice

4 ounces Gold Barbados rum

4 ounces Bacardi Limón

4 ounces maraschino liqueur

Melon balls, for garnish

Muddle or mash the fruit, lemon juice, and Simple Syrup in the bottom of a large open-mouth pitcher. If you don't have a bar muddler, a large wooden spoon will do fine. (The mashing or muddling step could also be done in a large bowl or pot using a potato masher, then transfer the ingredients to the large pitcher.) Add the remaining ingredients and stir well. For individual servings, strain the mixture into a cocktail shaker and shake well with ice. Strain into chilled cocktail glasses. Garnish each with a melon ball.

watermelon punch *♦

SERVES 12

I made a batch of this every day through the month of August at Blackbird Bar. Use the top third of the watermelon shell to create a stand for the melon punch bowl by placing it top up on a cutting board and making a 45-degree-angle cut all the way around the center where the stem attaches, creating a ring of watermelon about 5 or 6 inches across. Set this piece on a large plate as a stand and place the hollowed-out watermelon punch bowl on top.

Ripe round watermelon

4 ounces fresh lemon juice

6 ounces Triple Sec

8 ounces Bacardi Limón

4 ounces maraschino liqueur

Lemon wheels, for garnish

Sliced strawberries, for garnish

Cut the top third off the watermelon and hollow out the inside saving the melon and the shell. Be careful not to puncture the rind; it will be used to serve the punch. Mash the melon through a large chinois strainer to express the juice. You will need 46 ounces (5¾ cups) of juice. Add the other four ingredients to the watermelon juice and mix well. Chill and serve inside the hollowed-out watermelon.

Ladle the punch into goblets over ice. Garnish with lemon wheels and strawberry slices.

sangria ♦

SERVES 6

3 orange wheels

3 lemon wheels

3 lime wheels

2 ounces fresh lemon juice

2 ounces Simple Syrup

1 bottle dry Spanish red wine

3 ounces orange curaçao

6 ounces brandy or vodka

3 ounces white grape juice

3 ounces fresh orange juice

Club soda

Fresh seasonal fruit, for garnish

Place the orange, lemon, and lime wheels in the bottom of a large glass pitcher. Using a long wooden spoon or muddler, muddle them together with the lemon juice and Simple Syrup. Add the remaining ingredients and stir. Top with club soda and serve over ice in a large stemmed wineglass. Garnish with fresh seasonal fruit.

THE MOTHER OF ALL CURAÇAO: GRAND MARNIER

Grand Marnier, a blend of curaçao and Cognac, has been made by Marnier-Lapostolle since 1880. Grand Marnier has several bottlings, the Cordon Rouge being the standard-bearer of its label. There are anniversary bottlings for the one hundredth and the one hundred fiftieth anniversary of its creation, too. Traditionally, Grand Marnier was taken straight after a meal. But lately the marketing of the product has emphasized Grand Marnier in premium cocktails like the Cadillac Margarita (Grand Marnier Cordon Rouge, tequila, and lime juice) and the Millionaire's Margarita (Grand Marnier Centenaire, super-premium tequila, and lime juice).

coco's punch

3/4 ounces light rum

3/4 ounce añejo rum

1/2 ounce dark rum

1/4 ounce Malibu rum

2 ounces fresh orange juice

3 ounces pineapple juice

1/4 teaspoon grenadine

Dash of Angostura bitters

Maraschino cherry, for garnish

Orange slice, for garnish

Shake all the ingredients with ice and strain into a large goblet or a specialty drink glass. Garnish with the maraschino cherry and orange slice.

planter's punch *

SERVES 6

Shaking each individual drink just before serving adds life and flavor and makes the drink look great.

5 ounces dark rum

5 ounces light rum

3 ounces orange curaçao

12 ounces fresh orange juice

12 ounces pineapple juice

3 ounces Simple Syrup

3 ounces fresh lime juice

3 ounces grenadine

1 tablespoon Angostura bitters

Pineapple slices, for garnish

Orange slices, for garnish

Lime slices, for garnish

Mix all the ingredients in a large pitcher. Before serving, shake the drinks individually in a cocktail shaker and strain into a goblet filled three-quarters full with ice. Garnish with the pineapple, orange, and lime slices.

rainbow punch * +

3 ounces fresh orange juice

1/2 ounce fresh lime juice

3 ounces pineapple juice

1/2 ounce Simple Syrup

1/4 ounce grenadine

2 dashes of Angostura bitters

Splash of soda water

Cherry, for garnish

Orange slice, for garnish

Shake all the ingredients except the soda, and strain into an iced-tea glass. Top with soda. Garnish with the cherry and orange slice.

RAINBOW SOUR *

Pineau des Charentes has a wonderful bit of lore surrounding it. It is a *mistelle,* a combination of raw grape juice and some form of spirit; in the case of the Pineau des Charentes, the spirit is Cognac. The story is that a Cognac producer thought he was blending two Cognacs when he topped up a barrel in his cellar, but one of the barrels contained raw grape juice. He was sure he had destroyed a batch of good Cognac and put it aside and left it. A couple of years later, his cellar-master tasted it while checking barrels, and it had matured in an interesting way. The maker bottled it under the name Pineau des Charentes and a new product was born. Today several Cognac producers bottle a Pineau, perhaps using Cognac that is not suited for blending into their regular stocks. Pineau des Charentes is also known as Angelica.

1 ounce Pineau des Charentes

1 ounce Marie Brizard Apry

³/₄ ounce fresh lemon juice

¹/₂ ounce Simple Syrup

Cherry, for garnish

Orange slice, for garnish

Shake all the ingredients with ice and serve in a rocks glass. Garnish with the cherry and orange slice.

RED BEER

A mountain favorite in the Catskills.

> **Add 2 ounces of tomato juice to a draft lager beer.**

RED LION

This drink was rescued from the 1930s and has been used with great success by Grand Marnier for promotions. It was originally promoted by the Booths Gin Company after it won first place in their 1933 cocktail competition, and it was originally served in a glass rimmed with lemon and sugar.

1 ounce Grand Marnier

1 ounce dry gin

¹/₂ ounce fresh orange juice

¹/₂ ounce fresh lemon juice

Flamed orange peel (see page 58), for garnish

Shake well with ice and strain into a chilled martini glass. Garnish with the flamed orange peel.

RICARD TOMATE

A popular way to serve Ricard in France. Sounds awful, but it is surprisingly drinkable. It is important with this drink that the ice be added last to prevent an unpleasant film or scaling effect on the surface of the drink.

2 ounces Ricard

¹/₄ ounce grenadine

4 to 5 ounces water

Pour Ricard and grenadine into a highball glass. Add water and then the ice last to prevent a residue from forming on top of the drink.

RICKEYS

RICKEYS ARE TRADITIONALLY A DRY DRINK, BUT SYRUP OR SUGAR CAN BE ADDED. THE RICKEY TOOK ITS NAME FROM "COLONEL JOE" RICKEY, A LOBBYIST IN WASHINGTON IN THE LATE NINETEENTH CENTURY WHO REGULARLY DRANK WITH MEMBERS OF CONGRESS IN SHOEMAKER'S BAR. THE BARMAN WHO INVENTED THE DRINK LET COLONEL JOE TASTE IT, AND WHEN THE COLONEL CALLED FOR ANOTHER, HE CHRISTENED IT THE GIN RICKEY. ODDLY ENOUGH, COLONEL JOE LATER BECAME THE FIRST MAJOR IMPORTER OF LIMES TO THIS COUNTRY. THE EARLY RECIPE, WHICH FIRST APPEARED IN *MODERN MIXED DRINKS,* BY GEORGE KAPPELER, IN 1900, IS EXACTLY THE SAME AS OUR CONTEMPORARY RECIPE. THE GIN RICKEY IS A JUMPING-OFF POINT FOR MORE OF-THE-MOMENT, SEXY COCKTAILS.

gin rickey

1¹/₂ ounces gin

¹/₂ ounce fresh lime juice

5 ounces club soda

Lime wedge, for garnish

Mix all the ingredients in a highball glass with ice. Garnish with the lime wedge.

city rickey *

This is more of a tall, sparkling Cosmopolitan than a Rickey.

1¹/₂ ounces gin

¹/₂ ounce fresh lime juice

1 ounce Cointreau

Club soda

Cranberry juice

Orange slice, for garnish

Lime slice, for garnish

Pour gin, lime juice, and Cointreau into a highball three-quarters filled with ice. Fill with soda and cranberry and stir. Garnish with orange and lime.

stone rickey *

1¹/₂ ounces gin

¹/₂ ounce fresh lime juice

2 ounces fresh orange juice

1 ounce Simple Syrup

3 ounces club soda

Orange slice, for garnish

Pour the gin, lime juice, orange juice, and Simple Syrup in a highball glass three-quarters filled with ice. Fill with club soda and stir. Garnish with the orange slice.

lime rickey * +

This is the drinking man's nonalcoholic drink.

³/₄ ounce fresh lime juice

1 ounce Simple Syrup

3 dashes of Angostura bitters

Club soda

Lime-peel spiral (see page 59), for garnish

Build all the ingredients in a collins or iced-tea glass and top with soda. Garnish with a spiral piece of lime peel.

RITZ COCKTAIL *

This drink is my tribute to the Ritz Cocktails of Paris and Madrid.

1 ounce Cognac

1/2 ounce Cointreau

1/4 ounce maraschino liqueur

1/4 ounce fresh lemon juice

Champagne

Flamed orange peel (see page 58), for garnish

Stir the first four ingredients in a mixing glass. Strain into a martini glass and fill with Champagne. Garnish with the flamed orange peel.

ROB ROY

Bill Grimes, in his wonderful book *Straight Up or On the Rocks,* reveals the origin of the name of this scotch Manhattan: a Broadway show called *Rob Roy.* In the original *The Savoy Cocktail Book* (1930), Harry Craddock calls for equal parts of scotch, sweet vermouth, and dry vermouth, but that might be a tad sweet for today's drinker. This is also called Affinity.

2 1/2 ounces scotch

1 ounce Italian sweet vermouth

Dash of Angostura bitters

Lemon peel, for garnish

Pour all the ingredients over ice in a mixing glass and stir as you would a Martini. Strain into a chilled cocktail glass and garnish with the lemon peel.

Variation: Substitute a dash of orange bitters and a dash of Cointreau for the Angostura bitters to make a Green Briar.

ROSARITA *

3/4 ounce Triple Sec

3/4 ounce Alizé Red Passion

3/4 ounce tequila

Prepare in a rocks glass three-quarters full of ice, using the layering spoon on the rim of the glass. Pour slowly and carefully to prevent the layers from mixing. The ingredients are listed in the order they should be poured, the bottom layer listed first.

ROSARITA HIGHBALL *

1 1/2 ounces tequila

1/2 ounce cassis

1/4 ounce fresh lime juice

4 ounces ginger ale

Cucumber slice, for garnish

Shake the first three ingredients and strain into an ice-filled highball glass. Fill with ginger ale. Garnish with the slice of cucumber.

ROSETTA

One of my cocktail safaris led Tony Abou Ganin (of the Belagio Hotel in Las Vegas) and me to Daddy-O's Bar in Greenwich Village. Bartender Tony Debok invented this special cocktail for us.

1 1/2 ounces Stolichnaya Ohranj

1/2 ounce Cointreau

3/4 ounce Campari

1 ounce fresh orange juice

Flamed orange peel (see page 58), for garnish

Shake well with ice and strain into a chilled cocktail glass. Garnish with the flamed orange peel.

ROYAL COCKTAIL

Adapted from a recipe from the Embassy Club in Hollywood, from the 1930s.

1 1/2 ounces gin

3/4 ounce dry vermouth

3/4 ounce Peter Heering Cherry Heering

Flamed lemon peel (see page 58), for garnish

Stir with ice and strain into a chilled martini glass. Garnish with the flamed lemon peel.

ROYAL HAWAIIAN

One of my favorite drinks from the Royal Hawaiian Hotel in Honolulu. Although the hotel is still there, the bar no longer serves this cocktail, which was its signature drink in the fifties.

1 1/2 ounces gin

1/2 ounce fresh lemon juice

1 ounce pineapple juice

1/4 ounce orgeat

Shake all the ingredients with ice and strain into a small cocktail glass. No garnish.

ROYAL ROMANCE

I found this in the *Café Royal Cocktail Book* by W. J. Tarling. It won the 1934 Empire Cocktail Competition for its inventor, J. Perusine.

1 1/2 ounces gin

1/2 ounce Grand Marnier

1 ounce passion fruit juice or nectar

2 dashes of grenadine

Flamed orange peel (see page 58), for garnish

Shake all the ingredients with ice and strain into a chilled cocktail glass. Garnish with the flamed orange peel.

RUM RUNNER

1 lime piece

1 ounce light rum

1 ounce medium rum

2 ounces pineapple juice

1/2 ounce fresh lime juice

1 ounce Simple Syrup

1 small egg white

Dash of Peychaud's bitters

Dash of Angostura bitters

Tropical fruits, for garnish

Bruise the lime in the bottom of the mixing glass, add the remaining ingredients, and shake well with ice. Serve over ice in a tall or collins glass. Garnish with tropical fruits.

RUM SWIZZLE *

Those long Jamaican swizzles are hard to come by, but there is a solution. Go to the housewares store and buy a wooden spoon with a hole in the bowl of the spoon and a long handle. Put it between the palms of your hand and swizzle away. For a flavor twist, try using flavored syrups like Simple Syrup with vanilla beans or orgeat. Note: Orgeat is a milky almond syrup used extensively in baking; it is a favorite ingredient in tropical rum drinks.

1 1/2 ounces Barbados rum

3/4 ounce fresh lime juice

1 ounce Simple Syrup

Dash of Falernum (syrup made in Barbados that is flavored with citrus fruits and spices. It comes in two versions, one with about 11% alcohol and a nonalcoholic version that is exported to the United States.)

3 dashes of Angostura bitters

Lime wheel, for garnish

Swizzle the ingredients in a highball glass filled with crushed ice until they foam. Garnish with the lime wheel.

RUMTOPF

1 pound cherries, washed and pitted

1 pound seedless grapes

12 peaches, pitted and diced into 1-inch squares

12 plums pitted and diced into 1-inch squares

4 pints strawberries, washed and quartered

2 pounds sugar

1 liter medium rum

Add the cherries and grapes to a crockery pot with a top and bruise them with a potato masher to break the skin. Add the rest of the fruit, the sugar, and the spirits. Stir well, cover, and store in a cool place for 5 months. Serve alone or as a topping for ice cream or pastries.

RUSTY NAIL

2 ounces scotch

3/4 ounce Drambuie

Pour the scotch over ice and float the Drambuie on top. No garnish.

RYE CLUB COCKTAIL *

A cocktail like this, served over shaved ice, is referred to as a "mist." I created this for Fritz Maytag's malted rye Whiskey.

1¹/₂ ounces Old Potrero rye

1 ounce orange curaçao

Dash of orange bitters (or Angostura bitters)

Shake all the ingredients with ice and serve over shaved ice.

SALT-AND-PEPPER HIGHBALL *

I liked the name and the whole idea of the Salty Dog, but I found the recipe a bit boring. So I created my own salty drink with more flavor. See Salty Dog (below) for directions on rimming the glass.

1¹/₂ ounces gin

³/₄ ounce fresh lemon juice

1 ounce Simple Syrup

3 ounces fresh grapefruit juice

3 dashes of Angostura bitters

Fill a rimmed highball glass with ice. Shake all the ingredients with ice and strain into the prepared glass.

SALTY DOG

Lemon or lime piece, for rimming

Coarse salt, for rimming

1¹/₂ ounces vodka

Fresh grapefruit juice

Rim a highball glass by rubbing the lemon or lime piece around the outside rim of the glass to dampen it and then dusting the rim with coarse salt. (Do not use table salt.) Fill the glass with ice and build the drink. No garnish.

SANGRITA

In 1978, with eviction looming, I bought a 1969 Dodge Dart four-door sedan, with the famous slant-six engine, for a thousand bucks. I piled in with my girl-friend, Ann, my dog, Sally, and as many possessions as I could fit and headed West. After three weeks on the road, with time out for car repairs in Florida, a thirty-six-hour binge in New Orleans, and several frigid nights on a mountain in New Mexico, we made a sprint for the Pacific. We arrived in Santa Monica in the midst of the worst rainy season in years. When the rain subsided, we took a blustery walk on the beach and retired to the Wind and Sea Bar. It was cozy, friendly, and cheap. We blew in with the dog and our backpacks and were an immediate hit with the crowd of retired cops, cab drivers, and assorted neighborhood characters. Several of them were downing tequila shots with a spicy tomato chaser. I hadn't discovered tequila yet. But I later learned their drink was tequila and sangrita. After a few hours in the joint, we were assured of an apartment, a job, and the life-long friendship of all. We left, and I never saw or heard from any of them again. The recipe below is for the quick version; see page 89 for the more traditional version.

8 oranges, juiced (yields 8 to 10 ounces of juice)

3 limes, juiced (2¹/₂ ounces of juice)

1¹/₂ ounces Simple Syrup

12 ounces tomato juice

Tabasco sauce, to taste (about 6 drops)

4 dashes of white pepper

4 dashes of salt

Mix all the ingredients well. Serve as a shot alongside a shot of premium tequila, or serve as you would a Bloody Mary.

SAN SALVADOR

1¹/₂ ounces dark rum

1 ounce curaçao

¹/₂ ounce fresh lime juice

1¹/₂ ounces fresh orange juice

Orange slice, for garnish

Lime slice, for garnish

Shake all the ingredients with ice and strain into an ice-filled double old-fashioned glass. Garnish with the orange and lime.

SARATOGA COCKTAIL•

Edward Spencer lists this wonderful champagne cocktail in *The Flowing Bowl*. There was another cocktail called the Saratoga in the early twentieth century, pre-Prohibition, with applejack, sweet vermouth, and orange bitters. If pineapples are out of season or not sweet and ripe, use $1/2$ ounce pineapple syrup.

3 or 4 cubes of fresh pineapple, 1 inch square

2 fresh strawberries, plus more for garnish

$1/4$ ounce maraschino liqueur

3 dashes of Angostura bitters

$1/2$ ounce Simple Syrup

$1^1/2$ ounces Cognac

Lemon peel, for garnish

Muddle the fruit in the bottom of a mixing glass with the maraschino liqueur, bitters, and syrup. Add the Cognac and ice cubes and shake well. Strain over ice into a stem glass with ice and top with Champagne. Garnish with lemon peel.

SATAN'S WHISKERS

Adapted from an Embassy Club recipe from Hollywood, circa 1930. This is a sinfully rich version of the Bronx Cocktail, and like everything else in Hollywood, if it costs more it must be better.

1 ounce gin

$1/2$ ounce sweet vermouth

$1/2$ ounce dry vermouth

$1/2$ ounce Grand Marnier

1 ounce fresh orange juice

Dash of Angostura or orange bitters

Flamed orange peel (see page 58), for garnish

Shake all the ingredients with ice and strain into a chilled martini glass. Garnish with the flamed orange peel.

SAZERAC

This drink is based on a bitters created by Antoine Amédée Peychaud, who made a Cognac cocktail by mixing his bitters with Cognac. The most popular Cognac for many years in New Orleans was Sazerac de Forge et Fils. In 1859, John Schiller officially christened the Sazerac Cocktail in his newly opened bar, the Sazerac Coffee House. When John H. Handy took over the bar, he altered the famous drink and used whiskey instead of Cognac. I have my own twist on the Sazerac, a mix of Cognac and bourbon.

Splash of Ricard or Herbsaint

1 ounce VS Cognac

1 ounce rye whiskey

$1/2$ ounce Simple Syrup

2 dashes of Peychaud's bitters

2 dashes of Angostura bitters

Lemon peel, for garnish

Chill one rocks glass while preparing the drink in another. Splash the Ricard into the second glass and swirl it, then pour it out. Add the Cognac, rye, Simple Syrup, and the two kinds of bitters. Stir with ice cubes to chill. Strain into the chilled rocks glass and garnish with the lemon peel.

SCARLETT O'HARA

The Scarlett O'Hara was a promotion by the Ocean Spray Company in the fifties.

2 ounces Southern Comfort

$1/2$ ounce fresh lime juice

1 ounce cranberry juice

Shake all the ingredients with ice and strain into a small cocktail glass.

SCARLETT'S TORCH *

I created this in honor of the Olympic torch when it passed through New York on the way to Atlanta in 1996. For true Olympians, try a nonalcoholic version: 1 ounce peach purée instead of liqueur, and increase the orange and cranberry juices to 1 ounce each.

1 ounce bourbon

1/2 ounce Marie Brizard peach liqueur

1/4 ounce Simple Syrup

1/4 ounce fresh lemon juice

1/2 ounce cranberry juice

1/2 ounce fresh orange juice

Flamed orange peel (see page 58), for garnish

Shake all the ingredients with ice and strain into a cocktail glass. Garnish with the flamed orange peel.

SCORPINO

Julia Roberts's favorite drink.

2 ounces vodka

2 ounces cream

1 ounce Cointreau

1 big scoop of Italian lemon ice

Blend all the ingredients and serve.

SCORPION ♦

2 pineapple wedges

2 cherries

1 ounce rum

1 ounce brandy

3/4 ounce fresh lemon juice

1/2 ounce Simple Syrup

1 ounce fresh orange juice

1/2 ounce orgeat

Bruise 1 pineapple wedge and 1 cherry in the bottom of a mixing glass, add the rest of the ingredients, and shake well with ice. Strain into an ice-filled bucket or double old-fashioned glass. Garnish with the remaining pineapple and cherry.

SCREWDRIVER

This was one of the drinks that John Martin used to promote Smirnoff vodka after the Second World War. The name comes from the oilmen in Texas, Oklahoma, and California who stirred the vodka and OJ with their screwdrivers.

1 1/2 ounces vodka

5 ounces fresh orange juice

Orange slice, for garnish

Build over ice in a highball glass. Garnish with the orange slice.

SEA BREEZE

The Sea Breeze was created as a promotion by Ocean Spray Company in the sixties to take advantage of the growing popularity of vodka. They even participated in the release of a new spirit product called Tropico (not to be confused with today's Bacardi Tropico) that was a blend of Don Cossack vodka and cranberry juice. The Seagram Company used the Sea Breeze to promote its aged Ancient Golden Gin in the 1960s and set the stage for the tremendous popularity of the Cosmopolitan.

1 1/2 ounces vodka

4 ounces fresh grapefruit juice

1 1/2 ounces cranberry juice

Lime wedge, for garnish

Pour the vodka into an iced highball glass. Fill partially with the grapefruit juice and top with the cranberry juice. Garnish with the lime wedge.

SEVILLA *

I created the Sevilla at Jeroboam Restaurant in Dallas to complement their Onion and Cheddar soup.

3 ounces Stolichnaya Ohranj

3/4 ounce Lustau East India Solera Reserva Sherry

Flamed orange peel (see page 58), for garnish

Stir with ice to chill and strain into a chilled cocktail glass. Garnish with the flamed orange peel.

Clockwise from left: Coffee Cocktail, Sidecar, South Beach, and Rainbow Sour.

SEX ON THE BEACH

1½ ounces vodka

½ ounce Peachtree Schnapps

¼ ounce Chambord

2 ounces cranberry juice

2 ounces pineapple juice

Shake all the ingredients and strain into an iced highball glass.

SHANDYGAFF OR SHANDY

The modern recipe for this English and Australian favorite is a pint glass of lager beer mixed half and half with lemonade (lemonade in England refers to sparkling lemon-lime soda, similar to our 7-Up). But the original recipe from the time of Dickens was much more interesting.

½ pint ale

½ pint ginger beer

1 ounce orange curaçao

½ ounce fresh lemon juice

1 lemon zest, for garnish

Build ingredients in a mug and garnish with the lemon zest.

SHERRY COCKTAIL

Adapted from *The Savoy Cocktail Book,* by Harry Craddock (1930).

2½ ounces fino sherry

½ ounce Absente

½ ounce maraschino liqueur

Flamed orange peel (see page 58), for garnish

Shake all the ingredients well with ice and strain into a chilled cocktail glass. Garnish with the flamed orange peel.

SIDECAR

About twenty years ago, when I was working at the bar at the Hotel Bel-Air, I had just finished making a Sidecar one afternoon when an older gentleman looked at me and said, "You know what a real Sidecar is, son?" I thought I did until I heard him describe the recipe. After four years of tending bar, I finally began to collect proper recipes.

1 ounce brandy

1 ounce Cointreau

¾ ounce fresh lemon juice

Flamed orange peel (see page 58), for garnish

Shake all the ingredients with ice and strain into an iced old-fashioned glass. Garnish with the flamed orange peel.

Note: If served "up," strain into a small cocktail glass with a sugared rim.

SINGAPORE SLING

Created at the Long Bar in the Raffles Hotel in Singapore about 1915 by bartender Ngiam Tong Boon. The recipe varies from book to book. Robin Kelly O'Connor, the Bordeaux wine expert, faxed me this recipe from Raffles while staying there in 1990. I've never tasted a better version.

1½ ounces gin

½ ounce Peter Herring Cherry Heering

¼ ounce Cointreau

¼ ounce Bénédictine

2 ounces pineapple juice

Dash of Angostura bitters

2 dashes grenadine

½ ounce fresh lime juice

Club soda (optional)

Orange slice, for garnish

Cherry, for garnish

Shake all the ingredients except the soda with ice and strain into a highball glass. Top with soda. Garnish with the orange slice and cherry.

Note: All fruit punch–style drinks can be topped with soda as an option.

SINGAPORE SLING BY THE BATCH

Use a half-gallon container.

12 ounces gin

4 ounces Peter Heering Cherry Heering

2 ounces Cointreau

2 ounces Bénédictine

6 to 8 dashes of Angostura bitters

2 ounces fresh lime juice

Mix these ingredients in the container. Use 3 ounces of this mix per 3 ounces of pineapple juice to make 1 drink.

SCOTCH AND SODA

I can't imagine a cocktail book without the Scotch and Soda. From the day charged water was invented, it was adopted by the whiskey drinker to replace the water to dilute and liven up a glass of whiskey. There is even a song named after the drink! But I have a much more important reason to list the Scotch and Soda: It gives me the chance to tell the story about Jim Callaway, title holder for endurance cocktailing—"a real larger-than-death character," as his partner, Ron Holland, said when Jim was diagnosed with cancer.

In 1987, Jim had major surgery to remove a tumor from his brain. A week after surgery, he was back with us at the bar in Charley O's, bald head covered with a stocking cap, double scotch and a Diet Coke in front of him. Jim carefully instructed that if his wife walked through the door, whoever spied her first would pick up his scotch, take a large gulp, and set it down in front of himself.

Conversation carried on as we kept 360 degrees covered, but somehow in the blink of an eye, there was his wife, standing right behind Jim as he was raising the glass to his lips. We all sat there hopelessly wondering how he'd get out of this one. Seeing the panic in our eyes, Jim slammed down the scotch and choked out: "This is not my Diet Coke!"

SLIPPERY NIPPLE

3/4 ounce Baileys Irish Cream

3/4 ounce Sambuca

3/4 ounce brandy

Layer in a cordial glass as listed.

SLOE COMFORTABLE SCREW

1 ounce sloe gin

1 ounce Southern Comfort

4 ounces fresh orange juice

Orange slice, for garnish

Build in a highball glass. Garnish with an orange slice.

SLOE GIN FIZZ

1 ounce sloe gin

1 ounce gin

3/4 ounce fresh lemon juice

1 ounce Simple Syrup

3 to 4 ounces soda water or seltzer

Orange slice, for garnish

Cherry, for garnish

Shake the first four ingredients with ice and strain into an ice-filled highball glass. Top with soda and garnish with the orange and cherry.

SMITH AND KEARNS

2 ounces Kahlúa

3 ounces milk or half-and-half

Club soda

Build an iced highball glass and top with soda. Note: For a Colorado Bulldog, substitute Coca-Cola for the soda.

SOURS

THE SOUR DRINKS ARE THE BENCHMARK OF THE PROFES-
SIONAL BARTENDER AND ARE THE BIGGEST CHALLENGE
FOR THE AMATEUR. THE DIFFICULT FACTOR IS THE
VOLATILE FRESH LEMON AND LIME JUICE. FOLLOW THE
FORMULA BELOW FOR ALL YOUR SWEET-AND-SOUR
DRINKS—COLLINS, FIZZ, MARGARITA—AND THEY WILL
PLEASE 95 PERCENT OF THE PEOPLE; FOR THE 5 PERCENT
THAT REQUIRE A SWEETER DRINK, JUST KEEP A BOTTLE OF
SIMPLE SYRUP HANDY AND ADD AS NECESSARY. IN THE
NINETEENTH CENTURY, THE SOUR CATEGORY INCLUDED
"FIXES" THAT HAD THE SAME INGREDIENTS AS A SOUR BUT
WERE GARNISHED EXTRAVAGANTLY WITH FRESH SEA-
SONAL FRUIT.

sour

1¹/₂ to 2 ounces base liquor

³/₄ ounce sour ingredient

1 ounce sweet ingredient or ingredients

Shake all the ingredients very hard for a slow ten
count to create a really lively drink.

The other issue associated with sours is egg white.
The practice of adding egg white to create foam
is an unnecessary shortcut that leaves a trace
flavor some people find offensive. Leave out the
egg white and shake harder, and you'll get a
great-looking drink.

Whiskey Sour.

SOUTH BEACH *

I created this one for the Paddington Spirit Distribu-
tors Company in 1992 to find Campari cocktails that
were less bitter and would appeal to the American
palate. This one worked.

³/₄ ounce Campari

³/₄ ounce Amaretto

2 ounces fresh orange juice

¹/₂ ounce Simple Syrup, optional

Flamed orange peel (see page 58), for garnish

Shake all the ingredients with ice and strain
into a martini glass. Garnish with the flamed
orange peel.

SOUTH COAST COCKTAIL

SERVES 2

From *Recipes of American and Other Iced Drinks*, by Charlie Paul (1902).

2¹/₂ ounces full-bodied scotch

¹/₂ ounce curaçao

¹/₂ ounce fresh lemon juice

¹/₄ ounce Simple Syrup

2¹/₂ ounces soda water

2 flamed orange peels (see page 58), for garnish

Mix all the ingredients in a mixing glass with ice. Stir gently and strain into two chilled martini glasses. Garnish each with the flamed orange peel.

SOUTH OF THE BORDER *

1¹/₂ ounces Malibu coconut liqueur

¹/₂ ounce Amaretto

5 ounces pineapple juice

Shake all the ingredients and strain into a martini glass.

SOUTHSIDE ◆

This was the house drink of the Famous '21' Club for years—a kind of Mint Julep for the New England crowd.

2 sprigs of fresh mint

2 lime pieces

³/₄ ounce fresh lime juice

1 ounce Simple Syrup

2 ounces gin

3 or 4 ounces soda water

Muddle 1 of the mint sprigs with the limes, lime juice, and Simple Syrup in the bottom of a bar glass. Add the gin and shake well. Pour into a goblet over crushed ice and stir until the outside of the glass frosts. Top with soda water and garnish with the remaining sprig of mint.

SPARKLING HUNT PUNCH *

¹/₄ ounce white rum

¹/₂ ounce Amaretto di Saronno

¹/₂ ounce Marie Brizard Cherry liqueur

1 ounce fresh orange juice

3 ounces Champagne

Chill the first four ingredients and strain into a champagne glass. Top with the Champagne. No garnish.

SPRITZER

White wine with ice and club soda. Garnish with lemon peel.

STEEPLECHASE * ◆

My tribute to the horsey set and their famous cocktails. Thanks to Don Mell for the name.

3 or 4 mint leaves

¹/₄ ounce blackberry brandy

¹/₄ ounce orange curaçao

2 ounces bourbon

2 dashes of Angostura bitters

2 ounces fresh orange juice

1 sprig of fresh mint, for garnish

Muddle the mint leaves and the two liqueurs in the bottom of a mixing glass. Add the rest of the ingredients and shake with ice. Strain into a rocks glass and garnish with the sprig of mint.

STELLA'S ROSE *

2 ounces bourbon

2 dashes of grenadine

2 dashes of Peychaud's bitters

Flamed orange peel (see page 58), for garnish

Stir all the ingredients with ice and strain into a chilled martini glass. Garnish with the flamed orange peel.

STILLETTO

1 ounce Amaretto

1/2 ounce banana liqueur (I recommend Marie Brizard)

1 ounce fresh orange juice

1 ounce pineapple juice

Flamed orange peel (see page 58), for garnish

Shake all the ingredients well with ice and serve up in a chilled cocktail glass. Garnish with the flamed orange peel.

STINGER

The classic New York nightcap.

2 ounces Cognac or brandy

1 ounce white crème de menthe

Shake both ingredients with ice and strain into an old-fashioned glass filled with crushed ice.

STONE FENCE

Adapted from *Recipes of American and Other Iced Drinks,* by Charlie Paul (1902).

2 ounces Maker's Mark bourbon

5 ounces fresh apple cider

1/2 ounce fresh lemon juice

3 dashes of Simple Syrup, optional

Apple slice, for garnish

Cherry, for garnish

Build in a tumbler with ice. Garnish with an apple slice and Bourbon Cherries.

STONE SOUR

I don't know who coined the name first, but it came from California. As a matter of fact, Stone Sours were also called California Sours. Stone Sour just indicates the addition of a little fresh orange juice.

1 1/2 ounces Old Potrero rye

3/4 ounce fresh lemon juice

1 ounce Simple Syrup

1 ounce fresh orange juice

Orange slice, for garnish

Cherry, for garnish

Shake all the ingredients with ice and serve in a rocks glass over ice. Garnish with the orange slice and cherry.

STORK CLUB COCKTAIL

I had this beauty on my menu for years at the Rainbow Room, but credit goes to the great Nathaniel Cook. He sounds like a Revolutionary War hero, but he was chief barman at the legendary Stork Club.

1 1/2 ounces gin

1/2 ounce Triple Sec

1/4 ounce fresh lime juice

1 ounce fresh orange juice

Dash of Angostura bitters

Flamed orange peel (see page 58), for garnish

Shake all the ingredients well with ice and strain into a chilled martini glass. Garnish with the flamed orange peel.

STRAWBERRY DAIQUIRI, FROZEN

1 1/2 ounces light rum

1/2 ounce maraschino liqueur

2 ounces Simple Syrup

1 ounce fresh lime juice

5 strawberries, plus 1 for garnish

Blend all the ingredients with crushed ice and serve in a large goblet. Garnish with a strawberry.

SUFFERING BASTARD

A Mai Tai with orange juice.

1 1/2 ounces good medium rum

1 ounce overproof rum, such as Wray & Nephew
   or Bacardi 151

3/4 ounce orange curaçao

1/2 ounce orgeat

1 ounce fresh lime juice

2 ounces fresh orange juice

Lime slice, for garnish

Orange slice, for garnish

Shake all the ingredients well and strain into
an ice-filled double old-fashioned or Mai Tai
glass. Garnish with the lime and orange slices.

SUNDOWNER *

I created this one for Angostura bitters in 1993.

1 1/2 ounces Malibu Coconut Liqueur

5 ounces pineapple juice

2 dashes of Angostura bitters

Shake all the ingredients and strain into a
martini glass.

SUNFLOWER HIGHBALL

1 ounce Absolut

1 ounce Licor 43

5 ounces fresh orange juice

Freshly grated nutmeg, for dusting

Build over ice in a highball glass. Dust with
the nutmeg.

SUNSET BREEZE *

For a frozen drink, use 1 1/2 ounces of Simple Syrup
instead of 1/2 ounce. Blend all the ingredients with
3/4 cup of crushed ice and serve in a goblet.

1/2 ounce Absolut

1/2 ounce Absolut Citron

1 1/2 ounces Tropico

1/2 ounce fresh lime juice

1/2 ounce Peter Heering Cherry Heering

1/2 ounce Simple Syrup

Orange peel (see page 59), for garnish

Shake all the ingredients with ice and strain
into a martini glass. Garnish with the orange
peel.

SUNTORY COCKTAIL

The Suntory Distillery in Japan makes Midori, the
melon liqueur used in this cocktail.

1 1/2 ounces Absolut Citron

1 ounce Midori

1 ounce fresh grapefruit juice

Shake and strain into an iced martini glass.

SWIZZLE

The swizzle drinks are named after the Jamaican
swizzle—a stick about twelve inches long and very
thin with branches radiating out of one end that are
actually the root structure cut short. The swizzle is
surprisingly sturdy for what looks like a twig that
could easily be snapped in half. To use the thing, it is
placed in a tall drink with the root cluster in the drink
and is rotated rapidly between the palms, agitating
the drink as an electric mixer would.

1 1/2 ounces rum

1/4 ounce nonalcoholic Falernum (see page 181)

1/2 ounce fresh lime juice

1/2 ounce Simple Syrup

Dash of Angostura bitters

Lime piece, for garnish

Place all the ingredients in a tall glass with
crushed ice, swizzle, and garnish with the
lime piece.

TEQUILA SUNRISE

The original Tequila Sunrise appears in cocktail books in the 1940s and is made with sweetened fresh lemon juice instead of orange juice, and cassis instead of grenadine. (I found that recipe in *The Roving Bartender* by Bill Kelly, 1946.)

1$^1/_2$ ounces white tequila

4 or 5 ounces fresh orange juice

Grenadine

Ice a highball glass. Add the tequila, pour in fresh orange juice, and top off with a float of grenadine.

A LITTLE STINGER

In all my years tending bar at the Hotel Bel-Air, I can accurately say I never worked a day without seeing our most regular customer, Arnold Leader, a renowned Beverly Hills attorney. Arnold was always meticulously tailored and wore a handlebar mustache. And he often requested his favorite drink, J & B scotch on the rocks.

His usual routine began with lunch at Scandia and continued with drinks at the Tail of the Cock and then the Cock & Bull. Late afternoon found him at the hotel bar before he retreated to the dining room with his wife. On weekends he'd arrive at the bar in full riding gear, fresh from his morning ride. His storytelling abilities were matchless; his use of dramatic pauses, hushed tones, eye contact, and mock horror coupled with a well-oiled audience at the bar combined to create hours of amusement in the best tradition of saloon-dwelling spinners of tall tales.

Arnold's favorite story was when his wife, Sylvia, spoke to him about his drinking. She broke the subject gently at dinner one night: "Arnold, I realize how much pressure you're under...I know that midway through the morning sometimes you'll have a little taste in your office just to ease the growing tension, and then of course a pre-lunch Martini or two with a client is de rigeur, followed by something gentle with lunch. Then there's your three o'clock at Tail of the Cock, and of course it would be rude and unsociable not to have that scotch with a client or friend, and I know how much you need that drink at cocktail hour to celebrate the victories and wash away the defeats of the day...and then there is dinner with a nice bottle of wine, and I know sometimes, just before you go to bed you need a little Stinger or a Hot Toddy to send you off to sleep. But Arnold," she said sternly, "what I really can't tolerate is this constant sip, sip, sipping in between!"

TI PUNCH

In the French islands in the Caribbean, plantation owners would make their own punch from local rum, citrus fruits, and homemade sugar syrup. They called it Petite Punch, or Ti-punk, when shortened. This is the house drink all over the French West Indies. It is simple and fun, and you can play with the recipe. The basic ingredients are local rum, sugar syrup, and lime juice, but the variations are plentiful. Use your favorite rum, and use sugar syrup or spiced sugar syrup.

1$^1/_2$ ounces rum

$^1/_2$ ounce nonalcoholic Falernum (see page 181)

$^1/_2$ ounce Simple Syrup

$^3/_4$ ounce fresh lime juice

Lime wedge, for garnish

Shake all the ingredients well and strain into an iced old-fashioned glass. Garnish with a squeeze of the lime.

TOASTED ALMOND

Add vodka to make this a Roasted Almond or a Toasted Almond.

$^3/_4$ ounce Amaretto

$^3/_4$ ounce Kahlúa

2 ounces cream

Shake all the ingredients with ice and strain into a small cocktail glass.

TODDIES

IN HIS 1801 BOOK *THE AMERICAN HERBAL,* SAMUEL STERNS HAD THIS RECIPE FOR THE TODDY: WATER, RUM OR BRANDY, SUGAR AND NUTMEG. IT WAS CONSIDERED TO BE A SALUTARY (HEALTHY) BEVERAGE AND WAS ESPECIALLY POPULAR IN THE SUMMER.

In his 1862 *How To Mix Drinks,* Jerry Thomas lists toddies and slings together. He indicates that the only difference between them is a little grated nutmeg on top of a sling. Thomas served toddies and slings hot and cold and used only spirits, sugar, and water (except for the Apple Toddy, which is made with a baked apple). By the 1890s, lemon juice and lemon peel were introduced to the toddy and it was on its way to becoming a lemon-and-honey hot cure for colds, dispensed by mothers and grandmothers everywhere.

apple toddy

Jerry Thomas's original recipe.

In a bar glass:

$1/2$ **baked apple**

1 tablespoon fine white sugar

1 wine glass of cider brandy (applejack)

Whole nutmeg, for grating

Put the baked apple, sugar, and applejack in a glass or mug. Fill the glass two-thirds full of boiling water, and grate a little nutmeg on top. If there is a question whether the glass is tempered for extremes of hot and cold, place a silver spoon in the glass before adding the boiling water.

hot toddy

$1/2$ **ounce brandy, rum, or both**

1 teaspoon honey

$1/2$ **ounce fresh lemon juice**

Combine in a mug and fill with hot water or tea.

THE SPICE BOX

Colonial inns kept a spice box with equal parts of ground nutmeg, cinnamon, ginger, and orange peel. One teaspoon of the mix was used per drink for Flips and Toddlers.

TOM COLLINS

From the Planter's Hotel in St. Louis in the 1850s.

1 1/2 ounces gin

3/4 ounce fresh lemon juice

1 ounce Simple Syrup

4 ounces club soda

Orange slice, for garnish

Cherry, for garnish

Shake the first three ingredients with ice and strain into a collins glass. Add the soda and stir. Garnish with the orange slice and cherry.

TRINIDAD *

1 1/2 ounces Bacardi rum

4 dashes of Angostura bitters

5 ounces Coca-Cola

Lime wedge, for garnish

Build in a highball glass over ice and garnish with the lime wedge.

TROPICAL COCKTAIL

This is an alternative to a Daiquiri from the Ritz hotel in Paris.

2 ounces white rum

3/4 ounce orange curaçao

1/2 ounce fresh lime juice

Shake all the ingredients with ice and strain into a chilled martini glass.

TROPICAL HIGHBALL *

1 1/2 ounces Mount Gay rum

Dashes Angostura bitters

4 ounces ginger ale

Lime wedge, for garnish

Build over ice in a highball glass. Garnish with the lime wedge.

TROPICAL WHISKEY PUNCH * ◆

4 1-inch cubes of mango

2 lemon wedges (one for garnish)

2 pineapple wedges

1 ounce water

3/4 ounce Simple Syrup

2 ounces Crown Royal Canadian Whiskey

Pineapple wedge, for garnish

Lemon wedge, for garnish

Cherry, for garnish

Muddle all the ingredients except the whiskey in a bar glass. Add the whiskey and shake with ice. Strain into an ice-filled rocks glass and garnish with the pineapple, lemon, and cherry.

TUXEDO

An unusual martini from the Ritz hotel in Paris.

2 ounces gin

1 ounce dry vermouth

2 dashes of maraschino liqueur

2 dashes of Anisette

Stir the ingredients with ice and strain into a chilled martini glass.

TWENTIETH CENTURY

2 ounces gin

1/4 ounce white crème de cacao

1/2 ounce Lillet Blonde

1/4 ounce fresh lemon juice

Shake all the ingredients with ice and strain into a chilled martini glass.

209 EAST COCKTAIL *

Coat the rim of the glass with a mix of sugar and powdered strawberry, if you wish. To make powdered strawberry, roast strawberries in a low oven until they are crisp and dry and pulverize them with a mortar and pestle. Mix with superfine sugar.

1¹/₂ ounces Sauza Hornitos

1 ounce Cointreau

¹/₂ ounce Marie Brizard strawberry liqueur

1 ounce fresh lime juice

Shake all the ingredients with ice and strain into a chilled cocktail glass.

209 EAST COCKTAIL

One of the problems for night owls like me is finding the time to socialize with regular folks during non-working hours. One evening in 1995, I was mulling over this dilemma with my good friend Carl Butrum, and we decided the only solution was a party that would last all night, so that people could arrive at any time from six in the evening to six in the morning. The party would be dubbed "Straight on 'til Morning" and should be an annual event.

When I decided that I would create a special cocktail to celebrate the first "Straight on 'til Morning" party, Sharen Butrum requested that whatever it tasted like, the drink should be pink. This was because her living room was pink. And she thought pink would be festive. At least it gave me my creative direction. Pink called for fresh strawberries and strawberry liqueur. The resulting creation, named the "209 East," after their house on Forty-eighth Street, was such a hit that not only is it traditionally served at every "Straight on 'til Morning" party, but it became a featured item on the cocktail list at the Rainbow Room.

VALENCIA II

At the Roosevelt Hotel in Hollywood in the thirties, there was a variation on the Valentia Martini that is wonderful. Here it is.

¹/₂ ounce apricot brandy

1 ounce fresh orange juice

2 dashes of orange bitters

Champagne

Flamed orange peel (see page 58), for garnish

Shake the first three ingredients with ice and strain into a chilled champagne flute. Top with Champagne. Garnish with the flamed orange peel.

VELVET HAMMER

³/₄ ounce Triple Sec

³/₄ ounce white crème de cacao

2 ounces cream

Freshly grated nutmeg, for dusting

Shake all the ingredients well with ice and strain into a chilled cocktail or martini glass. Dust with the nutmeg.

VENDOME

The house drink of the Vendome Club, Hollywood, circa 1930.

1 ounce Red Dubonnet

1 ounce gin

1 ounce dry vermouth

Lemon peel, for garnish

Stir all the ingredients with ice and strain into a chilled cocktail glass. Garnish with the lemon peel.

VERMOUTH CASSIS

³/₄ ounce cassis

4 ounces dry vermouth

Twist of lemon, for garnish

Fill a white-wine glass three-fouths full of ice. Pour in the cassis and fill with the vermouth. Garnish with the lemon twist.

VIRGIN CHAMPAGNE COCKTAIL * +

Prepare the same as a regular Champagne Cocktail, with an Angostura-soaked sugar cube in a champagne glass, but substitute nonalcoholic sparkling wine.

VIRGIN KIR ROYALE * +

1/4 ounce raspberry syrup

5 ounces nonalcoholic sparkling wine

Lemon peel, for garnish

Raspberry, for garnish

Pour the raspberry syrup into a champagne flute and fill slowly with a sparkling nonalcoholic wine. Garnish with the lemon peel and raspberry.

VIRGIN ROYAL HAWAIIAN * +

The original Royal Hawaiian was the special drink of the Royal Hawaiian Hotel in Honolulu many years ago, and it was made with gin.

3 ounces pineapple juice

1/2 ounce orgeat

3/4 ounce fresh lemon juice

1/2 ounce Simple Syrup

Shake all the ingredients with ice and strain into a London dock glass. No garnish.

VODKA STINGER (WHITE SPIDER)

1 1/2 ounces vodka

3/4 ounce white crème de menthe

Shake well and strain into an ice-filled rocks glass.

WALDORF

Albert Stevens Crockett's *Old Waldorf Bar Days* (1931) calls for equal parts of absinthe, sweet vermouth, and whiskey. That might have been fine with true absinthe, which was unsweetened and very bitter, but it won't work with today's absinthe substitutes. This recipe is much more appealing.

1/4 ounce Ricard

2 ounces bourbon or rye whiskey

3/4 ounce sweet vermouth

2 dashes of Angostura bitters

Pour the Ricard into the mixing glass and swirl to coat the glass. Pour out the excess Ricard, then add the remaining ingredients over ice and stir. Strain into a chilled martini glass.

WARD EIGHT

Created in 1898 at the Locke-Ober Restaurant in Boston by Tom Hussion to celebrate the victory of Martin Lomasney, a member of Boston's Hendricks Club political machine, to the state legislature from the Eighth Ward. Lomasney ended up a Prohibitionist and was embarrassed that his ward was becoming famous because of a drink.

2 ounces bourbon whiskey

1 ounce Simple Syrup

3/4 ounce fresh lemon juice

1/4 ounce grenadine

Orange slice, for garnish

Cherry, for garnish

Shake all the ingredients with ice and strain into an old-fashioned glass or a special sour glass. Garnish with the orange slice and cherry.

Clockwise from top: Singapore Sling, Gin Sling, Valencia Martini, and Fitzgerald.

WHISKEY DAISY ♦

This is adapted from the original 1888 edition of the Harry Johnson's *Bartender's Manual*. What interested me was the illustration that went along with the drink, showing fruit at the bottom of the glass as if it had been muddled.

1 lime wedge

1/2 lemon, quartered

3/4 ounce Simple Syrup

1/2 ounce yellow Chartreuse

1 1/2 ounces American whiskey

Lemon wedge, for garnish

Lime wedge, for garnish

Cherry, for garnish

Muddle the first four ingredients in a mixing glass. Add the whiskey and shake well with ice. Strain into a highball glass filled with crushed ice. Garnish with the lemon, lime, and cherry.

WHISKEY PEACH SMASH * ♦

Canadian Club makes a sherry-barrel whiskey that works well in this recipe, but it will work equally well with other American whiskies.

4 small peach quarters

3 mint leaves

2 lemon pieces

1 ounce water

1/2 ounce Simple Syrup

2 ounces Canadian whiskey

1 sprig of fresh mint

Peach slice, for garnish

Muddle all the ingredients except the whiskey in a bar glass. Add the whiskey and shake with ice. Strain into an ice-filled rocks glass and garnish with the sprig of mint and the peach slice.

WHISKEY PLUSH *

I adapted this recipe from the White Plush, a drink of whiskey and milk, in *How to Mix Drinks* by Jerry Thomas (1862). The White Plush was named after a gullible New England buyer, as Thomas tells it, who was hustled by a couple of dry-goods salesmen in New York City. They convinced him he was drinking milk and seltzer, a popular local favorite. When the whiskey started to take hold, he knocked over his "milk" and stared at it a moment, then remarked, "Gee, it looks just like white plush." This prompted the two slicks to order "another yard of white plush for the gentleman" from the knowing bartender.

1 ounce Irish whiskey

1 ounce Baileys Irish Cream

1/2 ounce Simple Syrup

4 ounces milk or cream

4 dashes of Angostura bitters

Freshly grated nutmeg, for garnish

Shake all the ingredients well with ice and strain into a chilled wineglass. Garnish with the grated nutmeg.

WHISKEY SMASH * ♦

For a tasty alternative, try substituting orange curaçao for the Simple Syrup.

2 lemon pieces

2 to 3 mint leaves

3/4 ounce Simple Syrup

1 1/2 ounces Maker's Mark bourbon

1 ounce of water

Sprig of fresh mint

Muddle the lemon, mint leaves, water, and Simple Syrup in the bottom of a mixing glass. Add the bourbon and shake. Strain into an old-fashioned glass filled with crushed ice. Garnish with the mint sprig.

WHITE BAT *

1½ ounces Bacardi rum

½ ounce Kahlúa

1½ ounces milk or half-and-half

3 ounces Coca-Cola

Build all the ingredients in a tall glass over ice. Stir and serve with a straw.

WHITE LADY

From Harry Craddock's *Savoy Cocktail Book* (1934).

1½ ounces gin

1 ounce fresh lemon juice

1 ounce Cointreau

Shake all the ingredients with ice and strain into a cocktail glass.

WHITE TIGER'S MILK

Adapted from *How to Mix Drinks* by Jerry Thomas.

2 ounces applejack or Calvados

2 ounces Marie Brizard Apry

½ teaspoon Angostura bitters

2 ounces Simple Syrup

1 egg white, beaten stiff

½ pint whole milk

Freshly grated nutmeg, for dusting

Combine all the ingredients in a pitcher and whisk to blend. Chill and serve dusted with the nutmeg.

WONDER BRA *

The Wonder Bra folks commissioned the drink, they can call it whatever they want.

1½ ounces gin

¾ ounce Cointreau

1 ounce pineapple juice

Shake all the ingredients with ice and strain into a chilled cocktail glass.

YELLOW BIRD

2 ounces rum

½ ounce Triple Sec

½ ounce Galliano

¾ ounce fresh lime juice

Lime peel, for garnish

Shake all the ingredients with ice and strain into a chilled cocktail or martini glass. Garnish with the lime peel.

ZOMBIE

Created at Don the Beachcomber by Ernest Raymond Beaumont-Gantt; now you know why he went by the name Don. A float of overproof rum is optional.

½ ounce fresh lime juice

½ ounce fresh lemon juice

1½ ounces fresh orange juice

1½ ounces fresh passion fruit purée

¼ ounce grenadine

1 ounce orange curaçao or apricot brandy

1 ounce dark rum

1 ounce light rum

2 dashes of Angostura bitters

Sprig of fresh mint, for garnish

Seasonal fruit, for garnish

Add all the ingredients into a mixing glass and shake. Strain into a large glass and add the mint and seasonal fruit.

PART 3

THE RESOURCES OF THE COCKTAIL

PRODUCTS, SERVICES AND SOURCES

DRINK DATABASES

COCKTAIL.COM

www.cocktail.com

Paul Harrington's site has a database of drink recipes with links associated with each element of the recipe, so you can point on ice, glass, and vermouth on one recipe and get a detailed explanation of that particular aspect. He also has a cocktail-party-planner search engine in which you can mix and match a drink to your social setting.

www.cocktaildb.com

Martin Doudoroff and Ted Haigh (a.k.a. Dr. Cocktail) have developed an extensive database at cocktaildb.com, which also includes a bibliography, extensive recipe library cross-referenced by ingredients, and an active and regularly updated message board.

INSTRUCTIONAL VIDEO

BAR ESSENTIALS

Two-part hands-on training video with master mixologist Dale DeGroff demonstrating bartending techniques, methods, and the tools of the trade used in preparing classic cocktails. An essential training resource for bartenders, managers, and owners interested in achieving a high level of excellence in their beverage programs. This video is one in a complete library of training programs written and produced by the Food and Beverage Institute and teacher-approved by the internationally acclaimed faculty at the Culinary Institute of America. To order, call 1-800-285-8280 or 914-451-1278 or visit kingcocktail.com.

NOVELTY ITEMS

CHARMING PRODUCTS

www.Charmingproducts.com

The information that Cheryl Charming has accumulated on her charming and overflowing site appears as if it had been compiled by a staff of fifty. Cheryl has "surfed the endless summer to the ends of the World Wide Web to hook you up with the mother lode of cool bar-related products." Hundreds of links to bar-related apparel and tchotchkes. You're certain to find whatever it is you're looking for.

SHAKEN NOT STIRRED: A CELEBRATION OF THE MARTINI

www.martiniplace.com/book2.html

Steve Visakay's classic and antique cocktail shakers. Vintage Barware Identification & Value Guide

P.O. Box 1517

West Caldwell, NJ 07007

CORKSCREW.COM

www.corkscrew.com

All about corkscrews: new, old, antique, plus history, patents, and function.

K&L INTERNATIONAL MERCHANDISE CORP.

www.knl-international.com

20470 Yellow Brick Road, #5B

Walnut, CA 91789

Phone: 888-598-5588; fax: 909-598-3380

Good source for party knickknacks, including unique drink picks, straws, flags, umbrellas, fans, and fruit straws.

MARTINI MISTER

Now you can mist your martinis with the perfect vermouth atomizer.

Contact Joe Garrison at Garri52@aol.com

OXO GOOD GRIPS

A line of ergonomically designed bar tools, including channel knives, wine openers, paring knives, and bottle openers.

OXO International

1536 Beech St.

Terra Haute, IN 47804

Phone: 800-545-4411

ZOO PIKS INTERNATIONAL
www.zoopiks.com
Great for unusual animal "piks," drinking straws, or custom-printed napkins.

STIR STICKS & PICKS INTERNATIONAL
Phone: 1-877-STIRPIK or 416-675-2783
A good source for cocktail accessories.

CLASSES AND SEMINARS

Dale DeGroff's Mixology Class, at the Institute for Culinary Education (formerly Peter Kump's New York Cooking School) in New York City. Phone: 212-847-0700.
Dale DeGroff's Cocktail Safari™; for information go to: www.kingcocktail.com.

Gary Regan's Weekend Bartending Classes, Cornwall on the Hudson; for information go to: www.Ardentspirits.com.

NEWSLETTERS

HOT TRUB
Edited by Peter LaFrance and presented by *American Brewer & Distiller, Hot Trub* is a newsletter that posts items of special interest to the brewing and distilling community and media covering the beverage alcohol business. For more information, contact Peter at peter.lafrance@beerbasics.com.

COCKTAIL COMMUNIQUÉ
cocktailcommunique@yahoogroups.com
The *Cocktail Communiqué* is an informative weekly publication of Cocktail.com. For more information, contact Kari Astrid, executive editor, at www.cocktail.com or bartender@cocktail.com.

SPIRIT JOURNAL
www.spiritjournal.com
F. Paul Pacult's *Spirit Journal* is a quarterly newsletter covering spirits, wine, and beer. For subscription information, call 800-560-7273.

ARDENT SPIRITS
www.ardentspirits.com
Ardent Spirits is a free, quirky e-mail newsletter written and published by noted spirits authors Gary and Mardee

Regan. It focuses on spirits and cocktails and is available to anyone who sends an e-mail address to gary@ardentspirits.com.

MISCELLANEOUS BAR AND COCKTAIL SITES

KING COCKTAIL
www.kingcocktail.com
Yes, I'm shamelessly promoting my very own website. Learn more about bartending and mixology, classes and seminars, recipe lists, Cocktail Safari, and great ideas for your bar.

BEVACCESS
www.bevaccess.com
Together with Beverage Media Group, the BevAccess publishes the United State's premier beverage alcohol trade magazines, and also serves as the national office for the Beverage Network, delivering timely information to over 140,000 beverage alcohol licensees in 48 markets each month.

ALCOHOL REVIEWS
www.alcoholreviews.com
A monthly online beer, wine, spirits, and cocktails magazine dedicated to reviewing beverage alcohol products. An interesting part of the site is an online store where consumers can purchase wines, spirits, and barware.

DRINK BOY
www.drinkboy.com
Robert Hess offers an informative site that includes a products guide, classic cocktail recipes, tools, games, and articles.

ABOUT.COM
www.cocktails.about.com
Kathy Hamlin hosts this excellent site that includes a great newsletter, lively forums, historical articles, recipes, trivia, and more. Kathy Hamlin and Steve Visakay collaborated on a series of articles, *Collecting Cocktails,* in which you'll find information on everything from shakers to odd collectibles.

WEBTENDER
www.webtender.com
A great place for regularly updated drink forums, plus mixing terms, bar measurements, stocking your bar, and more.

WINEMAKERI INC.
www.winemakeri.com
In addition to being a source for quality alcohol-related products, this site sources unique, proprietary products to complement their catalog of winemaking, liqueur making, and brewing products. There's also a very good liqueur and spirits glossary.

FRUIT, MIXERS, JUICES, AND GARNISHES

AJ-Stephans Ginger Beer
10 Dewitt Road
Stoneham, MA 02180
Phone/Fax: 781-438-2221

ANGOSTURA BITTERS
www.angostura.com
Mixers, sauces, rums, and events.

BLENDEX
www.blendex.com
This Louisville, Kentucky-based company recently introduced a line of designer margarita salts in five different shades: Sunset Red, Tropical Green, Mediterranean Blue, Sunburst Yellow, and Fresh Orange. Call 1-800-BLENDEX or contact rpottinger@Blendex.com.

DR. MCGILLICUDDY'S
Distributed by the Sazerac Company, Dr. McGillicuddy's is a line of mint and vanilla schnapps as well as nonalcoholic root beer. Phone: 877-906-6409 (in New Orleans 504-849-6409); e-mail: info@sazerac.com.

FEE BROTHERS ORANGE BITTERS
Source for orange bitters and other difficult-to-find ingredients. Call 1-800-961-FEES. New York residents can call American Cappuccino, 718-767-6669. (Minimum order is four bottles.)

FRANCO'S COCKTAIL MIXES
Franco's, based in Pompano Beach, Florida, is the largest producer of margarita salt in the world and introduced the first colored margarita salt in 1990. Call 1-800-782-4508 or 954-782-7491; or e-mail FrancoCktl@aol.com.

GOURMET SODA PRODUCTS
www.popsoda.com

OUT BACK JUICE FACTORY
Along with the commonly used juices, they also source specialty and seasonal juices that are available upon request. Call 610-678-2400; or write 566 Penn Avenue, Sinking Spring, PA 19608.

SABLE AND ROSENFELD FOODS
www.sableandrosenfeld.com
A great gourmet-products source and maker of Tipsy Olives and Tipsy Onions, packed in French vermouth.

SAZERAC
www.sazerac.com/bitters.html
Here's where you order Peychaud's bitters, the original and unique New Orleans bitters, created in 1793. For a printable order form, call 504-849-6450.

SLUSH AT HOME
www.slush-at-home.com
A great source for fruit smoothies and frozen cocktail mixes, all made from real fruit. Call 1-800-762-2525; or write 1534 Pennsylvania Avenue, Monaca, PA 15061.

SUMPTUOUS SELECTIONS
This company, based in Rocky Hill, Connecticut, sources flavored, roasted sea salts for Margaritas, including mesquite smoked with lime, and caramelized orange and lemon. Call 1-800-987-8512 or 530-674-5530; or e-mail info@chilecauldron.com.

TRADER VIC'S
www.tradervics.com
From the originator of the Mai Tai cocktail, a wonderful source for mixers, batters, and syrups, including koko kreme syrup, orgeat syrup, grenadine syrup, rock candy syrup, maraschino syrup, passion fruit syrup, hot-buttered-rum batter, Tom and Jerry batter, and Kafe-la-te hot drink mix. Order online or call 877-762-4824.

TWANG

www.twang.com

The Twang Company of San Antonio, Texas, has introduced Twangarita Margarita Salts, which come in three flavors: lemon-lime, pickle, and a tart and spicy chili con limón. You can call them at 1-800-950-8095.

TRICKS AND ENTERTAINMENT

FLAIR BARTENDING

www.bartendingacademy.com

Olympic Bartending videos are available at this online store.

CHARMING BAR TRICKS

www.charmingbartricks.com

Lots going on at this site, including *Miss Charming's Book of Bar Amusements.*

BAR SUPPLIES

BIG TRAY

www.bigtray.com

A great site for bar supplies, from soup to nuts.

BAR SUPPLY WAREHOUSE

www.barsupplywarehouse.com

Has a great home-bar starter kit that includes a jigger, six plastic pourers, four-prong strainer, 28-ounce shaker tin, 16-ounce mixing glass, recipes, bar spoon, corkscrew, and metal ice scoop—all for $16.99.

A BEST KITCHEN

www.abestkitchen.com/store/bar

Reasonably priced items for your home bar; good, fast, and easy to navigate.

ALESSI BAR TOOLS

www.alessi.com

You can order these beautiful Alessi bar tools online, or check out the following retail stores:

The Conran Shop, 344 East 59th Street, New York, NY 10022; 212-755-9083

Moss, 146 Greene Street, New York, NY 10012; 212-226-2190

Museum of Contemporary Art, 220 E. Chicago Avenue, Chicago, IL; 312-397-4000

Chiasso, Water Tower Place, 835 N. Michigan Avenue, L2, Chicago, IL 60611; 312-280-1249

Diva, 8801 Beverly Boulevard, Los Angeles, CA 90048; 310-278-3191

Alessi San Francisco, 424 Sutter Street, San Francisco, CA 94108; 415-434-0403

Strings, Inc., 3425 W. 7th Street, Fort Worth, TX 76107; 817-336-8042

Adesso, 200 Boylston Street, Boston, MA 02116; 617-451-2212

Exit Art, 201 Gulf of Mexico Drive, Longboat Key, FL 34228; 941-387-7395

Exit Art, 5380 Gulf of Mexico Drive, Longboat Key, FL 34228; 941-383-4099

Galeria Lamartine, 421 Espanola Way, Miami Beach, FL 33139; 305-695-0903

BIASCO SUPPLY, INC.

Purveyor of KoldDraft ice machines. Call 718-993-8000 or e-mail vjbl@aol.com.

CHEF RESTAURANT SUPPLIES

Great selection, including Rachand juicers. Call 212-254-6644.

RESTAURANT DEPOT

www.restaurantdepot.com

A wholesaler of high-quality fresh, frozen, and dry food products; beverages; and equipment (including blenders like the Vita Mix that can be bought online without membership). Locations throughout the United States.

CO-RECT PRODUCTS

www.co-rectproducts.com

Catering mainly to retailers, Co-Rect products are carried by Sarkissian Bar Supply Co., 3132 Webster Avenue, New York, NY 10467; call 718-655-7125 or 798-2819.

RING MOLDS FOR ICE RINGS TO CHILL PUNCH

www.fantes.com

Go to ring molds and see savarin ring molds.

STORAGE SYSTEMS FOR LEFTOVER WINE AND FORTIFIED WINE AND OTHER WINE ACCESSORIES

www.amazon.com

Go to kitchen and housewares.

www.vintagecellars.com

MEASURES

UNUSUAL MEASURES

Here are conversions for unusual measures typically found in nineteenth-century recipes

Pony/Cordial = 1 ounce

Pousse-café glass = 1.5 ounces

Cocktail glass = 2 ounces

Gill = 4 ounces

Wineglass = 4 ounces

Small tumbler = 8 ounces

Large tumbler = 16 ounces

STANDARD U.S. BAR MEASUREMENTS

Pony = 1 ounce

1 ounce = 3 centiliters

Jigger, shot = 1.5 ounces

Mixing glass = 16 ounces

Splash = $^1/_2$ ounce

6 drops = 1 dash = $^1/_6$ teaspoon

OTHER MEASURES

6 drops = 1 dash

12 dashes = 1 teaspoon

1 teaspoon = $^1/_8$ ounce

2 teaspoons = $^1/_4$ ounce

1 tablespoon = $^1/_2$ ounce

2 tablespoons = 1 ounce

$^1/_4$ cup = 2 ounces

$^1/_2$ cup = 4 ounces

1 cup or $^1/_2$ pint = 8 ounces

2 cups or 1 pint = 16 ounces

4 cups, 2 pints or 1 quart = 32 ounces

BOTTLE SIZE MEASURES

Split = 187 ml = 6.4 ounces

Half bottle = 375 ml = 12.7 ounces

Fifth = 750 ml = 25.4 ounces

Liter = 33.8 ounces

Magnum =1.5 Liters = 2 wine bottles

Jeroboam = 3 liters = 4 wine bottles

Rehoboam = 6 wine bottles

Methuselah = 8 wine bottles

Salmanazar = 12 wine bottles

Balthazar = 16 wine bottles

Nebuchadnezzar = 20 wine bottles

Sovereign = 34 wine bottles

FRESH FRUIT EQUIVALENTS

APRICOT
8 to 12 fresh = 1 pound/3 cups sliced

BANANA
3 medium = 1 pound fresh = $1^1/_2$ cups mashed

CANTALOUPE
1 whole 3-pound cantaloupe/5 cups cubed

CHERRIES
1 pound fresh = $2^1/_3$ cups pitted

GRAPEFRUIT
1 medium = 1 pound fresh

JUNIPER BERRIES
4 berries = $^1/_2$ teaspoon crushed

KIWI
5 medium = $2^1/_3$ cups sliced

LEMONS
1 pound = 4 to 6 medium lemons = 1 cup juice

1 medium = 3 tablespoons juice

1 medium = 2 to 3 teaspoon grated peel

MANGOES
1 large = 1 pound = $1^3/_4$ cups diced

PASSION FRUIT
Approximately 3 = 2 ounces

5 to 6 whole = $^1/_2$ cup pulp

PEACHES
3 to 4 medium = 1 pound = 2 cups puréed

7 to 8 medium = 1 quart (4 cups) puréed

RASPBERRIES
1 pint = $^3/_4$ pound

STRAWBERRIES
12 large or 36 small = 1 pint = $1^2/_3$ cups puréed

1 cup whole = $^1/_2$ cup puréed

20 ounces frozen = $2^1/_4$ cups puréed

BASIC RECIPES

BROWN SUGAR SYRUP

1 pound dark brown sugar

16 ounces spring water

Mix the sugar and water in a saucepan and heat gently, stirring until the sugar dissolves. Remove from the heat. Cool and store in the refrigerator between uses; good for two weeks.

HONEY SYRUP

Honey is wonderful in drinks, but at full strength it is difficult to use. A practical way of preparing honey for use in drinks is to turn it into a thinner syrup, similar to simple syrup. Combine 1 part honey with 1 part warm water and stir until all the honey is dissolved. Store in the fridge.

SIMPLE SYRUP

Simple Syrup provides a drink with both volume and sweetness. Here's how to make it:

Fill a cork bottle halfway up with superfine sugar, the other half with water. Shake vigorously until most of the sugar dissolves, about 1 minute. It will remain cloudy for 5 minutes; after it clears shake again briefly and it is ready to use. Stored in the refrigerator between uses, Simple Syrup will last for several weeks.

SPICED SIMPLE SYRUP

Into 2 quarts of water put 1 cup of dried orange peels, a few cloves, and 1 cinnamon stick. Steep overnight. Pour it into a saucepan and add 1 cup of sugar. Bring to a boil, then remove immediately from the heat, strain, and cool before bottling.

HOMEMADE GRENADINE*

By Gary and Mardee Regan

"We use a levered citrus fruit juicer to get the juice from pomegranates, and find this to be a very good method. Each fruit should yield 2 to 3 ounces of juice. To every 3 ounces of juice, just add 1 ounce of Simple Syrup. That's all there is to it."

We can take Gary and Mardee's idea a step further. Cut a pomegranate in half and then cut each half in quarters. Take one of those quarters and cut it in half again, then remove the fruit from the skin and toss it into the bottom of a mixing glass. Add 1 ounce of Simple Syrup, a lemon or lime wedge, and 1 ounce of the juice of your choice—orange, grapefruit, cranberry, or a blend of juices. Muddle the mixture to release all the flavor and color, then add 1½ ounces of the white spirit of your choice—vodka, rum, or gin—and shake well with ice. Strain into a cocktail glass. The result will be wonderful, but that is just the beginning of the possibilities. Try adding other fruits like mango or blueberries before muddling and the possibilities multiply. Choose your own combinations and create some personal house specials.

APPLE VODKA

An original by bartender Audrey Saunders.

1 case McIntosh apples

1 case (12 liters) vodka, preferably Svedka

Halve the apples, then slice into quarters, a half case at a time. Add the first batch of apples to a 5-gallon container and top with 6 bottles of vodka. Cover with a lid or seal tightly with plastic wrap and tape. Repeat with the second batch of apples and the remaining vodka. Date the container and store in the refrigerator for 2 weeks. Strain the vodka through a cheesecloth and discard the apples, then funnel it back into the bottles. Store in the refrigerator.

GINGER BEER

This noncarbonated version can be mixed in a cocktail shaker, unlike any carbonated drink.

2$\frac{1}{2}$ pounds gingerroot, peeled and roughly chopped

4 limes

$\frac{3}{4}$ cup light brown sugar

Bring 2 gallons of water to a boil in a large pot, then remove from the flame. Meanwhile, pulse the ginger with a few drops of boiling water in a food processor until minced. Add the ginger to the hot water. With a spoon, remove the lime flesh and juice, and drop along with the peels into the water. Add the sugar, stir well, and cover for 1 hour. Strain through a fine chinois or cheesecloth and pour into nonplastic containers to cool. It will keep for a few weeks, but is best fresh; the ginger flavor diminishes over time.

HAND-WHIPPED IRISH-COFFEE CREAM

To speed up the whipping, chill a steel pitcher or bowl beforehand (or if it is possible, rest the pitcher in a container of ice while whipping).

1 pint heavy whipping cream

Whisk the cream until all the air bubbles disappear, but stop short of stiff. The cream should still pour slowly. Gently ladle or pour the cream on top of the coffee drink, taking care not to allow the cream to mix in with the coffee. If the cream mixes in it, this indicates either that the cream was underwhipped or the pour was too rapid. The end product should show a perfect definition between the black coffee and the white cream on top when viewed through an Irish-coffee glass.

Sweetened Whipped Cream: Add sugar to taste, 1 tablespoon at a time, while whipping. Also add 2 or 3 drops of vanilla extract per half pint of whipping cream.

PROOF IN THE NUMBERS: STANDARD ALCOHOL CONTENT

Gin . . . . .40% to 47%

Vodka . . . . .40% to 50%

Scotch, Blended 40%

Scotch, Single Malt . . . . .40% to 62%

Rum 40%

Overproof Rum . . . . .Up to 77%

Bourbon, Rye, and Blended Whiskey .40% to 45%

Bourbon, Special Bottlings . . . . .Up to 62%

Tequila . . . . .40%; it is rare but there are one or two at 50%

Flavored Spirits . . . . .30% to 40%
(Gin, Vodka, Rum, and Tequila)

Brandy, Armagnac, and Calvados . . . . .40%; some rare examples of 43%
and up to 50%

Fruit Brandy (Eau-de-Vie) . . . . .40% and 45%

Liqueurs and Cordials . . . . .Most range between 15% and 35%, but
selected cordials such as Chartreuse and
Absente are 55%

Apéritifs . . . . .16% to 30%

MIXING TERMS AND TECHNIQUES

BUILDING refers to preparing a drink in the glass in which it will be served, usually by pouring the ingredients in the order listed and then stirring.

BRUISE fruit with a bar muddler (or, in a pinch, a wooden spoon will do the job). Herbs like mint, verbena, and borage and spices like ginger are used more and more to flavor drinks. These too should be bruised first to release more flavor, but they should not be torn apart.

CREAM drinks should always be made with heavy cream—people expect the rich flavor. Substitute half-and-half or milk for dieters.

DISCARD the ice used to shake a drink and strain the drink over fresh ice unless the recipe indicates otherwise, as in the Caipirinha.

FLAG refers to the standard garnish of an orange slice and cherry. It is used in sours, old fashioneds, and many tropical drinks. A slice of fresh pineapple is sometimes added to the flag garnish.

FRAPPÉ AND MIST drinks are served over crushed or shaved ice.

IN AND OUT usually refers to a style of Martini preparation. A small amount of dry vermouth is dashed into the mixing glass over the ice, swirled around, and then tossed out. Then the gin or vodka is poured over the seasoned ice, stirred to chill, and strained into the serving glass.

MUDDLING is more vigorous than bruising. I bruise mint leaves to avoid tearing them in little pieces while still releasing some essence. I muddle limes in a Caipirinha more aggressively to extract the juice and the oil from the skin. This easy step can add so much to a cocktail, so keep your eye out for the small icon of a muddler next to certain recipes throughout the list.

NEAT DRINKS are served at room temperature without ice.

ON THE ROCKS indicates a drink served in an old-fashioned or rocks glass over ice.

ROLLING a drink is pouring the assembled ingredients back and forth between two large bar glasses to mix without agitating too much. This technique is used for drinks with tomato juice to avoid destroying the texture of the juice on the tongue.

SEASON a glass by dashing a small amount of the spirit you wish to season with, then rotating the glass and tossing out the excess.

SHAKING A DRINK is obvious: The ingredients and the ice are assembled in a cocktail shaker and shaken well, then strained into a serving glass.

SHAKING FRESH FRUIT in a cocktail will always improve the flavor. For example when shaking a Whiskey Sour, throw in an orange slice and a cherry, bruise the fruit with a muddler, and shake. Strain the drink, and always use fresh garnish unless the recipe indicates otherwise.

SHOOTERS are fun crowd pleasers, but they also present a dilemma to the host: They're invariably ordered when guests already have drinks in front of them, so how do you as a host provide a fun, recreational environment and at the same time serve in a responsible way? Here is how: All shooters should be $3/4$ ounce to 1 ounce, no larger. Buy special shot glasses just for shooters if they are popular. Choosing the right recipes will allow some control over the alcohol content. My trick was to take a really tasty cocktail like the Flamingo (page 115) and re-create it as a shot. The drink doesn't have a high alcohol content, and the recipe calls for a total liquid content of $4^{1}/2$ ounces. By adding another ounce of rum to this recipe and shaking well with ice, you have a very tasty new shot that will serve 6 people, taste great, and spread just 3 ounces of alcohol over 6 shots.

STIRRED drinks are assembled in the glass portion of a cocktail shaker with ice and stirred with a long cocktail spoon before being strained into a serving glass.

STRAIGHT-UP drinks are served chilled and strained of the ice in a chilled cocktail glass.

GLOSSARY

ABBOTT'S BITTERS
American-made bitters; discontinued after Prohibition.

ABRICOTINE
A liqueur made from ripe apricots, rather than natural or synthetic flavor of apricot.

ABSENTA, AJENJO
Spanish version of absinthe, discontinued to comply with EEC rules.

ABSENTE
A new absinthe-like product, sweeter than the original, that uses a wormwood called southwood.

ABSINTHE
A distillate originally based on grape eau-de-vie and steeped with or rectified with several herbals and botanicals, including hyssop, lemon balm, anise, Chinese aniseed, fennel, coriander, and other roots and herbs. An important ingredient, wormwood oil, was responsible for the nearly worldwide ban on absinthe when it was determined that it contained thujone, a strong drug that causes epileptic-type seizures when taken in large quantities. There is scientific agreement today that absinthe's high 130 proof was more problematic than the tiny amount of chemicals.

ADVOCAAT
Dutch term for "lawyer" is also the name of a Dutch liqueur made with egg yolk and brandy and flavored with vanilla, among other flavors.

AGAVE
A large plant indigenous to Mexico that looks like a cross between a giant pineapple and a cactus. The plant is actually a member of the lily family. There are hundreds of varieties of agave, cultivated and wild. The Weber Blue Agave is used to make tequila (see Blue Agave).

AGED (IN OAK)
The process of storing wine and spirits in oak barrels for a period of time to remove harsh flavor notes and add specific characteristics found in the wood. The age, previous use, and size of the barrels determine the oak effects. The barrels are often charred inside to introduce additional flavors from the caramelized sugars in the oak.

AGUARDIENTE
Literally translates as "burning water." It is the word used in Spanish-speaking countries for brandy.

AGUARDIENTE DE BAGACO
Portuguese brandy distilled from grape pomace; similar to Italian grappa or French marc.

AGUARDIENTE DE CANA
Spirit derived from sugarcane, such as cachaça or rum.

AGUARDIENTE DE COLOMBIA
An anise-flavored liqueur from Colombia.

AGUARDIENTE DE PALMA
A Philippine spirit derived from palm.

AKVAVIT, AKAVIT, AQUAVIT
Grain-based spirit made in Scandinavian countries, flavored with different herbs, the most common of which are caraway and fennel.

ALAMBIC OR ALEMBIC STILL
The original single-batch pot still, thought to have originated in China and been brought to the West by the Moors, who introduced it to Continental Europe on the Iberian Peninsula. The first distilling of any kind in Europe probably took place in Sherisch, which was the Moorish name for the town of Jerez de la Frontera. The root of the word is the Arabic word for still, *al-inbiq*.

ALCOHOL, ETHYL
Beverage alcohol widely believed to be derived from the Arabic word *al-kohl*. *Kohl*, however, was a fine powdered cosmetic used by Arabic women for eye shadow. I am still looking for the connection.

ALE
A beer made with yeast that floats to the top during fermentation. Ale is the oldest style of beer, usually made with less hops and served fresh without aging.

ALIZÉ GOLD, ALIZÉ RED PASSION
A 16% alcohol liqueur made in Cognac with passion fruit, water, and sugar. Cranberry is added to the Red Passion version.

AMARETTO
Almond- and apricot-flavored liqueur, originally made in Italy but now made in other countries as well.

AMARETTO DI SARONNO
Almond-flavored liqueur from Saronno, Italy. Legend has it that Bernardo Luini, a student of the Da Vinci School, was painting frescoes for the Marie della Grazie Cathedral and used as a model a young woman who worked at the inn where he stayed. She showed her gratitude by making him this sweet liqueur with almonds and apricots.

AMARO
Italian liqueurs made from grape eau-de-vie and bitter herbs, usually served after a meal as a *digestivo*.

AMER PICON
French bitter liqueur flavored with quinine, orange peel, gentian, and other bitter herbs; it is 39% alcohol. The French distiller-turned-soldier Gaetan Picon first made it for the French troops fighting in Algeria in 1837.

ANACREONTICS
The name adopted by a nineteenth-century London drinking club called the Anacreontic Society. There are two exceptional books that contain huge collections of verse inspired by drink, but sadly they are both out of print. One is called *Inspired by Drink* (edited by John Digby; 1988), and the other is *Merry Go Down* by Rab Noolas, (Mandrake Press, early twentieth century).

AÑEJO RUM
Rum aged in oak barrels; the aging requirements vary.

ANGOSTURA BITTERS
J. G. B. Siegert, a young German army doctor who volunteered to fight for Simón Bolívar and Venezuelan independence, first created Angostura bitters in 1824 as a stomach tonic for Bolívar's jungle-weary troops. His first production plant was in the town of Angostura, but when the government became unstable he moved offshore to the Island of Trinidad, where it remains to this day in Port of Spain. The formula for Angostura is secret, but the top flavor notes are cinnamon, allspice, and clove. Angostura is officially categorized as a food additive, even though it is 40% alcohol.

ANISETTE
A liqueur made in many countries but originally French that is flavored with aniseed.

APÉRITIF
A drink before the main meal to stimulate the palate, from the Latin word *aperire,* "to open." Apéritifs can encompass anything from wine; flavored, aromatized and fortified wines; cocktails; to Champagne.

APPLEJACK
Whiskey made from a mash of at least 51% apples that is fermented, then distilled. The Lairds company in New Jersey has been making applejack since colonial times, and thus the drink is sometimes referred to as Jersey Lightning. Applejack is usually bottled at 40% alcohol.

APRICOT BRANDY, FRUIT BRANDIES
Misnomer for a flavored neutral spirit, in this case apricot or any other fruit, that is then sweetened and bottled at 35% alcohol. See Brandy for the real deal.

APRY
A proprietary apricot liqueur by Marie Brizard.

AQUA VITAE
Literally means "water of life"; Latin for spirits.

ARAK, ARRACK, RAKI
A distillation originally made from date palm, now also from rice and sugarcane. Arak was the base for the first punch drinks in the seventeenth century, a tradition taken to England from India by British traders. Today it is made in the Middle East, India, and Southeast Asia.

ARMAGNAC
French brandy from the department of Gers in southern France. Single distilled in a special still, Armagnac is considered a stronger style than Cognac. There are three regions in Armagnac as defined by the AOC: Bas Armagnac (the best), Ténarèze, and Haut Armagnac.

AROMATIZED WINES
Wines that are flavored with herbs, spices, and fruits; examples include vermouth and other apéritif wines.

ARROPE
Grape juice boiled down and added to a concentrated wine to make Pedro Ximenez, a sweetener for amoroso-style sherry. Arrope is also added to whiskey for color.

AVERNA AMARO
A bittersweet Italian liqueur served as a digestivo; bottled at 34% alcohol. Like most of the bitter liqueurs of France and Italy, it is flavored with herbs and quinine from the bark of the cinchona tree.

BACARDI RUMS

The Bacardi Company, with headquarters in Hamilton, Bermuda, is the largest rum producer in the world, with distilleries in several countries. The overall company is called Bacardi Martin Group, formed in 1992, and together they produce brands, including the Martini & Rossi vermouths and apéritif. Bacardi originated in Cuba, but Fidel Castro nationalized the company in 1960 and the family began producing in Puerto Rico.

BACK

Water or soft drink served with or behind a drink of spirits. Classic nineteenth-century bar service called for a water back to be served with every alcoholic beverage.

BAGASSE

The fiber left after the juice has been removed from sugarcane; traditionally used in rum distilleries to fuel the fire in the still. Today it is used for insulation.

BAILEYS IRISH CREAM

A proprietary Irish liqueur made from fresh dairy cream, Irish whiskey, and sugar. Baileys was the first cream liqueur to solve the problem of separating and curdling.

BANANA LIQUEUR

Neutral alcohol flavored with natural or artificial banana flavor, sweetened with sugar, and bottled at between 25% and 35% alcohol.

BANANA RUM

Rum flavored with banana; Cruzan Rum from the American Virgin Islands makes a popular version.

BARBANCOURT

Haitian rum made from sugarcane juice, instead of molasses, whose reputation rests on French distilling techniques borrowed from Cognac. Today Barbancourt rum is distilled twice, first in a column and then in a pot still. All Barbancourt rum is aged in oak; Three Star is aged 4 years, Five Star is aged 8 years, and the Reserve du Domain is aged 15 years.

BAR SPOON

A long-handled spoon for stirring cocktails. Some are made in one piece with a twisted stainless handle to aid in twirling the spoon; others are made in two pieces, with a shaft that revolves inside a sleeve.

BARTENDER, BARMAN, DOCTOR, CHEMIST

The individual who prepares and serves alcoholic beverages across the bar in an on-premises establishment. Many nicknames have grown popular over the years, like chemist, which dates to the nineteenth century, when bartenders were responsible for manufacturing many of products they used. Doctor was another nickname that referred to the practice many neighborhood bartenders adopted of commenting on and even warning regular patrons of individual health problems.

BATHTUB GIN

Illegal gin made literally in the bathtub during Prohibition by adding juniper oil to grain alcohol.

BEHIND THE STICK

Slang for working behind the bar; the stick is the beer tap.

BENDER

Slang for a bout of heavy drinking.

BÉNÉDICTINE D.O.M.

A French liqueur, originally made by Benedictine monks, that dates back to the sixteenth century. The base is grape eau-de-vie from Cognac, which is flavored with herbs, citrus peel, and aromatics. "D.O.M." is a Benedictine indulgence for "God Most Good, Most Great." It is one of the higher-proof liqueurs at 40% alcohol.

BIBBER

English slang term for heavy drinker.

BLACKBERRY BRANDY

Misnomer for a flavored neutral spirit, in this case blackberry, that is then sweetened and bottled at 35% alcohol. See Brandy for the real deal.

BLENDED SCOTCH WHISKY (NO "E"), SCOTCH BLENDED

A blend of single-malt Scotch whiskies and mixed grain whisky. Made in Scotland, usually from 80% to 90% corn, with a small amount of barley. The grain whisky is distilled at 190 proof. The whiskies are aged separately, then blended and married for several months in casks before being reduced to bottling strength. With a couple of exceptions, blended scotch whisky is the best choice for cocktails.

BLENDED STRAIGHT WHISKEY

A blend of 100% straight whiskies of the same type, i.e., rye, bourbon, or corn, from different distillers or from different seasons within one distillery.

BLENDED WHISKEY

A minimum of 20% straight whiskies at 100 proof, blended with neutral-grain whiskey or light whiskey.

BLIND TIGER (BLIND PIG)

An attempt to circumvent the law and licensing procedures by giving away a "free" glass of booze to anyone who would pay to see the "Blind Tiger" or "Blind Pig."

BLUE AGAVE TEQUILA

100% Blue Agave tequila is distilled from the fermented sugars of the Weber Blue Agave plant only, and must be made and bottled in Mexico. Like all tequila, 100% Blue Agave tequila can be aged or unaged. Agave plants take eight to ten years to mature to the point where they can be used for tequila production, so the tequila made from 100% Agave is more expensive to produce than mixto or blended tequila.

BOLS COMPANY

Lucius Bols founded the Bols Company of Holland in 1575. It began as a gin distillery but expanded to develop many fruit liqueurs, including the famous orange liqueur curaçao, made with the bitter Curaçao oranges brought back from the New World. Many of the early *liqueuristes* from Europe learned their craft by studying at the Bols distillery. Bols also purchased grape eau-de-vie from all the big distilling regions, Armagnac, Cognac, and Jerez, to use in liqueur production.

BOLS ORANGE BITTERS

Bitters from Holland that are made from the bitter Curaçao orange by the Bols Company.

BONDED WHISKEY

Whiskey bottled "in bond" is stored in a government warehouse for anywhere between four and twenty years while it ages. It is not taxed until after it is bottled, a practice started in the nineteenth century to protect the whiskey maker from paying tax on spirits that evaporated during aging. Bonded whiskey is bottled at 100 proof, under government supervision.

BOONEKAMP BITTERS

Aromatic bitters from Holland.

BOOTHS GIN

Possibly the first of the London dry gin distillers, established in 1740. Today, Booths is made by license in the United States.

BOSTON SHAKER

A two-piece cocktail shaker comprised of a 16-ounce glass mixing glass half and a slightly larger metal half that fits over the glass half forming a seal.

BOURBON

American whiskey made from a mash of between 51% and 79% corn (a small amount of barley, then either rye or wheat fills out the rest of the mash), usually aged two years in charred oak barrels.

BRANCH

Water from a small spring-fed stream used for mixing with bourbon whiskey. Also known as ditch.

BRANDY

Distilled spirit derived from fermented fruit.

CACAO

See Crème de Cacao.

CACHAÇA

A sugarcane spirit made in Brazil, usually distilled from fresh-cut cane and usually bottled without oak aging.

CALISAY

Spanish bittersweet digestive.

CALVADOS

Calvados is an aged brandy made from a mash of up to 48 different apples in the Normandy region of France, in the Calvados Département. The finest Calvados is double distilled in a pot still, then aged for a minimum of 6 years.

CAMPARI

Italian spicy/bitter aperitivo based on quinine and colored with cochineal, developed in the 1860s by Gaspare Campari in Milan. Campari, bottled at 24% alcohol, is used in many well-known cocktails, such as the Negroni and Americano highball.

CARPANO, PUNT E MES

The Carpano family in Turin, Italy, was the first to make the proprietary spiced wines in the vermouth category, developed in the late eighteenth century. The name translates to "point and a half," referring to the recipe at the Carpano Café: one point of the wine and a half point of the mixer. There is another product from the Carpano label that is a relative newcomer to the American market, called Carpano Formula Antico, which is even spicier than the regular Carpano. Punt e Mes is good in cocktails like the Negroni and the Manhattan in place of the regular vermouth; but it has big flavor and should be used more sparingly.

CASSIS OR CRÈME DE CASSIS
A liqueur made from black currant that originated in the town of Dijon, in Burgundy, but is now made throughout France. It is wonderful in a drink called a Kir, a small amount of cassis in a glass of white table wine. The Kir Royale is the same drink made with Champagne.

CENTILITER (CL)
Measure used in European cocktail recipes, one hundredth of a liter. One ounce equals about 3 cl.

CHAMBORD
A proprietary raspberry liqueur made in France, Chambord was adopted by the disco generation as a cocktail ingredient in drinks like Sex on the Beach, the Brain Tumor, and the Purple Hooter.

CHAMPAGNE
A sparkling wine made in the Champagne region of northeast France, primarily from the Pinot Noir and Chardonnay grapes. After the first fermentation the special character of the wine is created during a second fermentation in the bottle, with the addition of sugar and yeast to create the famous bubbles. This process is called the *méthode champenoise,* or Champagne method, and it is the benchmark of style for sparkling wines—though the word "Champagne" can only be on wine made there. The major styles of Champagne are determined by sugar content, from the driest style *Brut* or *Natural* to *Extra Dry* to *Demi Sec,* and then the sweetest, *Doux.* Champagne is bottled as a vintage and nonvintage wine, the former of which must be made from no less than 80% grapes from the vintage date, and aged a minimum of 3 years.

CHARGED WATER
Water into which carbon dioxide has been injected. This was a nineteenth-century name.

CHARTREUSE
A French herbal liqueur made in two styles: yellow, bottled at 80 proof, and green, bottled at 110 proof. Originally made by Carthusian monks in Voirons, France, then in Tarragona, Spain, beginning in 1901, when a law was passed in France against production by the religious

order. Production has since returned to France. An aged version designated V.E.P. is also available.

CHERRY BRANDY
See Apricot Brandy.

CHERRY HEERING
A superior cherry liqueur made in Denmark from native cherries with an intense bittersweet flavor. Made by the house of Heering, it is a famous ingredient in the true Singapore Sling.

COBBLER
The cobblers were wine- or spirit-based drinks made with sugar and water over lots of shaved ice and decorated with a generous garnish of fresh fruit. Some cobblers were shaken with fruit, like the Whiskey Cobbler.

COCO LOPEZ
Coconut-flavored paste used for Piña Coladas; widely available in grocery stores.

COFFEE LIQUEUR
Made around the world, usually bottled between 25% and 30% alcohol. Two well-known brands are Kahlúa (see page 218), made in Mexico and Denmark, and Tia Maria, from Jamaica.

COINTREAU
A premium proprietary version of curaçao orange liqueur made in France. Its many cocktail applications include the Sidecar, Margarita, and White Lady.

CONGENERS
Impurities carried along with the molecules of alcohol vapor during distillation. They may derive from the base fruit or grain used in the original mash, or other organic chemicals encountered during the different stages of beverage alcohol production. The congeners are the elements that give a spirit its distinctive taste and aroma. The chemical bonds between the congeners and the alcohol vapor can be broken by repeated distillation at high temperatures.

CONTINUOUS OR PATENT STILL
The two-column still that was invented in Ireland by Aeneas Coffey in 1831.

CORDIAL GLASS
The original pony glass was only 1 ounce and it was shaped like a small version of a port or dessert wine glass. Today most bars serve a large portion and the pony is seldom used.

CORDIALS
Sweet liqueurs flavored with fruits, herbs, botanicals, and spices. The Bols Company in Holland was an early pioneer in developing fruit liqueurs and cordials, both of which words today are interchangeable. Most cordials are under 35% alcohol with some notable exceptions, such as Chartreuse (80 proof).

COURVOISIER VS
A proprietary Cognac rated Very Superior, which indicates a minimum of two years in oak for the youngest brandy in the blend.

CRÈME DE BANANA
Banana-flavored liqueur used in cocktails like the Banshee, Rum Runner, and Yellow Bird.

CRÈME DE CACAO, CRÈME DE CHOUAO
Liqueur made from cocoa beans, bottled in two styles, dark or clear, and bottled at 25% alcohol. Crème de Chouao is a sweeter version.

CRÈME DE FRAISES, FRAISES
Strawberry-flavored liqueur. Used in the 209 East Cocktail.

CRÈME DE FRAMBOISE
Raspberry-flavored liqueur.

CRÈME DE MENTHE
Mint-flavored liqueur made in two colors, green and clear (white). The green is traditionally served frappéd over crushed ice, and the white or clear is an ingredient in classics like the Stinger and the Grasshopper.

CRÈME DE NOYAUX
A low-proof almond-flavored liqueur that is used in the Pink Squirrel cocktail.

CRÈME DE PRUNELLE
A French liqueur made with wild plums, called sloe berries.

CRÈME YVETTE
An American violet-blossom liqueur that is rare if available at all; Crème de Violettes is the French version.

CRIADERA
The numbered layers of barrels in a solera aging room used in the production of sherry in Spain.

CRUSTA
A nineteenth-century drink created by Joseph Santina, a New Orleans saloon keeper, that featured a sugar-rimmed (crusted) stem glass garnished with a long spiral of lemon zest. The drink could be made with any spirits, the most common of which were gin, brandy, whiskey, and rum, mixed with lemon juice, Simple Syrup, bitters, and a sweet liqueur (such as maraschino), shaken and served over crushed ice.

CUPS
Wine-based drinks flavored with liqueurs, spirits, fruits, and herbs, iced and topped with seltzer.

CURAÇAO
A liqueur first made by the Bols Distillery in Holland from small bitter Curaçao oranges; now made in many countries, it comes in white, orange, and blue—the color being the only difference. Curaçao was a superior cocktail ingredient used in the early days of the cocktail, much the way vermouth was used later. Curaçao is a great match with rums, lime, and juices.

CYNAR
An Italian artichoke-flavored aperitivo.

DAMSON GIN
Misnomer for a liqueur flavored with damson plums.

DIASTASE
The enzyme that is formed in the barley kernel when it is germinated or malted. Diastase helps transform the starch in the grain into sugar.

DISTILLATION
The process of separating parts of a liquid mixture through evaporation and condensation. Distillation is used to produce concentrated beverage alcohol, called ethanol.

do.
Used in nineteenth-century cocktail recipe books and in general use for the "ditto."

DRACHM
Scottish for dram, or small quantity, with an apothecary's weight of $1/8$ ounce.

DRAMBUIE
A scotch-based sweet liqueur made with heather honey.

DUNDER
Unique to rum production in Jamaica, dunder employs mash from an earlier fermentation that is cultured and carried forward to the next batch of mash.

EARLY SHRUB
Rum, orange juice, and lemon juice served in London taverns.

EAU-DE-VIE
French for spirits, but more specifically, a type of brandy made from fermented mash of fruit; occasionally aged in oak barrels. Eau-de-vie has evolved to be defined as a group of unaged digestif brandies made from stone fruits and other fruits like raspberries and strawberries.

EBONY COGNAC
One of many Cognacs blended to be cigar friendly, which is to say heavy and dark with strong flavor, produced by A. De Fussigny.

EIGHTY-SIX
Slang for "out-of-stock" products behind the bar or customers who are barred from entering the premises. Thought to have originated during Prohibition at Chumley's, a bar at 86 Bedford Street in New York City, which did brisk business as a speakeasy.

ESTERS
Acid compounds resulting from distillation that give aroma to spirits.

ETHYL ALCOHOL
Beverage alcohol produced by the fermentation of a sugar solution.

FALERNUM
A sugar syrup from the island of Barbados flavored with almonds, lime, and spices; it comes in alcoholic and non-alcoholic versions. The alcoholic version is 11% by volume and is not available in the United States.

FEE BROTHERS
The Fee Brothers of Rochester, New York, have a line of bitters that includes peach, mint, aromatic, and orange.

FERMENTATION
A process that breaks down sugar molecules into carbon dioxide gas and ethyl alcohol. This change is accomplished by a micro-organism called yeast, that reproduces itself rapidly in a solution containing sugar.

FINO SHERRY
The driest style of sherry; popular pre-dinner apéritif wine in Spain.

FIX
A nineteenth-century drink made like a sour, but garnished extravagantly with fruits.

FIZZ
A spin-off of the Sour, made possible by the appearance of "charged water" in the mid-nineteenth century.

FLIP
Flips were originally colonial drinks made either with beer or rum, and some sweetener. The mixture was sometimes heated with a hot loggerhead, or fire iron with a ball on the end used to heat drinks from the fire. Flips became much more sophisticated in the cocktail age, when they were made with sugar, a whole egg, and sherry or some spirit, shaken very well and served in a cocktail glass.

FORBIDDEN FRUIT
An American liqueur made with grapefruit and other citrus fruits, sweetened with honey. No longer widely available.

FOR THE MONEY
A post prohibition–era expression indicating a larger serving. A waiter would order "two Cokes; one for the money," indicating to the bartender a larger serving and a Coke "back," which was free.

FORTIFIED WINES
Wines with alcohol added like port, vermouth, Madeira, and sherry.

FRANGELICO
A proprietary liqueur from Italy flavored with hazelnuts.

FRAPPÉ
Drink served over snow or crushed ice. They are also referred to as "mist," i.e. scotch mist.

FRUIT PURÉE
Fruit broken down to liquid by a food processor. Restaurants often use flash-frozen fruit purées as the base for sorbet. If you can find a retail source to buy them, they also make great cocktails

GALLIANO
An Italian herb liqueur made with unaged grape brandy. The Harvey Wallbanger cocktail put Galliano on every American bar about thirty years ago.

GILL
Wineglass measuring a 4-ounce pour in the nineteenth-century cocktail recipe books.

GIN
Grain spirit flavored with botanicals, specifically *genièvre* or juniper, and other flavors, including coriander, lemon peel, fennel, cassia, anise, almond, gingerroot, orange peel, and angelica. Created in the 1600s by a Dutch chemist, Dr. Franciscus Sylvius, experimenting with the therapeutic properties of juniper.

GINGER BEER
A spicy soft drink, usually carbonated, made from ginger-root; originated in Jamaica.

GINGER LIQUEUR
There is a ginger-flavored liqueur on the market from China called Canton Ginger Liqueur.

GLASS RAIL
The inside channel on a bar top used for dirty glasses and for cocktail tools. The channel should be four inches wide to accommodate a liquor bottle or mixing glass.

GODIVA LIQUEUR
An American proprietary chocolate and caramel liqueur. The name and the logo are licensed from the Belgian chocolate company of the same name.

GOLDSCHLAGER
A Swiss proprietary cinnamon liqueur, bottled at 87 proof, with 24-carat-gold flakes in the bottle.

GRAND MARNIER
A French proprietary orange and brandy liqueur that is made with Curaçao oranges. There are three levels widely available: Cordon Rouge (the standard); Centenaire (100th anniversary); and Cuvée du Cent Cinquantenaire (150th anniversary).

GRAPPA
Poor man's brandy, or so it was originally. Grappa is made from the leftover skins, seeds, and stems after grapes are pressed for wine. Grappa is usually unaged. Today grappa has become fashionable in fine-dining restaurants and is being made from a larger percentage of grape juice and bottled in expensive designer bottles.

GREEN CHARTREUSE
See Chartreuse.

GRENADINE
Sweet red syrup used in alcoholic and nonalcoholic drinks. The original flavor base was pomegranate, but many brands use artificial flavor. The real deal is still being made by Angostura (see Resources), among others.

GUINNESS STOUT
Top-fermenting Irish beer, almost black in color, as a result of the heavily kilned (toasted) malt used to make it. Irish stout is dry with a slight bitter aftertaste; English stout is sweeter.

HEADS
Volatile spirit from the beginning of a distillation run that are usually re-distilled or removed. Form the spirit.

HIMBEERGEIST
Eau-de-vie distilled from fruit and not aged or sweet-ened. These fruit brandies were traditionally made in Alsace, Germany, and Switzerland, but now they are made in the United States. They are served after a meal as a digestif, and range from 80 to 90 proof.

INFUSION
A process similar to making tea—but on a bigger scale. In beer and whiskey making, the grains and malted grains are soaked in hot water several times, often with increasingly higher temperatures, resulting in a sweet liquid called *wort*. Infusion is also used in the production of fruit liqueurs, where fruit and other flavors are steeped in brandy for any extended time. After infusion, the mixture is strained, lowered to bottle proof with water, sweetened with sugar syrup, and then bottled.

IRISH CREAM
A liqueur made from Irish whiskey, sugar, and fresh cream. See Baileys Irish Cream.

IRISH MIST
Irish whiskey liqueur made from a blend of four whiskies, two pot distilled and two grain, sweetened with three kinds of honey, including heather and clover.

IRISH WHISKEY
A triple-distilled whiskey from Ireland, thought to be the first whiskey. Irish whiskey is a blend of pot-stilled malt whiskey, pot-stilled unmalted barley whiskey, and column-stilled grain whiskey. Irish whiskey has a completely different character than its neighbor Scotland's whisky, mostly because the malt is not kilned or toasted with peat, so there is no smoky quality in the flavor.

JÄGERMEISTER

A German liqueur made from 56 herbs that has a bitter-sweet flavor. Although Jägermeister has been produced since 1878, in the past ten years it has sold more than all the years prior, because of its popularity as a shooter with beer here in the United States. 70 proof.

JULEP

A popular American drink that originated in the late eighteenth century and is still popular today. It was originally made with Cognac and peach brandies, but it evolved into a bourbon drink mixed with fresh mint and sugar, served in a frosted silver cup over shaved ice.

KAHLÚA

A proprietary coffee liqueur from Mexico, arguably the best known of the coffee liqueurs. All Kahlúa sold in the United States is made in Mexico, but Kahlúa sold in Europe is made under a license by the Peter Heering Company in Denmark.

KIWI-LIME LIQUOR

A sweet, New Zealand fruit liqueur.

LAST CALL

The traditional phrase in bars announcing the last round of drinks before closing.

LAYERED

Maintaining separate visible layers in a drink by slowly pouring over the back of a spoon held inside the glass. The most famous layered drinks are the Pousse Café after-dinner drinks.

LICOR 43

A proprietary Spanish liqueur with 43 herbal ingredients and grape eau-de-vie—though the resulting flavor is distinctly vanilla; it is bottled at 34% alcohol.

LILLET

Lillet or Lille is a French wine-based apéritif that is produced in two styles: Lillet Blanc and Lillet Rouge. The Blanc, or Blonde, is produced from Sauvignon Blanc and Semillon grapes mixed with a concentrate prepared by macerating several fruits in brandy. The rouge is made from Cabernet and Merlot grapes mixed with a similar concentrate. Lillet has a sweet, fruity taste and finds a home in several well-known cocktails, such as the Vesper, created for James Bond in *Casino Royale*. Referred to in older recipe books as Kina Lillet.

LIQUEURS

See Cordials.

MACERATION

The process of steeping a flavoring agent in water or alcohol, then either redistilling the resulting product or adding it to a larger batch for flavoring. The same flavoring agent will extract differently in water than in alcohol; alcohol tends to extract more bitter notes.

MADEIRA

Fortified sweet red wine from the Portuguese island of Madeira, it is aged in soleras, like the brandies of Spain. Madeira is reputed to be among the longest-lived wines in the world, lasting well over 100 years in some cases. The island of Madeira was often the last stop for ships sailing to the New World, and the barrels of wine were loaded for ballast as well as freight. The wine seemed to thrive in the steaming holds of the ships and had improved in flavor at the end of long voyages. Today Madeira makers recreate this "cooking" of the wine in a process called *estufagem,* whereby the temperature in the aging warehouses is raised to over 100°F to simulate the heat in the hold of a sailing vessel.

MAHOGANY

A slang word for a bar top.

MALTING

Germinating grain, usually barley or rye. (See Diastase).

MARASCHINO LIQUEUR

A sweet, clear liqueur made from marasca cherries and cherry pits. Maraschino was a popular ingredient in early punches and cocktails; it is almost never drunk straight. The talented bartenders of Cuba in the 1920s made maraschino popular by adding it to the Daiquiri recipe.

MARC

The skins and seeds left over from the pressing in wine-making in France. Marc is fermented and distilled into an unaged brandy of the same name, similar to grappa.

MARSALA

A fortified wine from Marsala, Sicily, it is more processed than the other great fortified wines from Portugal, Spain, and Madeira. After the base wine is made, concentrates of boiled-down wine and concentrated grape juice mixed with spirits are blended into the wine. The wine then begins its journey through the solera system for aging.

MESCAL

The general category of which tequila is a subcategory. To be clearer, all tequila is mescal but mescal is not tequila. Mescal is made primarily in Oaxaca, Mexico, from the espadin species of agave, and bottled with the infamous worm or gusano in the bottle. The worm has been retired of late, and premium mescals are now available from several makers, including Del Maguey and Encantado. Mescal has a smoky quality from the slow baking of the agave piña in clay ovens over hot rocks.

MIDORI
A proprietary melon liqueur from the Suntory distillery in Japan, it is popular in cocktails for the green color it brings to drinks, such as the Midori Margarita.

MINT BITTERS
See Fee Brothers.

MIST
Any spirit served over crushed ice.

MISTELLE
A blend of raw grape juice and spirits sometimes used as a base for apéritif fortified wines, such as vermouth, and sometimes bottled as a stand-alone product, as in Pineau des Charentes.

MIXTO
Mixto is a tequila that is at least 51% derived from the blue agave, but also contains sugars from cane or other sources.

MOUNT GAY RUM
Oldest brand of rum (1703), made by Abel and William Gay at the St. Lucy Estate on the Island of Barbados. Mount Gay is made from molasses and a very closely guarded yeast recipe. The rum is a blend of pot-still and continuous-still rums. The aging takes place in small barrels that are used a maximum of three times to avoid depletion and the aging lasts between 2 and 10 years. The blender takes over, exercising his art to marry the older and younger rums. Mount Gay produces four products: Eclipse Barbados Rum (standard) and the Premium White, both aged 2 years; Mount Gay Extra Old Rum, blended with a larger percentage of the 10-year-old rum; and the very rare Sugar Cane Brandy, which is not widely available.

MUDDLER
A wooden tool shaped like the grinding tool of a mortar and pestle (between 6 and 9 inches long) used to mash fruit and herbs with sugar or liqueur in the bottom of a bar mixing glass. This technique is essential for making Old Fashioneds and the Caipirinhas.

MULLED WINE
Wine cooked with spices and sugar.

NOSE
The aroma of a wine or spirit.

OJEN
Spanish anise-flavored liqueur.

OLD-FASHIONED GLASS
Holds 8 to 10 ounces in a short, stout shape. Often referred to as the "on the rocks" or simply "rocks" glass.

OLD POTRERO RYE
An unusual American rye whiskey made by the Anchor Distillery. It is made from malted rye and age for 2 years in new charred oak barrels and bottled at 61% alcohol.

OLD TOM GIN
A sweetened London dry-style gin very popular in the nineteenth century.

ON PREMISES (OP)
A trade term for a liquor business that serve spirits, wine, and beer by the glass, i.e., bars and restaurants.

ORANGE BITTERS
Alcohol-based bitters flavored with orange peel and other botanicals, made in the United States by the Fee Brothers in Rochester, New York, and in Europe by the Bols distillery. Orange bitters was a popular cocktail additive prior to Prohibition and was an ingredient in the first Dry Martini, but it was dropped in later recipes.

ORANGE CURAÇAO
See Curaçao.

ORANGE-FLOWER WATER
Water flavored with orange blossoms, used in baking and cooking. It is the critical ingredient in the famous New Orleans cocktail, the Ramos Gin Fizz.

ORGEAT OR ORGEAT SYRUP
A milky, sweet almond syrup used extensively in baking; also called orzata. Orgeat is the often forgotten ingredient in Victor Bergeron's classic Mai Tai cocktail.

OUZO
Greek anise-flavored liqueur.

PASSION FRUIT NECTAR
A sweet, thick juice made from sugar water and passion fruit. Fresh passion fruit is a wonderful addition to tropical cocktails, but it needs a lot of sweetening.

PEACH BITTERS
See Fee Brothers.

PEACH LIQUEUR

A fruit liqueur made from grape distillate and infused with fresh peaches.

PEACHTREE SCHNAPPS

This was the spirit that began the whole fruit schnapps craze; it is produced by DeKuyper. 30 proof.

PEPPER VODKA

Vodka made by steeping hot peppers in vodka.

PERFECT

A modifying term in cocktail recipes indicating a mix of half sweet and half dry vermouth, as in a Perfect Manhattan.

PERNOD

Created as an absinthe substitute. See Absinthe.

PERRY

Cider made from pears; or a combination of pears and apple.

PEYCHAUD'S BITTERS

Antoine Peychaud, owner of an apothecary shop in New Orleans, created an all-purpose flavoring and health tonic in 1793 from herbs and Caribbean spices that is believed to be the first commercial bitters in the Americas. He combined the bitters with French Cognac produced by Sazerac de Forge et Fils, and the beverage came to be known as a Sazerac.

PHYLLOXERA VASTATRIX

An American insect from the aphid family that was exported to Europe on root splicings that decimated wine-producing grapes in many countries. The aphids attack the roots, and American vines were resistant. Whiskey makers in Northern Europe and in the United States were the accidental benefactors of the disaster after the brandy makers in southern Europe were ruined.

PIMENTO LIQUEUR

Liqueur made in Jamaica from allspice berries. Available only sporadically in the United States.

PIMM'S CUPS

Pimm's cups were cocktail creations of James Pimm, a barman in London in the 1840s. In the 1870s former colleagues and customers used the formulas to create bottled cocktails under the name Pimm's. Like all cups, they are best served topped with something sparkling, such as seltzer, English lemonade, 7-Up, or Champagne. Pimm's cups were eventually made in six varieties: No. 1, gin based; No. 2, whiskey based; No. 3, brandy based; No. 4, rum based; No. 5, rye based; and No. 6, vodka based. In the United States only No. 1 is available, but in England No. 1 and No. 6 are still available.

PINEAU DES CHARENTES

A blend of raw grape juice and Cognac that is aged and bottled. Often served as an apéritif or mixed in cocktails; see Rainbow Sour, page 178.

POMEGRANATE MOLASSES

Thick syrup made from pomegranate juice, found in Middle Eastern grocery stores.

PONY GLASS

A small, stemmed glass measuring one ounce.

PORT

Fortified wine from the Douro Valley of Portugal; comes in several styles, including vintage, vintage character, ruby, tawny, and white. The grape varieties are numerous, including Touriga, Bastardo, Tinta Francisca, Tinta Cao, and Souzao.

PRUNELLE

Plum-flavored liqueur.

PUNCH

From the Persian word *panj,* or Hindi *panch,* meaning five (ingredients): spirit, sugar, lime juice, spice, and water. Similarly, an ancient Greek drink called *pentaploa* was also made with five ingredients: wine, honey, cheese, flour, and oil. Originated in India and popular in Colonial America and all over eighteenth-century Europe.

PUNT E MES

See Carpano.

RAMAZOTTI

Sometimes called "Amaro Felsina Ramazotti," it is made from 33 herbs and spices and has a bittersweet flavor. Produced by the same company in Milan since 1815.

REAL MCCOY

During Prohibition, Captain William J. McCoy operated a fleet of ships between the Caribbean and the East Coast of the United States, unloading bootleg and illegal spirits from overseas onto smaller boats while moored beyond the three-mile limit. His spirits were always high quality, hence the phrase "the real McCoy."

RECTIFYING

This is an often-misunderstood word because it can describe many different operations. Basically, it means to change a spirit in some way after it has been distilled. Those changes can include redistilling, adding flavor or color, and adding water to lower to bottle proof strength.

RED BULL

One of the first of the "energy-drink" soft drinks made with a heavy dose of caffeine and, according to the label, carbohydrates, sugar, and vitamins. These energy drinks are mixed with vodka and juices.

RED DUBONNET

French apéritif wine fortified with grape eau-de-vie, originally made in the nineteenth-century from the red wines of Roussillon, flavored with quinine, and used to protect soldiers from malaria in tropical colonial outposts.

RICARD, PERNOD

See Absinthe.

ROSE WATER

A food- and beverage-flavoring agent made by steeping rose petals in alcohol. Used extensively in the Middle East. Good in lemonade drinks.

RUBY PORT

See Port.

RUM

Made from molasses, sugarcane juice, or sugarcane syrup, it is considered the first spirit of the New World. First produced in Barbados and Jamaica, traditionally double distilled. Rhum Agricole is made from sugarcane juice, not molasses.

RUM SWIZZLE

Created at the Georgetown Club in British Guiana by putting rum, bitters, lime, and ice in a tumbler, then mixing it with a long swizzle stick until the outside of the glass frosts over.

RYE

Whiskey aged 2 years, with 51 to 100% rye in the mash.

SAINT RAPHAEL

An aromatized wine flavored with quinine, herbs, and spices. Used by the French government to protect their troops in Algeria from malaria.

SAKE

Japanese wine made from fermented rice.

SAMBUCA

Anise-based, licorice-flavored Italian after-dinner liqueur often taken with coffee. Black Sambuca was recently introduced to the American market under the names Opal Nera and Della Notte.

SANGAREE

An early colonial beverage made from wine, usually Madeira, water, and spices and served as a tall refresher in the summer. Mulled wine is a winter version of the sangaree served hot. The spices are boiled with water and the flavored water is added to the wine with sugar and served hot. The spices for mulled wine are nutmeg, cinnamon, mace, and clove. An egg version of mulled wine was popular in the nineteenth century, in which eggs were separated, beat very well with sugar, then beat together with a little water and whipped into the wine and spiced water as it was cooking. The spirit versions were floated with sweet wines like port and Madeira.

SANGRIA

A beverage originating in Spain made with red or white wine, sugar, and fruits and garnished with fresh fruits and berries.

SAZERAC

See Peychaud's Bitters.

SCHNAPPS

A Scandinavian and German term for strong, colorless spirits. Also known as snaps, they may be flavored or unflavored. It is also used as slang for any strong spirit. Today schnapps is a popular category of low-end fruit and spice spirits made by companies like DeKuyper, Mohawk, and Leroux.

SCOTCH

Whisky distilled in Scotland from malted barley.

SECRESTAT BITTERS

Popular French bitters that are no longer produced.

SHERRY

Spanish fortified wine from the province of Cádiz. Sherry has a long second fermentation during which the wine is in contact with the air and a yeast scum known as flor grows on top of the wine. The wines with the thickest layer of flor will be marked for fino, dryer with less alcohol added; and the wines with very little flor bloom on top will be marked for oloroso, fuller body with more alcohol added. All the sherry is fermented dry and some oloroso sherry is sweetened with Pedro Ximenez, a sweetened concentrated wine made by boiling down wine and adding *arrope* (boiled grape juice). Sherry is a blended wine that is aged by the solera system. The wine is preserved by the addition of alcohol distilled from local grapes. There are two broad categories of sherry: dry (fino) and fuller body, sometimes sweeter (oloroso)

SHOOTERS

One-ounce shots of cocktails or straight spirits like Jägermeister that are downed in one gulp.

SIMPLE SYRUP

Syrup made from mixing roughly equal parts sugar and water or more concentrated for baking applications.

SINGLE-MALT SCOTCH

A Scottish barley-based spirit produced by a single distillery in one season. Bottled straight or used as a blending agent in blended scotch.

SKIN

A category of drinks from the nineteenth century made with lemon juice, spirits, and hot water.

SLING

In the mid-nineteenth century a sling was described as a toddy (spirits, sugar, and water with nutmeg grated on top). The sling developed into a more complex cocktail with the addition of citrus juice and liqueur modifiers, like the early-twentieth-century Singapore Sling.

SLOE GIN

A misnomer for an American liqueur made from wild plums called sloe berries. It is not a style of gin.

SMALL BEER

Simply a beer that is low in alcohol.

SOLERA AGING

Spanish brandy and sherry are both aged in this system of barrels in the bottom layer of barrels is the *solara* and the other layers are called the *criaderas*. During the solera aging process, the wine or spirit is moved through the criaderas by blending younger wines or brandies in with older barrels. In this way the wine or brandy takes on an age character beyond its years, or, as the Spanish say, the old brandy teaches the young brandy.

SORGHUM

A type of grass grown in the Plains states, boiled down to make a type of molasses.

SOURS

Cocktails made with a strong, sweet, and a sour ingredient. Those ingredients can vary widely from one sour to

the next, but the proportions should remain the same. The proportions I have determined to appeal to the widest audience are ¾ part sour to 1 part sweet to 2 parts strong. (See Fix.)

SPANISH BRANDY

See Solera aging.

SPRITZER

A mix of white wine and club soda over ice.

STOLICHINAYA OHRANJ

Orange-flavored vodka from Russia. Russian vodka and Scandinavian Akvavit were the first flavored vodkas.

STRAWBERRY LIQUEUR

A liqueur made from the maceration of strawberries in a neutral spirit. See Liqueurs.

STREGA

Italian liqueur that is a blend of 70 different herbs and barks. Great over ice cream.

SUNTORY

The best-selling brand of Japanese whiskey; Suntory is also one of Japan's largest alcohol beverage companies.

SWEET VERMOUTH

See Vermouth.

SWIZZLE

See Rum Swizzle.

TAILS

Spirits from the end of a distilling run usually high in acrid fusel oils and removed by the distiller for re-distillation.

TAWNY PORT

Wood-aged port blended from several vintages and aged from 5 to 40 years in oak. Tawny starts out dark red like ruby or vintage ports, but the oldest ones take on the light copper color from which the name is derived.

TEQUILA

Produced in Mexico, derived from the Agave Tequiliana Weber Blue, one of the 400 varieties of the agave plant, a member of the lily family. Tequila comes in two main categories: Mixto and 100% Blue Agave. Mixto is at least 51% agave with other sugars added to the agave during fermentation, usually from cane. As the name indicates, 100% Blue Agave tequila is made only from agave. The three types of tequila are determined by age. Bianco or silver is bottled without aging in wood after resting in stainless tanks for up to 60 days. Reposado is rested but in wood for 60 days to a year, and añejo is aged a minimum of 1 year in wood. There is a minor category called dorado or gold that is colored with caramel, but not aged.

TIA MARIA
Coffee-flavored liqueur from Jamaica.

TISANE
Herbal infusions that do not contain tea leaves; often referred to as herbal teas.

TODDY
A sap derived from coconut, wild date, and palmyra trees. *Toddy* came to be known as a hot or cold beverage made of spirits, sugar, and water.

TONIC WATER
A carbonated water that contains quinine and sugar.

TRIPLE SEC
A liqueur made from the curaçao oranges, first in France but now produced in many countries. Triple Sec is mostly a mixer and is almost never taken straight.

TROPICO
A proprietary liqueur made with premium Bacardi Gold Rum and exotic fruit juices, including mango, passion fruit, guarana, and carambola; very mixable.

TUACA
An Italian sweet liqueur, flavored with citrus with a top vanilla note in the flavor.

UISGEBEATHA (CELTIC) OR USQUEBAUGH (GAELIC)
Literally translated to "water of life," the old word for whisky in the British Isles. Some believe the Celtic pronunciation led to the English word whisky.

UNDERBERG BITTERS
Aromatic bitters from Germany.

UNICUM BITTERS
Aromatic bitters from Austria.

VAT
The large containers in which whiskey is blended. Vatted malts are 100% single-malt whiskies blended together.

VERMOUTH
Fortified and flavored wines made in sweet or dry styles, used in cocktails and as an apéritif. The word originated from the German word for the wormwood plant, *wermuth*.

VODKA
From *voda* the Russian word for "water," vodka is distilled from grain and sometimes potatoes. It is mostly tasteless and odorless.

VS, VSOP, XO COGNAC
Very Special, and Very Special Old and Pale, and Extra Old are designations used in Cognac and Armagnac to indicate minimum aging for their brandies. The actual age for the three designations varies from maker to maker.

WHISKEY
From the Gaelic *uisqebaugh,* or "water of life," whiskey is made from grain that is ground into grist, then cooked with water to release starches. Malt is added to convert the starch into sugar, and then yeast to begin fermentation. The low-proof liquid after fermentation is called beer, which after distillation becomes whiskey.

WHITE CRÈME DE MENTHE
See Crème de Menthe.

WORMWOOD
This all-important herbal ingredient in absinthe is outlawed and is not used in the absinthe substitute products Ricard, Pernod, and Absente. Wormwood is still used as a flavoring in low-proof fortified and aromatized wines like vermouth. The Latin name for wormwood is *artemisia absinthium*. Later borrowed by Pernod as the name for its infamous outlawed spirit absinthe.

YELLOW CHARTREUSE
See Chartreuse.

YUKON JACK
Canadian whiskey slightly sweetened with honey.

ZUBROWKA
Vodka flavored with zubrowka grass.

BIBLIOGRAPHY

Barr, Andrew. *Drink: A Social History of America*. New York: Carroll & Graf Publishing, 1999.

Barty-King, Anton, and Hugh Massel. *Rum, Yesterday and Today*. London: Heidelberg Publishing, 1983.

Bergeron, Victor J. *Trader Vic's Rum Cookery & Drinkery*. New York: Doubleday, 1974.

Brown, John Hull. *Early American Beverages*. New York: Crown Books, 1966.

Carson, Gerald. *The Social History of Bourbon*. New York: Dodd, Mead & Company, 1963.

Cipriani, Arrigo. *Harry's Bar*. New York: Arcade Publishing, 1996.

Craddock, Harry. *The Savoy Cocktail Book*. London: Constable and Company, 1930.

Crockett, Albert Stevens. *Old Waldorf Bar Days*. New York: Aventine Press, 1931.

Cunningham, Stephen Kittredge. *The Bartender's Black Book*. Self-published, 1994.

David, Elizabeth. *Harvest of the Cold Months: The Social History of Ice and Ices*. New York: Viking Press, 1994.

Duffy, Patrick Gavin. *The Official Mixer's Manual*. New York: Alta Publications Inc., 1934

Edmunds, Lowell. *Martini, Straight Up: The Classic American Cocktail*. Baltimore: Johns Hopkins University Press, 1998.

Embury, David A. *The Fine Art of Mixing Drinks*. New York: Doubleday & Co., 1948.

de Fleury, R. *1800 and All That: Drinks Ancient and Modern*. 1937.

Foley, Peter Raymond. *The Ultimate Cocktail Book*. Foley Publishing, 1999.

Foley, Raymond and Jaclyn. *The Williams–Sonoma Bar Guide*. Williams–Sonoma/Time Life, 1999.

Gale, Hyman, and Gerald F. Marco. *The How and When*. Marco Importing Co., 1940.

Goodwin, Betty. *Hollywood du Jour*. Angel City Press, 1993.

Grimes, William. *Straight Up or On the Rocks*. New York: Simon & Schuster, 1993.

Haas, Irvin. *Inns and Taverns*. New York: Arco Publishing Co., 1972.

Haimo, Oscar. *Cocktail & Wine Digest*. 1945.

Hamilton, Edward. *The Complete Guide to Rum*. Chicago: Triumph Books, 1997.

Hills, Phillip. *Appreciating Whisky: The Connoisseur's Guide to Nosing, Tasting and Enjoying Scotch*. New York: HarperCollins, 2000.

Jeffs, Julian. *Little Dictionary of Drink*. London: Pelham Books, 1973.

Johnson, Harry. *New and Improved Bartender's Manual, or How to Mix Drinks of the Present Style,* 1888.

Jones, Andrew. *The Apéritif Companion*. New York: Knickerbocker Press, 1998.

Kappeler, George J. *Modern American Drinks*. Saafield Publishing Co., 1900.

Mason, Dexter. *The Art of Drinking*. Ferrar & Rinehart, Inc., 1930.

Meier, Frank. *The Artistry of Mixing Drinks*. Paris: Fryam Press, 1936.

Mendelsohn, Oscar A. *The Dictionary of Drink and Drinking*. Hawthorne Books, Inc., 1965.

Muckensturm, H.M. Louis. *Louis' Mixed Drinks*. Boston and New York: Caldwell Co., 1906.

Nowak, Barbara. *Cook It Right: The Comprehensive Source for Substitutions, Equivalents, and Cooking Tips*. Sandcastle Publishing, 1995.

Pacult, F. Paul. *Kindred Spirits*. New York: Hyperion, 1997.

Page, David and Barbara Shinn. *Recipes from Home*. New York: Artisan, 2001.

Paul, Charlie. *Recipes of American and Other Iced Drinks*. London: Farrow & Jackson Ltd., 1902.

Poister, John. *The New American Bartender's Guide*. Signet Book, 1999.

Pokhlebkin, William. *A History of Vodka*. London: Versoo, 1991.

The Practical Housewife: A Complete Encyclopedia of Domestic Economy and Family Medical Guide. Philadelphia: J. B. Lippincott and Company, 1860.

Price, Pamela Vandyke. *Dictionary of Wine and Spirits*. London: Northwood Books, 1980.

Ricket, Edward. *The Gentleman's Table Guide*. Published by the author, 1873.

Robert of the American Bar. *Cocktails and How to Mix Them*. London: Herbert Jenkins Ltd.

Schmidt, William. *The Flowing Bowl*. Charles L. Webster Co., 1891.

Schumann, Charles. *The Tropical Bar Book*. New York: Stewart, Tabori and Chang, 1989.

Spalding, Jill. *Blithe Spirits: A Toast to the Cocktail*. Washington, D.C.: Alvin Rosenbaum Projects, Inc., 1988.

Spencer, Edward. *The Flowing Bowl*. New York: Duffield & Co.

Strens, Samuel. *The American Herbal or Materia Medica,* 1801.

Tartling, W. J. *Café Royal Cocktail Book*. London: Pall Mall Ltd., 1937.

Taussig, Charles, *Rum, Romance and Rebellion*. London: William Jarrolds Publishers.

Thomas, Jerry. *The Bartender's Guide, or How to Mix All Kinds of Plain and Fancy Drinks*. New York: Dick & Fitzgerald Publishing, 1887.

Visakay, Stephen. *Vintage Bar Ware*. Schroeder Publishing Co., 1997.

Werner, M. R., *Tammany Hall*. Doubleday, Doran & Company, 1928.

SPECIAL THANKS...

To my wife, Jill, for her long hours of labor to help me make this book. You're number one, baby. To Anthony Giglio, for his invaluable assistance in making a readable book out of a bartender's rambling notes.

And to lots of others: the whole bar staff at the old Promenade Bar at the Rainbow Room for making one of the best bars in the world, Ron Holland for introducing me to the New York City Bar & Grill, Gerry Holland for his memory, Ray Wellington for putting me on the right track, John Hodgeman and Susan Ginsburg at Writers House for making the book a reality, Katie Workman and Chris Pavone of Clarkson Potter for all their assistance, Sharen Butrum for getting me into focus with the book (and Carl Butrum for getting me out of focus), and for the honor of making him his very last martini, Brian Rea for opening his library to me, Cynthia Fagen for giving me the King Cocktail moniker that's become my trademark, Don Gibbons and Kevin McGrinder at Minners Designs for providing glassware for the photos, at Hanely's Tavern, Brooklyn, New York—Harry, Zane, and Arnold—for the unforgettable stories, Bryan Cabrerra for rescuing our hard drive, Mrs. McKenna for the punch bowl, Steve Visakay for sharing his shaker collection, Fred McKibben of Grace for the photo venue, my family for all their love and meatballs, and my customers over the years for all their thirst and good cheer.

And special thanks to Joe Baum for taking me to a place where troubles melt like lemon drops. . . .

INDEX